实 用 汉 语 课 本

第 一 册

PRACTICAL CHINESE READER

ELEMENTARY COURSE

Book I

北 京 语 言 学 院

刘 珣 邓恩明 刘社会 编著

李培元 审订

THE COMMERCIAL PRESS

2006 Beijing

Published by the Commercial Press
36 Wanfujing Street, Beijing, China
Typeset by the Beijing Languages
Institute Printing House
Beijing, China
Distributed by China International Book Trading Corporation
35 Chegongzhuang Xilu, Beijing 100044, China
P.O. Box 399, Beijing, China

Printed in the People's Republic of China

前　言

　　《实用汉语课本》第一、二册共五十课，是供外国学生学习现代汉语用的基础阶段教材，也可以供外国人自学汉语使用。

　　这套教材的主要目的是培养学生在实际生活中运用汉语进行交际的能力，并为进一步学习汉语打下比较牢固的基础。本教材力求从汉语本身的特点出发，吸取不同的外语教学法的长处，通过句型替换、功能项目操练、语法分析等综合性的训练，来达到这一目标。

　　《实用汉语课本》的编写原则是：

　　1．本书所依据的是中国人所通用的、规范的、地道的现代汉语，首先介绍日常生活中最必需的、也是初学者在社会交际中急需掌握的活的语言材料。

　　2．本书不但要使读者掌握一定数量的常用语言形式，而且要具备在一定的情境中运用这些语言形式的能力。全书通过两个外国学生帕兰卡和古波在他们自己国家以及后来到中国学习汉语、跟中国朋友交往的情节，提供了一定的语言情境。第一册人物活动的场景不在中国——我们希望读者在他们自己国家的生活环境里也能进行汉语实践。

　　3．成年人学习外语，掌握必要的语音、语法规律并用来指导自己的语言实践，可以收到更好的效果。本书在强调语言实践的基础上，对基本的语音、语法知识也作了介绍。

　　4．要学好汉语，必须对中国的文化、历史和现实有所了解。本书（特别是从第二册开始）尽可能将语言和文化结合起来，通过有关中国社会、历史、名胜古迹、风土人情等题材学习汉语。

5. 每课的词汇、句型、扩展、语法、课文、阅读短文、练习等环节尽可能互相配合，加强词汇和句型的重现率。

由于学生的具体情况不同，教师在使用本教材时可根据教学对象的特点灵活掌握。教师可以全部或部分地使用书中所提供的材料，也可以自行确定教学环节的先后次序。

《实用汉语课本》的体例：

课文

大部分采用对话体，以利于基础阶段在听、说、读、写全面要求的基础上突出听和说的训练。

生词

除了必须掌握的生词外，每课的补充词供学生量力吸收。

注释

解释课文中的难句和某些词语的用法；补充说明已学的语法点；介绍必要的背景知识。有些难句中出现的新语法点，是以后将要重点学习的，本课只要求弄懂意思。

语音练习（前十二课）和语音语调

前十二课在学习会话和句型的同时，比较集中地进行语音和声调——重点是难音、难调——的训练，以打下较好的语音基础。第十二课以后，除继续巩固语音和声调外，还增加语调的练习。

会话练习（前十二课）和替换与扩展

在进行机械替换、能熟练地掌握基本句型的基础上，通过一定的情境扩展，进一步灵活运用所学句型。

语音（前十二课）和语法

介绍本课出现的主要语音点或语法点，不求全面系统，而是针对外国读者的难点和汉语本身的特点作必要的说明。每单元复习课中的语法小结，帮助读者归纳已学过的主要语法点。

阅读短文

重现已学过的词汇和句型，加强阅读练习并逐步培养口头、笔头成段表达的能力。

练习

通过各种练习形式，巩固主要语法点（包括每课注释部分介绍的一些词语用法）。希望读者充分利用本书的插图进行有情境的会话练习。

汉字

本书每课附有汉字笔顺表。在汉字练习本中对汉字的偏旁部首及字源、结构进行分析，并通过描写、临写等行之有效的办法帮助读者学习汉字。

《实用汉语课本》第一、二册在编写过程中得到北京语言学院汉语教师们很多帮助。我们期待使用本教材的国内外教师和读者提出宝贵意见，以便进一步修改这两册书并继续编写下一阶段教材。

本书的英文翻译：何培慧、熊文华、麦秀闲。插图：金亭亭、张志忠。

编　者
1981 年 2 月

3

INTRODUCTION

Practical Chinese Reader, with fifty lessons in its Book I & II, has been prepared for use with foreign learners in a course of elementary Chinese. It may also be used by foreigners who wish to teach themselves modern Chinese.

The *Reader* aims at enabling the learner to communicate in Chinese for everyday purposes, and at laying a solid foundation for further studies of the language. These aims are to be accomplished by means of pattern substitution, functional item drilling, grammatical analysis and various types of multiple-purpose exercises. The authors have tried to present the material through various effective foreign language teaching methods and in light of peculiarities of the Chinese language.

This course has been devised on the following principles:

1. The texts are prepared in standard, idiomatic modern Chinese in current use among native speakers; priority has been given to the most essential language items that the learner will need to express himself in Chinese in everyday social intercourse.

2. This course aims not only to teach the learner speech forms, but more importantly to enable him to use them freely in specific situations. The situations provided

centre around two foreign students, Palanka and Gubo, who studied Chinese first in their own country and then in China where they make friends with native speakers. Palanka and Gubo are represented in Book Ⅰ as living in other parts of the world, with a view to enabling the learner to use Chinese in his own country.

3. For adult learners it has proved profitable to their studies to observe carefully the basic rules of pronunciation and grammar. While the emphasis is on language practice, care has been taken to include information respecting Chinese phonetics and grammar.

4. In order to ensure good results in language study, some understanding of China's culture and history and present-day condition is neccessary. For this purpose, background information regarding Chinese society, history, scenic spots and historical sites, local customs and conditions has, where possible, been incorporated, especially in the texts of Book Ⅱ.

5. The vocabulary, sentence patterns and their extensions, grammar, texts, reading texts and exercises in each lesson are arranged in such a way as to ensure the recurrence of basic vocabulary and sentence patterns.

As students vary from place to place, the teacher is allowed considerable leeway to adapt the book to the needs of actual learners. He may use the whole or only part of the book, or change the order of presentation.

Guide to the Book:

TEXT—Most of the texts are written in the form of dialogues so as to facilitate audio-lingual practice while providing an overall grounding in elementary Chinese including reading and writing.

NEW WORDS—Apart from the required lexical items, an optional list of words and expressions is included in each lesson.

NOTES—Following each text are a number of notes that explain difficult sentences and expressions, give additional explanations about grammar items already covered and provide necessary background information. Some difficult sentences may contain grammar items that will be dealt with in later lessons, the students are merely required to understand these sentences.

PRONUNCIATION DRILLS (included in Lessons 1-12) & PRONUNCIATION and INTONATION—Apart from their focal task of providing practice in conversation and basic sentence patterns, the first twelve lessons contain a concentrated dose of drills in pronunciation and tones, with the emphasis on items that have proved difficult to foreign learners. This type of drill, which is meant to give the learner a reasonably good grounding in phonetics, continues through the rest of the lessons, with drills on intonation added.

CONVERSATION PRACTICE (included in Lessons 1-12) & SUBSTITUTION and EXTENSION—The mechanical

6

substitutional drills aim at giving the learner a proficient but formal mastery of the basic sentence patterns. These are followed by drills of a situational extension type, which aim at enabling the learner to use the sentence patterns with reasonable freedom.

PHONETICS (included in Lessons 1—12) & GRAMMAR—The phonetics and grammar items included in this book are not treated in an all-round and systematic manner, but are dealt with in a way that best solves the specific difficulties of the foreign learners; due attention has also been given to peculiarities of the Chinese language. The short grammatical summary included in the revision lesson following each unit recapitulates the items that have been taught up to that point.

READING TEXT—Texts of this kind are prepared to ensure the recurrence of some of the lexical items and sentence patterns already taught, and to develop the students' power of reading comprehension and consecutive speaking and writing.

EXERCISES—The various types of exercises are designed to consolidate the main grammar items covered, including the lexical items dealt with in the notes. It is hoped that students will make full use of the illustrations for situational oral practice.

CHARACTERS—A list of stroke-order of the characters is included in each lesson. The *Chinese Character Exercise Book* contains analyses of the components and structure of Chinese characters and etymological information, as well as various different types of character-writing exercises.

Grateful acknowledgements are due to teachers of the Beijing Languages Institute, who offered generous advice and assistance in the course of preparation of *Practical Chinese Reader* Book Ⅰ & Ⅱ. Teachers and students both at home and abroad are earnestly invited to offer criticisms and suggestions which will be invaluable to the revision of these two volumes and the preparation of future volumes.

These books are translated into English by He Peihui, Xiong Wenhua and Mei Xiuxian, and illustrated by Jin Tingting and Zhang Zhizhong.

Compilers
February 1981

8

目　录

CONTENTS

1

4

声　母 Initials　(z　c　s)

韵　母 Finals　ua　ia　iong

四、语　音 Phonetics

复韵母 Compound finals

5

day and hour

3. 名词谓语句 Sentences with a nominal predicate

六、语音语调 Pronunciation and Intonation

意群重音(2) Sense group stress (2)

一、课 文 Text 这束花儿真好看

二、注 释 Notes

助词"吧"(1) The modal particle "吧"(1)

副词"更" The adverb "更"

三、替换与扩展 Substitution and Extension

四、阅读短文 Reading Text 一张照片

五、语 法 Grammar

1. 形容词谓语句 Sentences with an adjectival predicate

2. 动词重叠 Reduplication of verbs

3. 动词、动词结构及双音节形容词作定语 Verbs, verbal constructions or disyllabic adjectives as attributives

六、语音语调 Pronunciation and Intonation

意群重音(3) Sense group stress (3)

词的重音(5) Word stress (6)

一、课 文 Text 后边有一个小花园

二、注 释 Notes

"的"字结构"作饭的" The "的" construction "作饭的"

三、替换与扩展 Substitution and Extension

四、阅读短文 Reading Text 古波的宿舍

五、语 法 Grammar

1. 方位词 Position words

2. 表示存在的句子 Sentences indicating existence

六、语音语调 Pronunciation and Intonation

10

12

action is going to take place in a short time

2. 语气助词"了"(2) The modal particle "了" (2)

3. 主谓谓语句 Sentences with a subject-predicate construction as its predicate

六、语音语调 Pronunciation and Intonation

句调 (5) Sentence tunes (5)

一、课 文 Text 布朗太太笑了

二、注 释 Notes

介词"离" The preposition "离"

代词"自己" The pronoun "自己"

三、看图说话 Talk About These Pictures

四、语法小结 A Brief Summary of Grammar

1. 四种句子 The four kinds of simple sentences

2. 动词谓语句(1) Sentences with a verbal predicate (1)

3. 动态助词"了"和语气助词"了"(1) The aspect particle "了" and the modal particle "了" (1)

4. 能愿动词 Optative verbs

第一课 Lesson 1

一、课文 Text

你 好

Pàlánkǎ: Gǔbō, nǐ hǎo!

Gǔbō, 你 好!

Gǔbō: Nǐ hǎo, Pàlánkǎ!
你 好, Pàlánkǎ!

生词 New Words

1. 你 (代) nǐ you (sing.)
2. 好 (形) hǎo good, well

专名 Proper Names

1. Gǔbō *a personal name*
2. Pàlánkǎ *a personal name*

二、注释 Notes

"你好!"

"How are you?" or "Good morning (good afternoon or good evening)."

这是汉语里常用的问候语，不论早上、中午、晚上见面时都可以用。对方的回答也是"你好"。

"你好" is a common greeting. It may be used in the morning, in the afternoon or in the evening. The answer to it from the person addressed is also "你好".

三、语音练习与会话练习
Pronunciation Drills and Conversation Practice

(一)

声母 Initials	b p g k h l n
韵母 Finals	a o l u ao an

2

1. 四声 The four tones

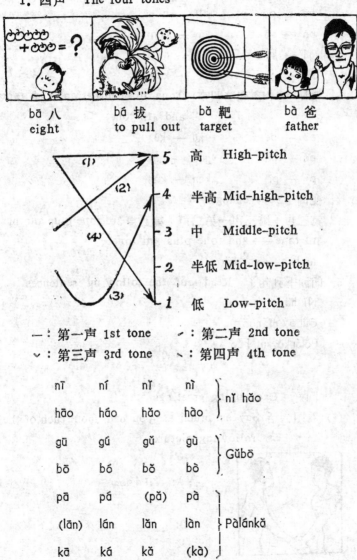

bā 八	bá 拔	bǎ 靶	bà 爸
eight	to pull out	target	father

5 高 High-pitch
4 半高 Mid-high-pitch
3 中 Middle-pitch
2 半低 Mid-low-pitch
1 低 Low-pitch

一: 第一声 1st tone ／: 第二声 2nd tone
ˇ: 第三声 3rd tone ＼: 第四声 4th tone

| nī | ní | nǐ | nì | ⎱ nǐ hǎo |
| hāo | háo | hǎo | hào | ⎰ |

| gū | gú | gǔ | gù | ⎱ Gǔbō |
| bō | bó | bǒ | bò | ⎰ |

pā	pá	(pǎ)	pà	⎱
(lān)	lán	lǎn	làn	⎬ Pàlánkǎ
kā	ká	kǎ	(kà)	⎰

3

2. 辨音　Sound discrimination

bō — pō　　　lǐ — nǐ

pà — bà　　　lán — nán

gǔ — kǔ　　　hǔ — gǔ

kǎ — gǎ　　　hǎ — kǎ

3. 辨调(第一声和第四声)　Tone discrimination　(1st tone and 4th tone)

bō — bò　　　kū — kù

pā — pà　　　gāo — gào

pī — pì　　　kān — kàn

4. 变调　Tone changes

第三声＋第三声→第二声＋第三声 3rd tone plus another 3rd tone —→ 2nd tone plus 3rd tone

nǐ hǎo —→ní hǎo

5. 朗读下列句子　Read out the following sentences

Nǐ hǎo.

Gǔbō, nǐ hǎo.

Pàlánkǎ, nǐ hǎo.

(二)

问好　Exchanging greetings

(1) 看图会话 Say as much as you can about each of the following pictures:

A:　Nǐ hǎo.

B:　_____.

A: _____ :

B: Nǐ hǎo。

(2) Pàlánkǎ 和 Gǔbō 互相问好 Imagine yourselves to be
Palanka and Gubo and greet each other
Gǔbō: Pàlánkǎ, nǐ hǎo| Pàlánkǎ: Nǐ hǎo, Gǔbō。
Pàlánkǎ: _____| Gǔbō: _____ 。

(3) 分组互相问好 Practise the greeting in pairs。

四、语音 Phonetics

1. 声母和韵母 Initials and finals

现代汉语普通话有 400 多个基本音节。汉语的音节大多数是
由声母和韵母拼合而成的，音节开头的辅音是声母，其余部分是
韵母。例如：ba, 其中 b 是声母，a 是韵母。

There are more than 400 basic syllables in the common
speech of modern Chinese. A syllable in Chinese is usually composed of an initial, which is a consonant that begins
the syllable, and a final, which covers the rest of the syllable. In the syllable "ba", for instance, "b" is an initial and
"a" is a final.

汉语的声母都是由一个辅音来充当的。汉语的韵母有的是单
元音（叫单韵母，如 a），有的是复合元音（叫复韵母，如 ao），
有的是元音加鼻辅音（叫鼻韵母，如 an）。

The initial of a Chinese syllable is always a consonant.

The final is a vowel, which may be a simple vowel (known as a "simple final", e.g. "a"), a compound vowel (known as a "compound final", e.g. "ao") or a vowel followed by a nasal consonant (known as a "nasal final", e.g. "an").

现代汉语共有 21 个声母， 38 个韵母。一个音节可以只有韵母，没有声母，但不能没有韵母。

In modern Chinese, there are altogether 21 initials and 38 finals. A syllable can stand without an initial, but no syllable will do without a final.

2. 发音要领 How to pronounce these initials and finals

声母 b[p] g[k] Initials b[p] and g[k]

是不送气清塞音，声带不振动。

These are both unaspirated plosives, and they are voiceless consonants, i.e., the vocal cords do not vibrate in pronouncing them.

声母 p[p'] k[k'] Initials p[p'] and k[k']

是送气清塞音，声带不振动，但必须用力吐出气流。

These are voiceless plosives, but they are aspirated, i.e., they are followed by a puff of suddenly released breath.

复韵母 ao[au] Compound final ao[au]

舌位由 a 向 o 方向自然移动。前面的 a 比单元音 a 舌位靠后，发得长而响亮；后面的 o 要念得轻、短、模糊，舌位也较高，介于 o 与 u 之间。

"ao" is produced by natully moving the tongue from "a" in the direction of "o". The tongue-position for "a" in "ao" is a little more to the back than that for the simple vowel "a". "a" is pronounced both longer and louder than "o", which is pronounced much less distinctly, with the tongue a little higher than in the case of the simple vowel "a".

鼻韵母 an[an] Nasal final an[an]

是一个舌尖鼻韵母。先发 a, 舌位比单元音 a 靠前, 紧跟着舌尖抵向齿龈, 同时软颚下垂, 让气流从鼻腔流出。

This is an alveolar nasal final, produced by pronouncing "a" first, with the tongue-position a little more to the front than in the case of the simple vowel "a", then raising the tip of the tongue against the gum and lowering the soft palate at the same time to let the air out through the nasal cavity.

3. 声调 Tones

汉语是有声调的语言。声调有区别意义的作用, 相同的音节, 声调不同意义也不同。北京语音有四个基本声调, 分别用声调符号"一 (第一声)、ˊ (第二声)、ˇ (第三声)、ˋ (第四声)"表示。

Chinese is a language with different tones that are capable of differenciating meanings. A syllable, when pronounced in a different tone, has a different meaning even if it is composed of the same initial and final. In the Beijing dialect there are four basic tones, represented respectively by the following tone-graphs: " — " (the 1st tone), " ˊ " (the 2nd tone), " ˇ " (the 3rd tone) and " ˋ " (the 4th tone).

当一个音节只有一个元音时, 声调符号标在元音上 (元音 I 上有调号时要去掉 I 上的点, 如 nǐ)。一个音节的韵母有两个或两个以上的元音时, 声调符号要标在其中的主要元音上, 即开口度最大的元音上, 如 hǎo。

When a syllable contains a single vowel only, the tone-graph is placed directly above the vowel sound. (The dot over the vowel "i" should be dropped if the tone-graph is placed above it, as in "nǐ".) When the final of a syllable is composed of two or more vowels (that is, when it is a diphthong or triphthong), the tone-graph should be placed above the main vowel (namely the one pronounced with the mouth widest open), e.g. "hǎo".

4. 变调　Tone changes

两个第三声紧密连在一起时，前一个音节应读成第二声（调号仍用"ˇ"），如 nǐ hǎo 的实际读音为 ní hǎo。

A 3rd tone, when immediately followed by another 3rd tone, should be pronounced in the 2nd tone, but with the tone-graph "ˇ" remaining unchanged. "nǐ hǎo", for example, becomes "ní hǎo" in actual pronunciation.

汉字笔顺表　Table of Stroke-order of Chinese Characters

1	你	亻	（ノ 亻）
		尔	（ノ ㇇）
		小	（亅 亅 小）
2	好	女	（㇛ 女 女）
		子	（㇇ 了 子）

8

The Chinese Language

What is usually referred to as Chinese is in fact the language of China's largest nationality, the Hans. It is the main language spoken in China and one of the world's major languages, ranking among the official as well as working languages at the United Nations and other international organs.

The Chinese language is one of the oldest languages in the world, its earliest written records going as far back as more than 3,000 years ago. During this long period of time, Chinese has seen constant development, but its grammar, vocabulary and writing system have in the main retained their basic features. What we propose to teach in this textbook is what is known as "the common speech", the kind of modern Chinese with "the Beijing speech sounds as the standard sounds, the Northern dialect as the basic dialect and modern classic works written in the vernacular as its grammatical models"

第二课 Lesson 2

一、课文 Text

你 好 吗

Gŭbō:　　Nǐ hǎo ma?
你 好 吗?

Pàlánkǎ:　Wǒ hěn hǎo, nǐ ne?
我 很 好, 你 呢?

Gŭbō:　　Yě hěn hǎo.
也 很 好。

生词 New Words

1. 吗　　（助）ma　　　*an interrogative particle*
2. 我　　（代）wǒ　　　I, me
3. 很　　（副）hěn　　　very
4. 呢　　（助）ne　　　*a modal particle*
5. 也　　（副）yě　　　also, too

二、注释 Notes

1.“你好吗？”

"How are you?"

这也是问候用语。回答一般是“我很好”之类的套语。

"你好吗？" is also a common greeting, and one of the commonly used answers is "我很好".

2.“你呢？”

"And (how are) you?"

3.“也很好。”

"(I'm) very well, too."

这个句子省略了主语“我”。汉语口语中当语言环境清楚时，主语常常省略。课文中的“我很好”也可省略为“很好”。

"也很好" is an elliptical sentence in which the subject "我" is omitted. In colloquial speech in Chinese, subjects of this kind are often omitted if the context leaves no room for misunderstanding. "我很好" in the text can also be further shortened to "很好".

11

三、语音练习与会话练习
Pronunciation Drills and Conversation Practice

(一)

```
声母  Initial   m
韵母  Finals    e  uo  ie  en
```

1. 四声 The four tones

nī   ní   nǐ   nì ⎤
hāo   háo   hǎo   hào ⎬ nǐ hǎo ma
mā   má   mǎ   mà ⎦

wō   wó   wǒ   wò

(nē)   né   (ně)   nè — nǐ ne

(hēn)   hén   hěn   hèn

yē   yé   yě   yè — yě hěn hǎo

2. 辨音 Sound discrimination

hé — hén   biē — piē
le — liè   bèn — pèn
kǎn — kěn   gē — kē
mō — māo   guò — kuò

3. 变调 Tone changes
半三声 Half 3rd tone   māo
Nǐ   ne?

12

Hǎo ma?

Gǔbō

三声变二声　A 3rd tone changing into a 2nd tone

Nǐ hǎo. (Ní hǎo.)

Hěn hǎo. (Hén hǎo.)

Wǒ hěn hǎo. (Wó hén hǎo.)

Yě hǎo. (Yé hǎo.)

Yě hěn hǎo. (Yé hén hǎo.)

(二)

问好　Exchanging greetings

(1) A: Nǐ hǎo ma?

B: _____, ___?

A: Yě hěn hǎo.

(2) A: Nǐ hǎo ma?

B: _____。

A: Gǔbō ne?

B: _____。

(3) A: Gǔbō hǎo ma?

B: _____。

A: Pàlánkǎ ne?

B: _____。

四、语音　Phonetics

1．发音要领　How to pronounce these finals

单韵母 e[ɤ]　Simple final e[ɤ]

是一个舌位半高、不圆唇的后元音。先发 o，舌位保持不变，然后唇由圆变扁，即可发出 "e"。

e[ɤ] is a back, unrounded vowel, formed with the tongue in a mid-high position. It is produced by pronouncing "o" first, then changing from lip rounding to lip spreading, but with the tongue-position remaining the same.

复韵母 ie[iɛ] Compound final ie[iɛ]

这里的 e 是另一个极少单独使用的单韵母 ê[ɛ]（口半开，嘴角展开，舌尖抵下齿背）。发 ie 时，先发 i，很快就滑向 ê。ê 比 i 更响亮、更长。

The "e" in "ie" is a simple final "ê" [ɛ] which is seldom used alone (with the mouth half-open, the corners of the mouth spread wide, the tip of the tongue against the back of the lower teeth). "ie" is produced by pronouncing "i" first, then promptly sliding in the direction of "ê", which is pronounced louder and longer than "i".

复韵母 uo[uo] Compound final uo[uo]

先发 u 音，很快滑向 o，o 比 u 要发得更响、更长。

It is produced by pronouncing "u" first, then promptly sliding in the direction of "o", which is pronounced louder and longer than "u".

2. 轻声 Neutral tone

普通话里有一些音节读得又轻又短，叫作轻声。轻声不标调号。如：Nǐ ne? Hǎo ma?

In the Chinese common speech there are a number of syllables which are unstressed and take a feeble tone. This is known as the neutral tone which is shown by the absence of a tone-graph, as in "Nǐ ne?" and "Hǎo ma?".

3. 半三声 Half 3rd tone

14

第三声在第一、二、四声和绝大部分轻声字前边时，要读成半三声，就是只读原来第三声的前一半降调。完全的第三声在实际语言中使用的机会较少（只有在单独念或后边有较大的停顿时才读第三声），大部分情况下都变为半三声。半三声仍用第三声调号。

A 3rd tone, when followed by a 1st, 2nd or 4th tone or most neutral tones, usually becomes a half 3rd tone, that is, the tone that only falls but does not rise. The 3rd tone is seldom used in full unless it occurs as an independent tone or when followed by a long pause. In most cases it is changed into a half 3rd tone, but with its tone-graph unchanged.

4．拼写规则 Rules of phonetic spelling

i 在一个音节开头时必须写成 y，如 ie→ye。i 单独成音节时要写成 yi，如 yī。

At the beginning of a syllable, "i" is written as "y", e.g. "ie→ye". "i" is written as "yi" when it forms a syllable all by itself, e.g. "yī".

u 在一个音节开头时必须写成 w，如 uo→wo。u 单独成音节时要写成 wu，如 wǔ。

At the beginning of a syllable, "u" is written as "w", e.g. "uo→wo". "u" is written as "wu" when it forms a syllable all by itself, e.g. "wǔ".

五、语法 Grammar

1．汉语的词序 The word order in a Chinese sentence

汉语语法的最大特点是没有人称、时态、性、数、格等形态变化。作为一种语法手段，词序起着非常重要的作用。

The Chinese language is characterized by its total lack of inflectional endings employed by other languages to express person, tense, gender, number and case. Word order, or the arrangement of words, in a sentence, is thus an extremely important means in expressing the various grammatical relationships.

汉语词序，一般都是主语在前，谓语在后。例如：

A Chinese sentence usually begins with the subject followed by the predicate. E.g.

你好。

我很好。

（我）也很好。

这三个句子的"你"、"我"是主语，"好"是谓语主要成分。副词"也"、"很"作状语，修饰谓语形容词"好"。副词必须放在它所修饰的词语（动词或形容词等）的前边。

In the three sentences above, "你" and "我" are the subjects while "好" is the main element of the predicates. The adverbs "也" and "好" function as adverbial adjuncts to qualify the predicative adjective "好". In Chinese, an adverb must precede what it qualifies (usually a verb or an adjective).

2．用"吗"的疑问句　Questions with the interrogative particle "吗"

在陈述句句尾加上表示疑问语气的助词"吗"，就成了汉语的一般疑问句，这种疑问句跟它的答句的词序完全一样。例如：

16

When the interrogative particle "吗" is added at the end of a declarative sentence, it becomes a general question. The word order of such a question is exactly the same as that of the answer to it. E.g.

你好。

你好吗？

我很好。

汉字笔顺表 Table of Stroke-order of Chinese Characters

1	吗	口 (丨 ㄇ 口)		嗎
		马 (ㄱ 马 马)		
2	我	ノ 二 于 手 我 我 我		
3	很	彳 (丿 彡 彳)		
		艮 (ㄱ コ ヨ 𠃜 艮 艮)		
4	呢	口		
		尼	尸 (ㄱ コ 尸)	
			匕 (ノ 匕)	
5	也	ㄱ 乜 也		

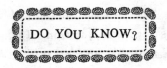

Chinese Characters

Chinese, which is formed of characters, is among the world's oldest written languages. Generally speaking, each character stands for a meaningful syllable. The total number of Chinese characters is estimated at more than 50,000 of which only 5,000—8,000 are in common use. Of these merely 3,000 are used for everyday purposes.

The Chinese characters in use today developed from the pictographs cut on oracle bones dating from over 3,000 years ago and the pictographs found on ancient bronze vessels dating a little later. In the course of their history of develop-

甲骨文	⊙	𝔇				
钟鼎文						
篆书						
隶书	日	月	火	水	羊	马
楷书	日	月	火	水	羊	马

18

ment, Chinese characters evolved from pictographs into characters formed of strokes, with their structures very much simpler. Most of the present-day Chinese characters are known as pictophonetic characters, each formed of two elements, with one indicating the meaning and the other the sound.

Chinese characters have made great contributions to the long history of the Chinese nation and Chinese culture, and Chinese calligraphy is a highly developed art. But Chinese characters have serious drawbacks. It is very difficult to learn, to read and to write and still more difficult to memorize. Reforms should be carried out to make the characters easier.

第三课 Lesson 3

一、课文 Text

你 忙 吗

Gǔbō: Nǐ máng ma?
你 忙 吗?

Pàlánkǎ: (Wǒ) bù máng.
（我）不 忙。

Gǔbō: Nǐ gēge hǎo ma?
你 哥哥 好 吗?

Pàlánkǎ: Tā hěn hǎo.
他 很 好。

Nǐ gēge、 nǐ dìdi hǎo ma?
你 哥哥、你 弟弟 好 吗?

Gǔbō: Tāmen dōu hěn hǎo.
他们 都 很 好。

生词 New Words

1. 忙　　　（形）máng　　　busy
2. 不　　　（副）bù　　　　not, no
3. 哥哥　　（名）gēge　　　elder brother
4. 他　　　（代）tā　　　　he, him
5. 弟弟　　（名）dìdi　　　younger brother
6. 他们　　（代）tāmen　　they, them
7. 都　　　（副）dōu　　　all

二、注释 Notes

1. "你哥哥好吗?"

汉语人称代词可以直接放在表示亲属的名词前作定语，表示领属关系。例如"你弟弟"、"我哥哥"、"他弟弟"等。

In Chinese, a personal pronoun can be put immediately before nouns indicating family relationships as an attributive to show possession, e.g. "你弟弟", "我哥哥" and "他弟弟" etc.

2. "他们都很好。"

"They are all very well."

"都"必须放在主语之后，谓语动词或形容词之前。副词"都"不能放在主语前，不能说"都他们很好"。

The adverb "都" must follow the subject but precede the predicative verb or predicative adjective. It is never found before the subject and it is wrong to say "都他们很好"。

三、语音练习与会话练习
Pronunciation Drills and Conversation Practice

(一)

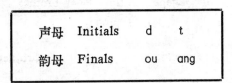

声母	Initials	d	t
韵母	Finals	ou	ang

1. 四声　The four tones

  gē　　gé　　gě　　gè —— gēge

  dī　　dí　　dǐ　　dì —— dìdi

  tā　　tá　　tǎ　　tà ⎫
  mēn　mén　(měn)　mèn ⎭ tāmen

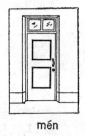

mén

  (māng) máng　mǎng　(màng) —— bù máng

  dōu　dóu　dǒu　dòu —— dōu hěn hǎo

2. 辨音　Sound discrimination

  dì — tì　　　　　kē — gē

  dā — tā　　　　　kǒu — gǒu

  bǎng — pǎng　　　tōu — dōu

  bù — pù　　　　　hěn — kěn

3. 辨调(第四声和第二声) Tone discrimination (4th tone
　　　　　　　　　　　　　　and 2nd tone)

22

dì — dí   mò — mó
bù — bú   tàng — táng
mèn — mén   hòu — hóu

4. 变调——半三声 Tone changes—half 3rd tone

nǐ gēge   wǒ gēge
nǐ dìdi   wǒ dìdi
Nǐ máng ma?   Wǒ bù máng.

5. 四声和轻声 The four tones and neutral tone

Nǐ gēge hǎo ma?   Tā gēge máng ma?
Tā dìdi hǎo ma?   Nǐ dìdi máng ma?
Tāmen hǎo ma?   Tāmen máng ma?

(二)

问候 Exchanging greetings

(1) A: Nǐ hǎo ma?
    B: _____。

    A: Nǐ gēge hǎo ma?
    B: _____。

    A: Tā máng ma?
    B: _____。

    A: Nǐmen dōu máng ma?
    B: _____。

(2) A: Nǐ dìdi máng ma?
    B: _____。

    A: Tā hǎo ma?
    B: _____。

    A: Nǐ dìdi yě hǎo ma?

B: _____.

A: Tāmen dōu hǎo ma?

B: _____.

(3) A: Nǐ máng ma?

B: _____.

A: Pàlánkǎ máng ma?

B: _____.

A: Pàlánkǎ hǎo ma?

B: _____.

(4) A: Nǐ hǎo!

B: _____!

A: Nǐ máng ma?

B: _____._____?

A: Yě bù máng.

A: _____?

B: Hěn máng. Nǐ ne?

A: _____.

A: Gǔbō máng ma?

B: _____.

A: Pàlánkǎ ne?

B: _____.

(5) A: Tā gēge hǎo ma?

B: _____.

A: Tā dìdi ne?

B: _____.

四、语音 Phonetics

1. 发音要领 How to pronounce these finals

复韵母 ou[əu] Compound final ou[əu]

前面的 o 不象单发 o 音时唇那么圆，要念得长而响亮，后面的 u 要念得轻、短、模糊，嘴唇也比单发 u 时要放松些。

In pronouncing the "o" in "ou", the lips are not so rounded as in the case of the simple final "o". Moreover, "o" is pronounced long and loud whereas "u" is pronounced light, short and somewhat indistinct with the lips a little laxer than for the simple final "u".

鼻韵母 ɑng[aŋ] Nasal final ɑng[aŋ]

这是一个舌根鼻韵母。先发舌位靠后一点的 ɑ，紧跟着舌头往后缩，舌根抵向软腭，同时软腭下垂，让气流从鼻腔里出来。

ɑng[aŋ] is a velar nasal final. It is produced by pronouncing "ɑ" first, with the tongue-position a little more to the back, then promptly retracting the tongue backward, with the root of the tongue against the soft palate, and lowering the soft palate at the same time to let the air out through the nasal cavity.

2. 送气音和不送气音 The aspirated and unaspirated

声母 b, p, d[t], t[t'], g, k（和以后将要学到的 zh, ch; j, q; z, c）是几组相对应的不送气音和送气音。每组两个辅音的发音部位完全一样，只是在发 p, t, k（以及 ch, q, c）时气流用力吐出，称为"送气音"，而发 b, d, g（以及 zh, j, z）时气流爆发而出，不送气，称为"不送气音"。读者在发音时可用一张小纸片放在嘴前边，试验有无气流喷出。

The unaspirated "b" and aspirated "p" are pronounced in exactly the same manner as regards tongue-positions. So are "d"[t] and "t"[t'], "c" and "k" (and "zh" and "ch", "j" and "q" and "z" and "c" to be introduced in later lessons): The only difference is that, in pronouncing the aspirated "p, t, k (and ch, q and c as well)", the air is puffed out strongly, whereas with the unaspirated "b, d, g (and zh, j and z)" the air is let out with a pop through the lips. Learners can put a small piece of paper in front of the mouth to see if the puffing is properly done or not.

注意：汉语不送气音也是清辅音，发音时声带不振动。

Note that in Chinese, the unaspirated are also voiceless consonants. The vocal cords do not vibrate when they are pronounced.

五、语法 Grammar

形容词谓语句 Sentences with an adjectival predicate
谓语主要成分是形容词的句子叫形容词谓语句，如：

A sentence in which the main element of the predicate is an adjective is known as a sentence with an adjectival predicate. E.g.

我很好。

他很忙。

他们都很好。

26

形容词谓语句的否定形式是在形容词前加上否定副词"不"，如："我不忙。"

Sentences of this kind are made negative by putting the adverb "不" before the predicative adjective, as in "我不忙"：

*

名词或代词 Nouns or pronouns	副　词 Adverbs	形　容　词 Adjectives	助　词 Particle
我 你 我	很 不	好。 好 忙。	吗？

* 本书语法部分的表格，只归纳了基础阶段常用的句式。

Tables in the grammar sections of this book include only those sentence patterns dealt with in the initial stage.

汉字笔顺表　Table of Stroke–order of
Chinese Characters

1	忙	忄 （丶 丶 忄）	
		亡 （丶 ㇗ 亡）	
2	不	一 フ 不 不	
3	哥	可 （一 ㅜ 可）	
		可	
4	他	亻	
		也	
5	弟	丷 （丶 丷）	
		弔 （㇀ ㇕ 弓 弔 弟）	
6	们	亻	們
		门 （丶 丨 门）	
7	都	者 丿 （一 ㅓ 土 耂）	
		日 （丨 冂 冃 日）	
		阝 （㇌ 阝）	

28

第 四 课 Lesson 4

一、课文 Text

这 是 我 朋 友

Pàlánkǎ: Zhè shì wǒ bàba.

这 是 我 爸爸。

Zhè shì wǒ māma.

这 是 我 妈妈。

Zhè shì wǒ péngyou—Gǔbō.

这 是 我 朋友—Gǔbō。

Gǔbō: Nǐmen hǎo!

你们 好！

Bàba: Nǐ hǎo!
Māma:

你 好！

生词 New Words

1. 这 (代) zhè this
2. 是 (动) shì to be
3. 朋友 (名) péngyou friend
4. 爸爸 (名) bàba father
5. 妈妈 (名) māma mother
6. 你们 (代) nǐmen you (pl.)

二、注释　Notes

1. "这是我爸爸。"

   "This is my father."

   给别人作介绍时常用"这是……"（"是"字轻读）。如果是自我介绍，就说"我是……"。

   The expression "这是…" is usually used to introduce one person to another, and the expression "我是…" is used when one introduces oneself. "是" in both expressions is pronounced light.

2. "你们好。"

   如果对方不止一个人，向他们问好时用"你们好"。

   "你们好" is used to greet more than one person.

三、语音练习与会话练习
Pronunciation Drills and Conversation Practice

(一)

声母	Initials	zh	sh	
韵母	Finals	-i[ʅ]	Iou(-Iu)	eng

1. 四声和轻声 The four tones and neutral tone

   zhē　zhé　zhě　zhè ⎫
   shī　shí　shǐ　shì ⎬ zhè shì
   bā　bá　bǎ　bà —— bàba

mā   má   mǎ   mà —— māma

pēng   péng   pěng   pèng } péngyou
yōu   yóu   yǒu   yòu

2. 辨音 Sound discrimination

zhēn — zhēng   dàng — dēng

shuō — shōu   zhǐ — zhě

liú — lóu   shé — shí

3. 辨调(第二声和第一声) Tone discrimination (2nd tone and 1st tone)

péng — pēng   shé — shē

zhí — zhī   zhóu — zhōu

shéng — shēng   shén — shēn

4. 变调——半三声 Tone changes—half 3rd tone

wǒ māma   nǐ māma

wǒ gēge   nǐ gēge

wǒ péngyou   nǐ péngyou

wǒ dìdi   nǐ dìdi

wǒ bàba   nǐ bàba

wǒmen   nǐmen

hǎo ma   nǐ ne

5. 朗读下列词语：Read out the following phrases:

tā māma   tā péngyou

tā bàba   tā hǎo

(二)

1. 辨认人或物 Identifying people or objects

Gǔbō: Zhè shì wǒ bàba,

zhè shì wǒ māma.

Pàlánkǎ: Zhè shì tā bàba,

zhè shì tā māma.

Gǔbō: _____,

_____.

Pàlánkǎ: _____,

_____.

A: _____.

B: _____.

2. 给别人介绍 Introducing one person to another

A: Zhè shì _____.

Zhè shì _____.

B: Nǐ hǎo!

C: Nǐ hǎo!

3. 向别人介绍自己 Introducing oneself

A: Nǐ hǎo, wǒ shì _____.

33

B: Nǐ hǎo, wǒ shì＿＿＿＿＿＿＿＿＿。

4. 问好 Greeting each other

(1)

A: ＿＿＿＿＿＿＿＿。

B: ＿＿＿＿＿＿＿＿。

A: ＿＿＿＿＿＿＿＿。

B.C.D: ＿＿＿＿＿＿＿＿。

(2) Nǐ bàba máng ma?
Wǒ bàba hěn máng。

māma
péngyou

(3) A: Nǐ bàba hǎo ma?
B: Tā hěn hǎo.
A: Nǐ māma ne?
B: Tā yě hěn hǎo。

gēge,	dìdi
māma,	péngyou
dìdi,	péngyou

(4) A: Nǐ máng ma?
B: Wǒ bù máng。
A: Nǐ péngyou máng ma?
B: Tā ＿＿＿＿ bù máng。
A: Nǐ gēge、nǐ dìdi ne?
B: Tāmen ＿＿＿＿ bù máng。

34

四、语音　Phonetics

发音要领 How to pronounce these initials and finals

声母 zh[tʂ] Initial zh[tʂ]

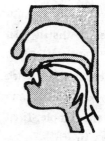

是舌尖后阻不送气的清塞擦音。发音时舌尖一定要上卷，顶住硬腭前端，气流从舌尖与硬腭间冲开一条窄缝，摩擦而出。声带不振动。

The initial zh [tʂ] is a blade-palatal, unaspirated voiceless affricate. It is produced by curling the tip of the tongue and raising it against the front part of the hard palate, allowing a narrow opening between the tongue-tip and the hard palate for the air to squeeze out. The vocal cords do not vibrate in pronouncing it.

声母 sh[ʂ] Initial sh[ʂ]

是舌尖后阻的清擦音，发音时舌尖上卷接近硬腭前端，形成缝隙，气流摩擦而出。声带不振动。

The initial sh[ʂ] is a blade-palatal voiceless fricative. It is produced by curling the tip of the tongue and raising it to the hard palate, leaving a narrow opening between them to allow the air to squeeze out through it. The vocal cords do not vibrate in pronouncing it.

单韵母 -i [ʅ] Simple final -i [ʅ]

zh, sh（及下两课将要学到的 ch, r）等声母后面的舌尖后元

音韵母 [ɿ]，用字母 I 来表示（为跟 I[i]区别，单写时可写作 "-I"）。在读 zhI, shI 等音节时要注意：当发出前边的辅音后，舌头不要移动，不要把 -I 读成单韵母 I[i]。单韵母 I 永远不能出现在 zh, ch, sh, r 之后。

The letter "I" is used to stand for the blade-palatale vowel [ɿ] after the initials "sh, zh" (and "ch" and "r" to be introduced in the next two lessons).In order to distinguish the simple final "I[ɿ]" from the simple final "I[i]", "I[ɿ]" is written as "-I" when it stands alone. In pronouncing such syllables as "zhI" and "chI", the tongue is kept still, and care must be taken not to pronounce it as the simple final "I[i]" which is never found after "zh, ch, sh" or "r";

复韵母 Iou[iau] Compound final Iou[iau]

舌位由 I 降到 o，再由 o 升到 u。iou 在跟声母相拼时简写为 Iu，调号标在后一元音上，如 IiÚ。

The compound final "Iou[iau]" is produced by first lowering the tongue from the position of "I" to that for "o", then raising the tongue fom the position of "o" to that of "u". The compound final "Iou" is written as "Iu" when it comes after an initial and the tone-graph is placed on the last element, e.g. "IiÚ".

汉字笔顺表 **Table of Stroke-order of Chinese Characters**

1	这	文 (丶 一 亠 文)	這
		辶 (丶 讠 辶)	

2	是	日	
		疋 (一 丁 下 开 疋)	
3	爸	父 (ˊ ˋ ハ ク 父)	
		巴 (フ 刀 コ 巴)	
4	妈	女	媽
		马	
5	朋	月 ( ) 刀 月 月)	
		月	
6	友	𠂇 (一 𠂇)	
		又 (フ 又)	

*   *   *

DO YOU KNOW?

Scheme for the Chinese Phonetic Alphabet

"The Scheme for the Chinese Phonetic Alphabet", which was adopted at the First Plenary Session of the First National People's Congress of the People's Republic of China on February 21, 1958, is a set of symbols used to transliterate Chinese characters and combine the speech sounds of the com-

37

mon speech into syllables. The scheme makes use of the Latin alphabet, modified to meet the needs of the Chinese language. The scheme, which will form the foundation for the creation of a Chinese alphabetic system of writing, is being used throughout the country to facilitate the learning of Chinese characters, help unify pronunciation and popularize the common speech. The scheme has for years been used among foreign learners of Chinese as well and has been found much useful and helpful.

第 五 课 Lesson 5

一、课文 Text

你 妈 妈 是 大 夫 吗

Gǔbō:　　Zhè　shì　nǐ　de　chē　ma?
这　是　你　的　车　吗？

Pàlánkǎ:　Zhè　bú　shì　wǒ　de　chē,
这　不　是　我　的　车，

zhè shì wǒ māma de chē.

这 是 我 妈妈 的 车。

Gǔbō: Nà shì tā de shū ma?

那 是 她 的 书 吗?

Pàlánkǎ: Nà shì tā de shū.

那 是 她 的 书。

Gǔbō: Nǐ māma shì dàifu ma?

你 妈妈 是 大夫 吗?

Pàlánkǎ: Shì, tā shì dàifu.

是, 她 是 大夫。

生词 New Words

1. 大夫　　(名) dàifu　　doctor
2. 的　　　(助) de　　　*a structural particle*
3. 车　　　(名) chē　　　vehicle
4. 那　　　(代) nà　　　that
5. 她　　　(代) tā　　　she, her

6. 书　　　(名) shū　　　　　book

1. bào　　　　(名)　　　　newspaper
2. zhǐ　　　　(名)　　　　paper
3. chǐ　　　　(名)　　　　ruler
4. bǐ　　　　(名)　　　　pen, pencil, writing brush

二、注释　Notes

1. "这是你的车吗？"

"Is this your car?"

"车"是各种车辆的总称。在一定的语言环境里，也可以具体指汽车、火车、自行车等。本课是指小汽车。

"车" is a general term for land vehicles of all kinds. In different context, it may refer to a motor-car, a train or a bicycle. In the present lesson "车" refers to a sedan.

2. "那是她的书吗？"

"Is that her book?"

第三人称"tā"有两个汉字：一个是"他"，代表男性；一个是"她"，代表女性。

In Chinese, there are two different characters for the singular third person pronoun "tā": one is "他" denoting a male person, the other is "她" denoting a female person. Both "他" and "她" are sounded exactly the same.

三、语音练习与会话练习
Pronunciation Drills and Conversation Practice

(一)

声母	Initials	(zh)	ch	(sh)	f
韵母	Final	ɑi			

1. 四声 The four tones

chē   ché   chě   chè

bū   bú   bǔ   bù ——— bú shì

nā   ná   nǎ   nà

shū   shú   shǔ   shù

dāi   dái   dǎi   dài

fū   fú   fǔ   fù   } dàifu

2. 辨音 Sound discrimination

zhǐ — chǐ   bǐ — pǐ

bào — pào   gāi — kāi

zhái — chái   chóu — shóu

3. 辨调（第四声和第一声） Tone discrimination (4th
                                    tone and 1st tone)

chè — chē   chǐ — chī

dài — dāi   fèn — fēn

shù — shū   chàng — chāng

4. 变调——半三声和轻声 Tone changes — half 3rd tone
                                    and neutral tone

nǐ de shū   nǐmen de chē
wǒ de shū   wǒmen de chē
tā de shū   tāmen de chē

5. 朗读下列句子：Read out the following sentences:

(1) A: Nǐ gēge shì dàifu ma?

B: Wǒ gēge bú shì dàifu,

wǒ péngyou shì dàifu.

(2) A: Nà shì nǐ de shū ma?

B: Nà bú shì wǒ de shū,

nà shì wǒ dìdi de shū.

(二)

1. 辨认人或物 Identifying people or objects

(1) A: Zhè shì shū ma?

B: _____。

A: Nà shì bǐ ma?

B: _____。

A: Nà shì bào ma?

B: _____

(2) A: Zhè shì nǐ de chē ma?
    B: Zhè bú shì wǒ de chē.
       Zhè shì tā de chē.

shū	bǐ
chǐ	zhǐ

(3) A: Nà shì tā gēge ma?
    B: Nà bú shì tā gēge.
       Nà shì tā péngyou.

dìdi
bàba

(4) A: Tā shì nǐ péngyou ma?
    B: Tā bú shì wǒ péngyou.
       Tā shì wǒ māma de péngyou.

gēge
dìdi
bàba

2. 询问职业 Asking about someone's occupation
    A: Nǐ shì dàifu ma?
    B: Shì, wǒ shì dàifu.

tā	tāmen
nǐmen	nǐ bàba

四、语音 Phonetics

1. 发音要领 How to pronounce the initial and final
声母 ch [tʂʻ]   Initial ch [tʂʻ]
是跟 zh相对的送气音。

44

The initial "ch[tʂʻ]" is the correspondent aspirated to the unaspirated "zh".

复韵母 ɑi[ai] Compound final ɑi[ai]

前面的 ɑ 比单发 ɑ 时的舌位偏前，是个前元音，要念得长而响亮。后面的 i 要念得轻、短、模糊。

The compound final "ɑi[ai]" is produced by first articulating "ɑ", a front vowel pronounced long and loud with the tongue-position a little more to the front than for "ɑ" as an independent final, then gliding in the direction of "i" which is pronounced light, short and somewhat indistinct.

2．"不"的声调　Tones of "不"

"不"单用或在第一、二、三声前读第四声，在第四声（或由第四声变来的轻声）前读第二声，如：bù máng, bù hǎo, bú shì。

"不" is pronounced in the 4th tone when it stands by itself or precedes a 1st, 2nd or 3rd tone, but is pronounced in the 2nd tone when it precedes another 4th tone (or a neutral tone that is originally a 4th tone), e.g. "bù máng", "bù hǎo", "bú shì".

五、语法　Grammar

1．"是"字句(1)　"是" sentence type (1)

动词"是"和其它词或短语一起构成谓语的句子叫"是"字句，"是"字一般轻读。"是"字句的否定形式是在"是"前加"不"。

A sentence in which the predicate is made up of the verb "是" and one other word or phrase is known as a "是" sentence. In a "是" sentence, the verb "是" is usually pronounced light. Such a sentence is made negative by putting "不"

in front of "是".

名词或代词 Nouns or pronouns	副　词 Adverb	动词"是" Verb "是"	名词或代词 Nouns or pronouns	助　词 Particle
这 这 那	不	是 是 是	你的车 我的车。 她的书。	吗?

2. 表领属关系的定语　Attributives showing possession

代词、名词作定语表示领属关系时，后面要加结构助词"的"。如"你的车"、"她的书"、"妈妈的车"。

When a noun or a pronoun is used attributively to show possession, it must take after it the structural particle "的", as in "你的车", "她的书" and "妈妈的车".

人称代词作定语，如果中心语是表示亲友等社会关系或集体、单位等的名词时，定语后可以不用"的"。如"我爸爸"、"你哥哥"。

When a personal pronoun is used attributively to show possession, it is used without "的" if the qualified word denotes a family relationship or a unit of which the speaker (or the person spoken to or of) is a member, e.g. "我爸爸", "你哥哥".

定语一定要放在它所修饰的中心语的前边。

In Chinese, an attributive must precede what it qualifies.

46

汉字笔顺表 Table of Stroke-order of Chinese Characters

1	的	白（′ 亻 白 白 白）	
		勺（′ 勹 勺）	
2	车	一 𠂉 左 车	車
3	那	月（丁 ㇇ 习 月）	
		阝	
4	她	女	
		也	
5	书	㇕ ㇆ 书 书	書
6	大	一 ナ 大	
7	夫	一 二 夫 夫	

第六课 Lesson 6

一、课文 Text

他是哪国人

Pàlánkǎ: Nà shì shéi?

那 是 谁?

Gǔbō: Nà shì wǒmen lǎoshī.

那 是 我们 老师。

Pàlánkǎ: Tā shì nǎ guó rén?

他 是 哪 国 人?

Gǔbō: Tā shì Zhōngguó rén.

他 是 Zhōngguó 人。

Pàlánkǎ: Tā shì Hànyǔ lǎoshī ma?

他 是 汉语 老师 吗?

Gǔbō: Tā shì Hànyǔ lǎoshī.

他 是 汉语 老师。

生词 New Words

1. 哪　　　(代) nǎ　　　　which
2. 国　　　(名) guó　　　country, state
3. 人　　　(名) rén　　　person
4. 谁　　　(代) shéi　　　who
5. 我们　　(代) wǒmen　　we, us
6. 老师　　(名) lǎoshī　　teacher
7. 汉语　　(名) Hànyǔ　　Chinese (language)

专名　Proper Names

Zhōngguó　　　　　　　China

补充词　Supplementary Words

1. Déguó　　　　(专名)　　Germany
2. Fǎguó　　　　(专名)　　France
3. Měiguó　　　　(专名)　　the United States of America
4. Mǎlǐ　　　　　(专名)　　Mali
5. Rìběn　　　　　(专名)　　Japan

二、注释　Notes

1. "那是谁?"

   "Who is that person?"

2. "他是哪国人?"

   "What's his nationality?"

3. "他是 Zhōngguó 人。"

   "He is a Chinese."

汉语里表示"某国人"一般在国名后加"人"。

To express the idea of "a certain person of a certain nationality", Chinese requires the addition of the word "人" to the name of the country.

4. "他是汉语老师吗?"

   "Is he a teacher of Chinese?"

"汉语老师"是指"教汉语的老师"。

"汉语老师" means "a teacher who teaches Chinese".

三、语音练习与会话练习
Pronunciation Drills and Conversation Practice

(一)

声母 Initials (zh ch sh) r

韵母 Finals u ei ong

1. 四声 The four tones

zhōng zhóng zhǒng zhòng ⎫
guō   guó   guǒ   guò   ⎬ Zhōngguó rén
(rēn) rén   rěn   rèn   ⎭

hān   hán   hǎn   hàn ⎫
yū   yú   yǔ   yù ⎬ Hànyǔ

lāo   láo   lǎo   lào —— lǎoshī

2. 辨音 Sound discrimination

bēi — pēi

lái — léi

rǎo — shǎo

nǔ — nǔ

lù — lù

róng — réng

zhǐ — chǐ — shǐ — rǐ

zhè — chè — shè — rè

3. 辨调（第一声和第二声）Tone discrimination (1st tone and 2nd tone)

guō — guó   tōng — tóng

rāng — ráng   fēi — féi

chōng — chóng   yū — yú

4. 变调——半三声和轻声 Tone changes——half 3rd tone and neutral tone

wǒmen lǎoshī   wǒ gēge

nǐmen lǎoshī   nǐ dìdi

tāmen lǎoshī   tā péngyou

5. 朗读下列词语：Read out the following words and phrases:

nǎ guó rén   Měiguó rén

Déguó rén   Mǎlǐ rén

Fǎguó rén   Rìběn rén

Zhōngguó rén

（二）

1. 辨认人或物 Identifying people or objects

(1)

A: Tā shì shéi?

B: _____.

A: Tā shì shéi?

B: _____.

A: Tā shì shéi?　　　　A: Tā shì shéi?

B: ＿＿＿＿＿＿。　　　B: ＿＿＿＿＿＿。

(2) A: Nà shì shéi?

B: Nà shì wǒmen lǎoshī.

nǐmen	tāmen
Hànyǔ	Zhōngguó

2. 询问国籍 Asking about nationalities

(1)

A: Tā shì nǎ guó rén?　　A: ＿＿＿＿＿＿?

B: ＿＿＿＿＿＿。　　　B: Tā shì Rìběn rén.

A: Tā shì nǎ guó rén?　　A: Tā shì nǎ guó rén?

B: ＿＿＿＿＿＿＿＿.　　B: ＿＿＿＿＿＿＿＿。

(2) A: Nǐ hǎo.

　　B: Nǐ hǎo.

　　A: Nǐ shì nǎ guó rén?

　　B: Wǒ shì ＿＿＿＿＿rén. Nǐ ne?

　　A: Wǒ shì ＿＿＿＿＿rén.

(3) A: Nǐ shì nǎ guó rén?

　　B: Wǒ shì ＿＿＿＿＿rén.

　　A: Tā yě shì ＿＿＿＿＿rén ma?

　　B: Tā yě shì ＿＿＿＿＿rén.

　　A: Nǐmen dōu shì ＿＿＿＿＿rén ma?

　　B: Wǒmen dōu shì ＿＿＿＿＿rén.

四、语音　Phonetics

1. 发音要领 How to pronounce these initial and finals

声母 r[ʐ] Initial r[ʐ]

发音部位跟 sh 一样，但 r 是浊擦音，有轻微摩擦，声带振动。

The initial "r[ʐ]" is a voiced fricative, pronounced in the same way as "sh", but with a very slight friction. The vocal cords vibrate.

单韵母 ü[y] Simple final ü[y]

先发 i 音，舌位保持不变，然后将嘴唇撮成小圆孔，就能发出 ü。

The simple final "ü[y]" is produced by first articulating "i", then rounding and protruding the lips as much as possible, leaving a very small opening, but with the tongue kept still.

复韵母 ei[ei] Compound final ei[ei]

前边的 e 读 [e]，念得长而响亮，后边的 i 念得轻、短、模糊。

The "e" in "ei" is pronounced as [e]. "e" is pronounced both long and loud whereas "i" is pronounced light, short and indistinct.

鼻韵母 ong[uŋ] Nasal final ong[uŋ]

先发 o，开口度比单元音 o 略小，接近 u 的发音，紧跟着舌头后缩，舌根抵向软腭，同时软腭下垂，让气流从鼻腔出去。

The nasal final "ong[uŋ]" is produced by first pronouncing "o", with the opening of the mouth somewhat smaller than in the case of the simple vowel "o" but about the same as for "u", then promptly retracting the tongue backward to press the back of the tongue against the soft palate and lowering the soft palate at the same time to let the air out through the nasal cavity.

2. 拼写规则 Rules of phonetic spelling

ü 自成音节或在一个音节开头时，写成 yu，如 Hànyǔ。

When forming a syllable by itself or when occuring at the beginning of a syllable, "ü" is written as "yu", as in "Hànyǔ".

汉字笔顺表 Table of Stroke-order of Chinese Characters

1	哪	口						
		那						
2	国	囗	冂 国 国					國
		玉 （一 二 干 王 玉）						
3	人	丿 人						
4	谁	讠 （丶 讠）						誰
		隹 （亻 亻 伫 仹 仹 隹 隹）						
5	老	耂						
		匕						
6	师	刂 （丿 刂）						師
		帀	一					
			巾 （丨 冂 巾）					
7	汉	氵 （丶 冫 氵）						漢
		又						

56

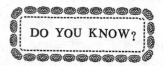

8	语	讠		語
		吾	五 (一 丁 丐 五)	
			口	

China's Dialect Areas

The Chinese language has eight major dialects. The eight dialect areas are: North China (for the Northern dialect), Jiangsu-Zhejiang (for the Wu dialect), Hunan (for the Hunan dialect), Jiangxi (for the Jiangxi dialect), Kejia (for the Kejia dialect, a form of Chinese spoken by descendants of northerners who moved to Guangdong and nearby provinces centuries ago), northern Fujian (for the northern Fujian dialect), southern Fujian (for the southern Fujian dialect) and Guangdong (for the Yue, another name of Guangdong Province, dialect). Of all the Chinese-speaking population, about 70% speak the Northern dialect, which is the reason why it has been made the basis of the common speech.

The vocabulary and grammar are basically the same in all the dialects, the chief difference being in pronunciation. In order to remove barries caused by dialectal differences and to facilitate and bring about a further political, cultural and economic development, a nation-wide campaign has been started to popularize the common speech.

第七课 Lesson 7

一、课文 Text

这是什么地图

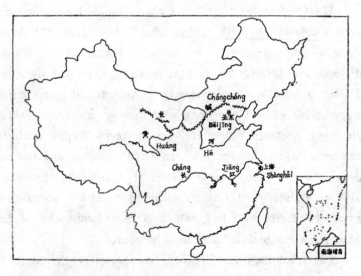

Zhè shì shéi de dìtú?

这 是 谁 的 地图？

Zhè shì Gǔbō de dìtú.

这 是 Gǔbō 的 地图。

Zhè shì shénme dìtú?

这 是 什么 地图？

Zhè shì Zhōngguó dìtú.

这 是 Zhōngguó 地图。

Nǐ kàn, zhè shì Běijīng, nà shì Shànghǎi.

你 看, 这 是 Běijīng, 那 是 Shànghǎi。

Zhè shì Cháng Jiāng ma?

这 是 Cháng Jiāng 吗？

Bú shì, zhè shì Huáng Hé, nà shì Cháng Jiāng.

不 是, 这 是 Huáng Hé, 那 是 Cháng Jiāng。

Zhè shì shénme?

这 是 什么？

Zhè shì Chángchéng.

这 是 Chángchéng。

生词　New Words

1. 什么　（代）shénme　　what
2. 地图　（名）dìtú　　map
3. 看　（动）kàn　　to see, to look, to have a look, to read, to watch

专名　Proper Names

1. Běijīng　　Beijing

2. Shànghǎi   Shanghai
3. Cháng Jiāng   the Changjiang (Yangtze) River
4. Huáng Hé   the Huanghe (Yellow) River
5. Chángchéng   the Great Wall

补充词 Supplementary Words

1. shìjiè   (名)   world
2. Ōu Zhōu   (专名)   Europe
3. Fēi Zhōu   (专名)   Africa
4. Dàyáng Zhōu   (专名)   Oceania
5. Nán Měi Zhōu   (专名)   South America

二、注释 Notes

1. "这是谁的地图?"
   "Whose map is this?"
2. "这是什么地图?"
   "What map is this?"
3. "你看。"
   "Look (you)."

三、语音练习与会话练习
Pronunciation Drills and Conversation Practice

(一)

声母 Initial	j		
韵母 Finals	ing	iang	uang

1. 四声　The four tones

jīng　　jíng　　jǐng　　jìng　——　Běijīng

jiāng　　jiáng　　jiǎng　　jiàng　——　Cháng Jiāng

huāng　　huáng　　huǎng　　huàng　——　Huáng Hé

chāng　　cháng　　chǎng　　chàng　——　Chángchéng

shēn　　shén　　shěn　　shèn　——　shénme

2. 辨音　Sound discrimination

bīng — pīng　　　　láng — liáng

zhuāng — chuāng　　rén — réng

bǎo — pǎo　　　　　dōu — diū

kōng — gōng　　　　nán — náng

tiē — diē　　　　　yǔ — wǔ

guò — kuò　　　　　máng — méng

3. 辨调（第二声和第三声）Tone discrimination (2nd tone and 3rd tone)

chuáng — chuǎng　　hái — hǎi

fáng — fǎng　　　　méi — měi

yáng — yǎng　　　　jié — jiě

4. 变调　Tone changes

(1) nǐ hǎo　　　　　(3) nǐ de chē

　　hěn hǎo　　　　　　　wǒ de dìtú

　　yě hǎo

(2) nǐ dìdi　　　　　(4) nǎ guó rén

　　wǒ péngyou　　　　　 Fǎguó rén

　　wǒmen lǎoshī　　　　 Měiguó rén

　　nǐmen lǎoshī

(二)

1. 辨认人或物 Identifying people or objects

(1)

 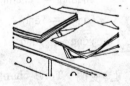

A: Zhè shì shénme?　　A: Nà shì shénme?

B: Zhè shì _____ 。　　B: Nà shì _____ 。

(2) A: Zhè shì shéi de chē?

B: Zhè shì <u>wǒ</u> de chē.

tā	dàifu
lǎoshī	tā péngyou

(3) A: Nà shì shénme dìtú?

B: Nà shì Zhōngguó dìtú.

Běijīng	Fēi Zhōu
shìjiè	Dàyáng Zhōu
Ōu Zhōu	Nán Měi Zhōu

2. 询问职业、国籍 Asking about occupations and nationalities

(1) 回答下列问题: Answer the following questions:

Pàlánkǎ shì shéi?

Pàlánkǎ de māma shì lǎoshī ma?

Nà shì Pàlánkǎ de chē ma?

Nà shì shéi de chē?

Tā shì lǎoshī ma?

Shéi shì nǐmen lǎoshī?

Hànyǔ lǎoshī shì Měiguó rén ma?

Hànyǔ lǎoshī shì nǎ guó rén?

(2) 朗读下列对话: Read out the following dialogue:

A: Nǐ máng ma?

B: Bù máng, nǐ ne?

A: Wǒ hěn máng. Nǐ bàba、māma hǎo ma?

B: Tāmen dōu hěn hǎo.

A: Nà shì shéi?

B: Nà shì Pàlánkǎ de bàba.

A: Tā yě shì dàifu ma?

B: Bú shì, tā shì lǎoshī.

A: Tā shì shéi?

B: Tā shì Gǔbō de lǎoshī.

A: Tā shì Zhōngguó rén ma?

B: Shì, tā shì Zhōngguó rén.

(3) 看图进行对话（用上括号内的词）：Make up dialogues on each of the following pictures, using the words given in brackets:

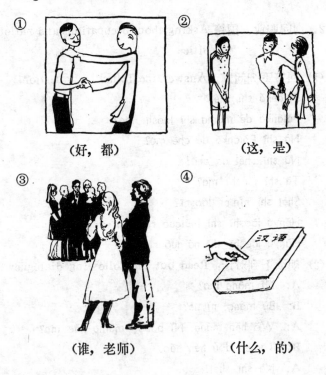

① （好，都）

② （这，是）

③ （谁，老师）

④ （什么，的）

四、语音 Phonetics

发音要领 How to pronounce the initial

64

声母 j[tɕ] Initial j[tɕ]

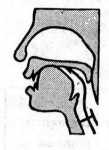

舌面前部贴紧硬腭,舌尖顶下齿背,然后气流冲开一条窄缝摩擦而出。声带不振动。

The initial j[tɕ] is produced by first raising the front of the tongue to the hard palate and pressing the tip of the tongue against the back of the lower teeth, then loosing the tongue to let the air squeeze out through the channel between the tongue and hard palate. The vocal cords do not vibrate in pronouncing this sound.

五、语法 Grammar

1. 用疑问代词的问句 Questions with an interrogative pronoun

汉语用疑问代词的问句,其词序跟陈述句一样。把陈述句中需要提问的部分改成疑问代词,就成了疑问句。例如:

In Chinese, a question with an interrogative pronoun has the same word order as that of a declarative sentence. Questions of this kind can be formed by substituting an interrogative pronoun for the word or phrase in the declarative sentence to be asked about. E.g.

他是 Gŭbō。——他是谁?

她是大夫。——谁是大夫?

这是书。——这是什么?

65

那是我的书。——那是谁的书？

他是 Zhōngguó 人。——他是哪国人？

2. 代词 Pronouns

人　称　代　词 Personal pronouns	疑问代词 Interrogative pronouns	指示代词 Demonstrative pronouns
我　你　他　她 我们 你们 他们 她们	谁什么哪	这　那

汉字笔顺表 Table of Stroke–order of Chinese Characters

1	什	亻				
		十（一 十）				
2	么	丿	厶	么		麼
3	地	土	（一 十 土）			
		也				
4	图	囗				圖
		冬	夂	（丿 ク 夂）		
			冫	（丶 冫）		

66

| 5 | 看 | 手 (一 二 三 手) |
| | | 目 (丨 冂 冃 目 目) |

*   *   *

DO YOU KNOW?

Beijing, Shanghai, the Changjiang (Yangtze) River, the Huanghe (Yellow) River and the Great Wall

Beijing is the capital of the People's Republic of China, the country's chief political, economic and cultural centre.

Shanghai is China's biggest city, and her largest industrial centre as well.

The Changjiang (Yangtze) River, whose total length is 6,300 kilometres, is the longest river in China and one of the longest rivers in the world.

The Huanghe (Yellow) River is the second largest with a total length of 5,464 kilometres. The Huanghe valley was the cradle of the ancient Chinese civilization.

The Great Wall, which was built over 2,000 years ago, is one of the world's wonders in ancient architecture. Its total length is more than 2,500 kilometres, but quite a number of places are made up of several walls, the actual length comes to over 6,000 kilometres (more than 12,000 *li*). And for this reason it is also known as the "Great Wall of Ten Thousand *li*).

第八课 Lesson 8

一、课文 Text

请 喝 茶

Gǔbō:　Wáng Lǎoshī, nín hǎo!
　　　　王　老师，　您　好！

Wáng:　Nǐ hǎo, qǐng jìn!
　　　　你　好，请　进！

Gǔbō: Zhè shì wǒ

这 是 我

péngyou—Pàlánkǎ.

朋友—Pàlánkǎ。

Wáng: Huānyíng, huānyíng.

欢迎，欢迎。

Qǐng hē chá.

请 喝 茶。

Pàlánkǎ: Xièxie.

谢谢。

Wáng: Bú kèqi. Nǐ xī yān ma?

不 客气。你 吸 烟 吗？

Pàlánkǎ: Wǒ bù xī yān.

我 不 吸 烟。

生词 **New Words**

1. 请 (动) qǐng   please

2. 喝 (动) hē   to drink

3. 茶 (名) chá   tea

4. 您 (代) nín   *polite form of "你"*

5. 进 (动) jìn   to enter, to come in

6. 欢迎	(动) huānyíng	to welcome
7. 谢谢	(动) xièxie	to thank
8. 客气	(形) kèqi	polite, courteous
9. 吸烟	xī yān	to smoke

专名 Proper Names

Wáng   *a surname*

补充词 Supplementary Words

1. kāfēi	(名)	coffee
2. píjiǔ	(名)	beer
3. niúnǎi	(名)	milk
4. xiānsheng	(名)	Mr., sir, gentleman
5. tàitɑi	(名)	Mrs., madame

二、注释 Notes

1. "Wáng 老师, 您好!"

汉语的习惯, 姓氏必须放在称呼的前边。如"王大夫"、"丁
先生"。

In Chinese, the surname precedes instead of following
any form of address, e.g. "Wáng Dàifu", "Dīng Xiānsheng (Mr.
Ding)".

"您"是第二人称代词"你"的尊称。通常对老年人或长辈讲话
称"您", 如"您好"。为了表示礼貌, 对与自己年龄相仿的人, 特

70

别是在初次见面时也可用"您"称呼。

"您" is the polite form of the pronoun for the second person singular "你". It is normally used to address one's elders and betters, as in "您好". For the sake of politeness or courtesy it is also used to address someone of one's own age, especially when meeting him or her for the first time.

2．"请进！"

"Come in, please."

"请……"是一种比较客气的表示请求的用语。

"请…" is an expression of polite request.

3．"不客气。"

别人对自己表示感谢时可以回答"不客气"。

"不客气" is used in polite reply to expressions of thanks from others.

4．"你吸烟吗？"

"Do you smoke?"

三、语音练习与会话练习
Pronunciation Drills and Conversation Practice

（一）

声母 Initials	(j)	q	x
韵母 Finals	in	ian	uan

1．四声　The four tones

qīng	qíng	qǐng	qìng
jīn	jín	jǐn	jìn

} qǐng jìn

xiē	xié	xiě	xiè——xièxie

xī	xí	xǐ	xì
yān	yán	yǎn	yàn

} xī yān

kē	ké	kě	kè
qī	qí	qǐ	qì

} kèqi

huān	huán	huǎn	huàn
yīng	yíng	yǐng	yìng

} huānyíng

2. 声调组合 Combinations of tones

" — " + " — "	" — " + " ╱ "	" — " + " ╲ "
xī yān	Zhōngguó	qiānbǐ (pencil)
kāfēi	huānyíng	tīngxiě (to have dictation)

" — " + " ╲ "	" — " + " o * "
jīqì (machine)	tāmen
jīngjù (Beijing opera)	xiānsheng

3. 变调——半三声 Tone changes——half 3rd tone

qǐng jìn

qǐng hē chá

---

* "o" 在本课及以后各课的"声调组合"中都代表轻声。

"o" in the "Combinations of Tones" of this lesson and the later lessons stands for the neutral tone.

qǐng xī yān

4. 读下列双音节词语： Read out the following disyllabic
words:

kàn jiàn (to see)　　xiūxi (to rest)

niánqīng (young)　　qǐ chuáng (to get up)

xǐhuan (to like)　　shíxí (to practise)

diànyǐng (film, movie)　　duànliàn (to take exercise)

yínháng (bank)　　jīnnián (this year)

5. 多音节连读： Try to pronounce the following polysyl-
lables in quick succession:

Wǒ niàn.　　(I'll read it.)

Nǐmen tīng.　　(You'll listen, please.)

Gēn wǒ niàn.　　(Read it after me.)

Qǐng nǐ niàn.　　(You please read it.)

Hěn hǎo.　　(Very good.)

(二)

招待客人 Entertaining a guest

(1) A: Wáng Lǎoshī, nín hǎo！

B: Huānyíng, huānyíng.

Qǐng jìn！

Wáng Dàifu
Qián Tàitai
Jīn Xiānsheng

(2) A: Nín hē shénme?

B: Wǒ hē kāfēi.

chá　　niúnǎi
píjiǔ

73

(3) A: Jīn Xiānsheng, qǐng hē chá.

B: Xièxie.

A: Bú kèqi.

> kāfēi
> píjiǔ

(4) A: Nǐ xī yān ma?

B: Xièxie, wǒ bù xī(yān).

> hē chá   hē píjiǔ
> hē niúnǎi

(5) A: Wáng Lǎoshī shì nǎ guó rén?

B: Wáng Lǎoshī shì Zhōngguó rén.

> Wáng Dàifu
> Jīn Lǎoshī
> Jiāng Xiānsheng

四、语音 Phonetics

1. 发音要领 How to pronounce these initials

声母 q[tɕʻ] Initial q[tɕʻ]

是跟 j 相对的送气音。

The initial "q[tɕʻ]" is the correspondent aspirated to the unaspirated "j".

声母 x[ɕ] Initial x[ɕ]

74

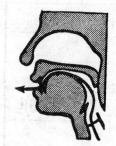

x

舌面前部靠近硬腭，形成一条窄缝，气流摩擦而出。声带不振动。

The initial "x[ɕ]" is produced by raising the front of the tongue to (but not touching) the hard palate leaving a narrow opening through which the air escapes causing audible friction. The vocal cords do not vibrate in producing this sound.

2．拼写规则 Rules of phonetic spelling

in，ing 自成音节时分别写成 yin，ying。

When forming syllables by themselves, "in" and "ing" are written as "yin" and "ying" respectively.

汉字笔顺表 Table of Stroke–order of Chinese Characters

1	请	讠		请
		青	圭（一 二 圭 圭）	
			月（丿 刀 月 月）	
2	喝	口		
		曷	日（丨 冂 日 日）	
			匃（丿 勹 勹 匃 匃）	
3	茶	艹（一 十 艹）		

75

		余	人	
			示（一 千 示 示）	
4	您	你		
			心（丶 心 心 心）	
5	进	井（一 二 丰 井）		進
		辶		
6	欢	又		歡
		欠	ケ（丿 ケ）	
			人	
7	迎	卬	丨（丶 丨）	
			卩（丁 卩）	
		辶		
8	谢	讠		謝
		射	身（丿 亻 门 门 自 身 身）	
		寸（一 十 寸）		
9	客	宀（丶 丷 宀）		
		各	夂	
			口	
10	气	丿 仁 仨 气		氣

76

11	吸	口	
		及 (ノ 乃 及)	
12	烟	火 (丶 丿 丷 火)	煙
		因 口	
		大	

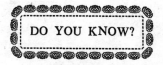

DO YOU KNOW?

The Complex and Simplified Forms
of Chinese Characters

The ultimate aim of the reform being carried out in the Chinese writing system is to gradually replace the ideograms with a phonetic writing system. Before this can be done, the characters should first of all be simplified and the number of strokes of the characters reduced so as to relieve much of the burden of both users and learners of Chinese. The simplification of Chinese characters is twofold: reduction of the number of the characters (mainly through the elimination of the complex variants) and reduction of the nuwber of the strokes of which a complex character is composed (by the popularization of the simplified characters).

This simplification conforms entirely to the general tendency of development of the Chinese characters towards greater simplicity. The simplified forms, as compared with their complex equivalents, are much easier to learn, to memorize, to read and to write. A very few examples will help to show the advantages of the simplified over the complex forms: "们(們)", "妈(媽)", "欢(歡)" and "进(進)". The simplified forms used in this textbook are all among those published by the Government of the People's Republic of China. (For the readers' convenience, the original complex eduivalents of the simplified characters are also given in the book.)

第九课 Lesson 9

一、课文 Text

您 贵 姓

Pàlánkǎ: Qǐngwèn, nín shì Zhōngguó rén ma?

请问, 您 是 Zhōngguó 人 吗?

Dīng Yún: Shì, wǒ shì Zhōngguó liúxuéshēng.

是, 我 是 Zhōngguó 留学生。

Pàlánkǎ: Nín guì xìng?

您 贵 姓?

Dīng Yún: Wǒ xìng Dīng, wǒ jiào Dīng Yún:

我 姓 Dīng, 我 叫 Dīng Yún。

Pàlánkǎ: Wǒ jiào Pàlánkǎ, shì Wàiyǔ Xuéyuàn de

我 叫 Pàlánkǎ, 是 外语 学院 的

xuésheng. Wǒ xuéxí Hànyǔ.

学生。 我 学习 汉语。

生词 New Words

1. 贵姓   guì xìng   What's your name? May I ask your name?

2. 请问 (动) qǐngwèn   May I ask…?

    问   (动) wèn   to ask

3. 留学生 (名) liúxuéshēng   a student who studies abroad

4. 姓   (动、名) xìng   (one's) surname is…, surname

80

5. 叫	(动)	jiào	to call, to be called
6. 外语	(名)	wàiyǔ	foreign language
7. 学院	(名)	xuéyuàn	college, institute
8. 学生	(名)	xuésheng	student
9. 学习	(动)	xuéxí	to study, to learn
学	(动)	xué	to study, to learn

专名 Proper Names

Dīng Yún   *a personal name*

补充词 Supplementary Words

1. xiǎojie	(名)	miss
2. nǚshì	(名)	*a polite form of address to a woman*, lady, madam
3. tóngzhǐ	(名)	comrade
4. Cháoxiǎn	(专名)	Korea
5. Yīngguó	(专名)	Britain

二、注释 Notes

1. "请问"

"May I ask…?" or "Excuse me, but…."

这是向别人提出问题时的一种客气的套语。

It is a polite form of inquiry, used to ask someone

something.

2．"您贵姓?"

"What's your surname?"

这是询问对方姓氏的一种客气的提问法。回答时可以只说自己的姓"我姓……"，也可以说自己的全名"我叫……"。

It is a polite way of asking someone's surname. The person thus asked may give just his or her surname, i.e. "我姓…" or his or her name in full, i.e. "我叫…".

3．"我姓 Dīng, 我叫 Dīng Yún。"

"My surname is Ding, and my name is Ding Yun."

三、语音练习与会话练习
Pronunciation Drills and Conversation Practice

(一)

声母	Initials	(j	q	x)
韵母	Finals	iao		
		uei (-ui)	uai	uen (-un)
		üe	üan	ün

1．四声 The four tones

jiāo   jiáo   jiǎo   jiào

xīng   xíng   xǐng   xìng

wēn   wén   wěn   wèn — qǐngwèn

guī   guí   guǐ   guì — guì xìng

xuē   xué   xuě   xuè ⎫
shēng   shéng   shěng   shèng ⎬ xuésheng

liū   liú   liǔ   liù — liúxuéshēng

wāi   wái   wǎi   wài — wàiyǔ

yuān   yuán   yuǎn   yuàn — xuéyuàn

xī   xí   xǐ   xì — xuéxí

2. 声调组合 Combinations of tones

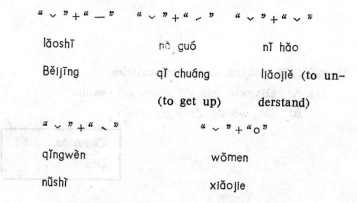

"ˇ" + "ˉ"   "ˇ" + "ˊ"   "ˇ" + "ˇ"

lǎoshī   nǎ guó   nǐ hǎo

Běijīng   qǐ chuáng   liǎojiě (to un-

                  (to get up)   derstand)

"ˇ" + "ˋ"   "ˇ" + "o"

qǐngwèn   wǒmen

nǚshì   xiǎojie

3. 读下列双音节词 Read out the following dissyllabic words:

juéxīn (determination)   yuànyì (to be willing)

yúkuài (happy, pleasant)   huídá (to answer)

wèntí (question, problem)   yīnyuè (music)

zhǔnbèi (to prepare)   jiàoshì (classroom)

kèwén (text)   Lǔ Xùn (Lu Xun)

4. 多音节连读 Try to pronounce the following poly-syllables in quick succession:

niàn kèwén (to read aloud the text)

kàn kèwén (to read the text)

wèn wèntí (to ask questions)

huídá wèntí (to answer questions)

Wǒ wèn. (I'll ask a question.)

Nǐmen huídá. (You answer it.)

Duì bu duì? (Is it right or wrong?)

Duì. (It is right.)

(二)

1. 询问国籍 Asking about nationalities

  (1) A: Qǐngwèn, nín shì <u>Zhōngguó</u> rén ma?

  B: Shì, wǒ shì Zhōngguó rén.

Cháoxiǎn	Mǎlǐ
Déguó	

  (2) A: Qǐngwèn, nín shì <u>Rìběn</u> rén ma?

  B: Bù, wǒ shì <u>Zhōngguó</u> rén.

Zhōngguó,	Cháoxiǎn
Fǎguó,	Yīngguó
Yīngguó,	Měiguó

2. 询问姓名 Asking about surnames and names

  (1) A: Qǐngwèn dàifu, nín guì xìng?

  B: Wǒ xìng_____, jiào_____。

  A: Wǒ jiào_____。

```
xiǎojiě        nǚshì
xiānsheng   tóngzhì
tàitai
```

(2) A: Qǐngwèn, nín shì <u>Wáng Xiānsheng</u> ma?

    B: Shì.

    A: Nín hǎo.

```
Dīng Xiǎojiě   Wáng Nǚshì
Jīn Lǎoshī     Zhāng Tóngzhì
```

(3) A: Tā xìng shénme?   A: Tā jiào shénme?

    B: Tā xìng_____.   B: Tā jiào_____。

四、语音 Phonetics

1. 发音要领 How to pronounce the compound final
复韵母 üe[yɛ] Compound final üe[yɛ]

先发 ü 然后很快滑向 ê，注意 ê 比 ü 更响亮、更长。

The compound final "üe [yɛ]" is produced by articulat-ing "ü" first, then promptly gliding to "ê". "ê" should be pronounced much louder and longer than "ü".

2. 拼写规则 Rules of phonetic spelling

uei, uen 前面加声母时写成 ui, un。ui 跟声母相拼，调号标在 i 上。

"uei" and "uen", when preceded by an initial, are writ-ten as "ui" and "un" respectively. When "ui" comes after an initial, the tone-graph is placed above "i".

ü及由ü开头的韵母和 j, q, x 相拼时，ü上的两点省去,如:
xuéxí。

When "ü" and the finals that begin with "ü" appear after "j", "q" or "x", "ü" is written as "u", with the two dots omitted, e.g. "xuéxí":

汉字笔顺表 Table of Stroke-order of Chinese Characters

1	贵	中 (丶 冂 口 中)		貴
		一		
		贝 (丨 冂 贝 贝)		
2	姓	女		
		生 (丿 ㇛ 二 牛 生)		
3	问	门		問
		口		
4	留	𠂊 (丿 ㇇ ㇇)		
		刀 (𠃌 刀)		
		田 (丨 冂 曰 田 田)		
5	学	䒑 (丶 丷 丷 䒑)		學
		子		
6	生			

7	叫	口		
		丩（乚 丩）		
8	外	夕（ノ ㇏ 夕）		
		卜（丨 卜）		
9	院	阝		
	完	宀		
		元（一 二 テ 元）		
10	习	乛 习 习		習

第十课 Lesson 10

一、课文 Text

她住多少号

Pàlánkǎ: Qǐngwèn, Dīng Yún
请问，Dīng Yún

zài ma?
在 吗？

Zhōngguó Tā bú zài, qǐng
xuésheng: 她不在，请

zuò.
坐。

Pàlánkǎ: Xièxie. Tā zài
谢谢。她在

nǎr?
哪儿？

Zhōngguó Tā zài sùshè.
xuésheng: 她在宿舍。

Pàlánkǎ: Tā zhù duōshao hào?
她住多少号？

Zhōngguó	Sìcéng	sìèrsān	hào:

Zhōngguó xuésheng: 四层 四二三 号。

Pàlánkǎ: Xièxie nǐ.

谢谢 你。

* * *

líng	yī	èr	sān	sì	wǔ

〇 一 二 三 四 五

生词 New Words

1. 在 (动、介) zài to be at (a place), in, at

2. 坐 (动) zuò to sit, to take a seat

3. 哪儿 (代) nǎr where

4. 宿舍 (名) sùshè dormitory

5. 住 (动) zhù to live

6. 多少 (代) duōshao how many, how much, what

7. 号 (名) hào number

8. 四 (数) sì four

9. 层 (量) céng *a measure word*, storey

10. 二 (数) èr two

11. 三 (数) sān three

12. ○	（数）líng	zero
13. 一	（数）yī	one
14. 五	（数）wǔ	five

补充词 Supplementary Words

1. yīyuàn	（名）	hospital
2. cèsuǒ	（名）	toilet, latrine, lavatory, W.C.
3. zhèr	（代）	here
4. nàr	（代）	there

二、注释　Notes

1. "Dīng Yún 在吗?"

    "Is Ding Yun here?"

    这里"在"是动词。

    "在" here is a verb.

2. "她住多少号?"

    "What's her room number?"

3. "四层四二三号。"

    "No. 423, 3rd floor."

    按中国习惯，楼的层数从地面上第一层算起。

    By the Chinese reckoning, the different storeys of a building are numbered from the very ground level up.

三、语音练习与会话练习

Pronunciation Drills and Conversation Practice

(一)

声母 Initials	z	c	s
韵母 Finals	-ı[ı]	er	

1. 四声 The four tones

zāı	(záı)	zǎı	zàı	—	zàı ma
zuō	zuó	zuǒ	zuò	—	qǐng zuò
cēng	céng	(cěng)	cèng		
sī	sí	sǐ	sì	—	sì céng
sū	sú	(sǔ)	sù	—	sù shè
sān	sán	sǎn	sàn		
(ēr)	ér	ěr	èr		
duō	duó	duǒ	duò		} duōshao
shāo	sháo	shǎo	shào		

2. 声调组合 Combinations of tones

" ╱ " + " — "　　　　　" ╱ " + " ╱ "　　　　　" ╱ " + " ╲ "

Cháng Jiāng　　　　xuéxí　　　　　　Cháoxiǎn

túshū(books)　　　　Chángchéng　　　cáichǎn

　　　　　　　　　　　　　　　　　　　(property)

91

" ˊ " + " ˋ "   " ˊ " + "o"

xuéyuàn   péngyou
búcuò (not bad)   érzi

3. 韵母 er 和儿化韵 Final "er" and retroflex final

èr	érzi (son)
nǎr	ěrduo (ear)
nǎr	nǚ'ér (daughter)
zhèr	wánr (to play)

4. 读下列双音节词 Read out the following dissyllabic words:

zìjǐ (self)   cuòwu (mistake, error)

qúnzi (skirt)   cóngcǐ (from now on)

xǐzǎo (to take a bath)   cānguān (to visit)

qīzi (wife)   Hànzì (Chinese character)

shēngcí (new word)   Sūlián (the Soviet Union)

5. 多音节连读 Try to pronounce the following polysyl-lables in quick succession:

shuō Hànyǔ (to speak Chinese)

niàn shēngcí (to read aloud new words)

xiě Hànzì (to write Chinese characters)

tīng lùyīn (to listen to recordings)

zuò liànxí (to do exercises)

fānyì jùzi (to translate sentences)

jiǎng yǔfǎ (to explain grammar)

Dǒng bu dǒng? (Do you understand?)

Dǒng. (Yes, I do.)

(二)

1. 找人 Asking for someone

   (1) A: Dīng Yún zài ma?

       B: Zài. Qǐng jìn.

| Wáng Nǚshì |
| Dīng Xiǎojie |
| Jīn Dàifu |

   (2) A: Qǐngwèn, Dīng Yún zài ma?

       B: Tā bú zài.

       A: Tā zài nǎr?

       B: Tā zài sùshè.

| yīyuàn |
| xuéyuàn |
| nàr |

2. 问住址 Asking about addresses

   (1) A: Nǐ zhù nǎr?

       B: Wǒ zhù zhèr.

       A: Nǐ zhù duōshao hào?

       B: Wǒ zhù sìcéng sìsān'èr hào.

```
2 — 201
èr—èrlíngyī
4 — 425
sì—sìèrwǔ
```

(2) A: Nín guì xìng?

    B: Wǒ xìng Dīng, jiào Dīng Yún。

    A: Nín zhù nǎr?

    B: Wǒ zhù <u>yīèrwǔ hào</u>。

```
422
sìèrèr
124
yīèrsì
```

3. 问路 Asking the way

    A: Qǐngwèn, <u>Wàiyǔ Xuéyuàn</u> zài nǎr?

    B: Zài nàr.

```
sùshè
yīyuàn
cèsuǒ
```

四、语音 Phonetics

1. 发音要领 How to pronounce these initials and finals

    声母 z[ts] Initial z[ts]

94

z

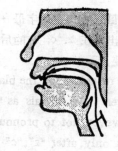

舌尖平伸，抵上齿背，然后气流冲开一条窄缝，摩擦而出。声带不振动。

The initial "z[ts]" is produced by first pressing the tip of the tongue against the back of the upper teeth, then lowering it to let the air squeeze out through the narrow opening thus made. It is unaspirated. The vocal cords do not vibrate when producing this sound.

声母 c[ts'] Initial c[ts']

c

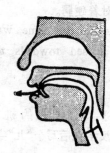

是跟 z 相对应的送气音。

The initial "c[ts']" is an aspirated consonant corresponding to the unaspirated "z".

声母 s[s] Initial s[s]

s

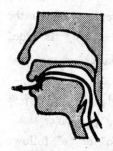

舌尖靠近上齿背，构成窄缝，气流摩擦而出，声带不振动。

The initial "s[s]" is produced by pressing the tip of the tongue to (but not against) the back of the upper teeth, forming a narrow opening through which the air escapes causing audible friction. The vocal cords do not vibrate when producing it.

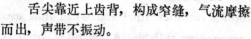

95

单韵母 -ı [ʅ] Simple final -ı[ʅ]

z, c, s 等声母后面的舌尖前元音韵母 [ʅ]，也用字母 -ı 来表示（注意，不要把它读成 [i]）。它只出现在 z, c, s 的后边。不能跟任何其他声母相拼，也不能单独使用。

The letter "-i" is sometimes used to stand for the blade-alveolar vowel [ʅ] when it occurs after such initials as "z", "c" and "s". (Care must be taken, however, not to pronounce "-i" as [i].) The sound "-i[ʅ]" comes only after "z", "c" and "s". It never comes after any other initials, nor does it occur as an independent final.

单韵母 er[ər] Simple final er[ər]

在发出单元音 e[ə] 时，把舌头卷起来对着硬腭。

The simple final "er[ər]" is produced in the same way as "e", but with the tongue curled and raised towards the hard palate.

2. 儿化韵 Retroflex final

韵母 er 有时跟其他韵母结合成儿化韵母。儿化韵母的拼写法是在原韵母之后加 "r"，汉字写法是在原汉字之后写个 "儿" 字，如 wánr（玩儿）。

The final "er" is sometimes attached to another final to form a retroflex final and when thus used, it is no longer an independent syllable. A retroflex final is represented by the letter "r" added to the final. In actual writing, "儿" is added to the character in question, as in "wánr（玩儿）"：

3. 拼写规则 Rules of phonetic spelling

a, o, e 开头的音节连接在其他音节后面时，为了使音节界限清楚，不致混淆，要用隔音符号 " ' " 隔开，例如 nǚ'er。

When a syllable beginning with "a", "o" or "e" follows

another syllable in such an ambiguous way that division of the two syllables could be confused, it is essential to put a dividing mark " ' " in between, e.g. "nǚ'er".

五、语法 Grammar

动词谓语句 Sentences with a verbal predicate

谓语的主要成分是动词的句子叫动词谓语句。动词谓语句的一种否定形式是在动词前加上副词"不"，表示"经常不"、"不愿意"、"将不"等意思。

A sentence with a verbal predicate is one in which the main element of the predicate is a verb. One way to make such a sentence negative is to put the adverb "不" before the predicative verb, indicating "One does not, will not do something or is not willing to do something":

名词或代词 Nouns or pronouns	副　词 Adverb	动　词 Verbs	助　词 Particle
Dīng Yún （她） 她	 不	在 在。 在。	吗？

动词如果带有宾语，宾语一般在动词的后边。

The object, if the verb takes one, usually comes after the verb.

名词或代词 Nouns or pronouns	副　词 Adverb	动　词 Verbs	名词或代词 Nouns or pronouns	助　词 Particle
你		吸	烟	吗？
我	不	吸	烟。	
我		学习	汉语。	
我		叫	Pàlánkǎ。	

汉字笔顺表 Table of Stroke-order of Chinese Characters

1	在	犭（一 ナ 犭）			
		土（一 十 土）			
2	坐	人			
		人			
		土			
3	儿	丿 儿			兒

98

4	宿	宀			
		佰	亻		
			百	一	
				白	
5	舍	人			
		舌	千	（一 二 千）	
			口		
6	住	亻			
		主	（、 一 二 午 主）		
7	多	夕	（ノ ク 夕）		
		夕			
8	少	丨 丨 小 少			
9	号	口			號
		丂	（一 丂）		
10	四	丨 冂 四 四 四			
11	层	尸			層
		云	（一 二 云 云）		
12	二	一 二			
13	三	一 二 三			

14	○	
15	一	
16	五	

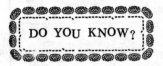

DO YOU KNOW?

China's Minority Nationalities
and Their Languages

China is a country of many nationalities, with 94% of her population belonging to the Han nationality. Apart from the Hans, there are more than 50 other nationalities such as the Monggols (Mongolians), the Huis, the Zangs (Tibetans), the Uygurs (Uighurs), the Miaos, the Yis, the Zhuangs, the Buyis, the Koreans, the Mans (Manchus) and the Gaoshans.

All of China's minority nationalities have languages of their own(some have their own written languages) with the exception only of the Hui, Man and She nationalities who use Chinese or the language of the Hans. The Chinese Constitution stipulates that all the nationalities of China have the freedom to use and further develop their spoken and written languages. In order to rapidly develop the culture and education of the minority nationalities, the government has helped the Zhuang, Miao, Jingpo and other minority nationalities to devise their own written languages based on the Latin alphabet or to improve their existing writing system.

cation of the minority nationalities, the government has help-
of the Zhuang, Miao, Dong and other minority nationalities
to devise their own written languages based on the Latin
alphabet or to improve their existing writing system.

第十一课 Lesson 11

一、课文 Text

谢 谢 你

Dīng Yún: Huán nǐ huàbào, xièxie.
还 你 画报，谢谢。

Pàlánkǎ: Bú xiè. Nà shì Hànyǔ cídiǎn ma?
不 谢。那 是 汉语 词典 吗？

Dīng Yún: (Nà) shì Hànyǔ cídiǎn.
（那）是 汉语 词典。

Pàlánkǎ: Nǐ xiànzài yòng ma?
你 现在 用 吗?

Dīng Yún: Bú yòng. Nǐ yòng ma?
不 用。 你 用 吗?

Pàlánkǎ: Wǒ yòng yíxiàr.
我 用 一下儿。

Dīng Yún: Hǎo.
好。

Pàlánkǎ: Xièxie nǐ.
谢谢 你。

Dīng Yún: Bú kèqi.
不 客气。

Pàlánkǎ: Zàijiàn!
再见!

Dīng Yún: Zàijiàn!
再见!

* * *

liù qī bā jiǔ shí
六 七 八 九 十

生词 New Words

1。还　　　（动）huán　　　to return

103

2. 画报	(名)	huàbào	pictorial
3. 词典	(名)	cídiǎn	dictionary
4. 现在	(名)	xiànzài	now, nowadays
5. 用	(动)	yòng	to use, to make use of
6. 一下儿		yíxiàr	a little while
7. 再见	(动)	zàijiàn	to say good-bye, to bid farewell to
8. 六	(数)	liù	six
9. 七	(数)	qī	seven
10. 八	(数)	bā	eight
11. 九	(数)	jiǔ	nine
12. 十	(数)	shí	ten

补充词　Supplementary Words

1. zázhì	(名)		magazine
2. diànhuà	(名)		telephone, telephone call
3. běnzi	(名)		note-book, exercise-book
4. yǔsǎn	(名)		umbrella

二、注释　Notes

1. "还你画报。"

"Here is the pictorial (I borrowed from you)."

104

2. "我用一下儿。"

"May I use it for a while?"

"一下儿"在这里表示时间不长。

"一下儿" here means "a little while" or "a short time";

三、语音练习与会话练习
Pronunciation Drills and Conversation Practice

(一)

声母 Initials	(z c s)
韵母 Finals	ua ia iong

1. 四声 The four tones

zāi	(zái)	zǎi	zài	—	zàijiàn
cī	cí	cǐ	cì	—	cídiǎn
huā	huá	(huǎ)	huà	—	huàbào
xiā	xiá	(xiǎ)	xià	—	yíxiàr
yōng	yóng	yǒng	yòng		

2. 声调组合 Combinations of tones

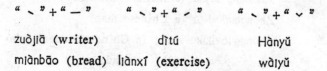

" ˋ " + " — "   " ˋ " + " ˊ "   " ˋ " + " ˇ "

zuòjiā (writer)   dìtú   Hànyǔ

miànbāo (bread) liànxí (exercise)   wàiyǔ

$$ \text{``} \diagdown \text{''} + \text{``} \diagdown \text{''} \qquad\qquad \text{``} \diagdown \text{''} + \text{``} \circ \text{''} $$

huàbào   xièxie

zàijiàn   tàitai

3. 儿化韵 Retroflex final

huār (flower)   yìdiǎnr (a little, a bit)

yíxiàr   yíhuìr (in a moment)

4. 读下列双音节词 Read out the following dissyllabic
words:

cānjiā (to take part in)   bǐsài (competition, match)

zhuōzi (table)   cèyàn (test, quiz)

cāochǎng (sports-field)   Yà Zhōu (Asia)

cíqì (porcelain)   huá bīng (to skate, skating)

yǒngyuǎn (forever)   xióngmāo (panda)

5. 多音节连读 Try to pronounce the following polysyl-
lables in quick succession:

Hànyǔ cídiǎn (Chinese dictionary)

Hànyǔ lǎoshī (a teacher of Chinese)

wàiyǔ xuéyuàn (institute of foreign languages)

xuésheng sùshè (students' dormitory)

Zhōngguó dìtú (a Chinese map)

Zhōngguó liúxuéshēng (a Chinese student who studies
abroad)

(二)

1. 道谢 Expressing one's thanks to someone

(1)

A: _____ .

B: _____ .

(2) A: Qǐng zuò .
   B: Xièxie.
   A: Bú kèqi.

jìn
hē chá
hē kāfēi

(3) A: Huán nǐ dìtú .
   　　 Xièxie nǐ.
   B: Bú xiè.

shū	cídiǎn
bǐ	běnzi
zázhì	yǔsǎn

2. 告别 Saying good-bye to someone

A: _____ .

B: _____ .

3. 问电话号 Asking about telephone numbers

A: Qǐngwèn, nǐ de diànhuà
hào shì duōshao?

B: èrliùbāqīwǔjiǔ.

> 728064
> qīèrbālíngliùsì
> 870492
> bāqīlíngsìjiǔèr

四、语音 Phonetics

复韵母 Compound finals

在 ia[ia], ie, ua[ua] uo, üe 等复韵母中，后一元音比前一元音响亮，响度逐渐变大。第二个元音表示复元音的终点。

The second elements in such compound finals as "ia[ia]", "ie", "ua[ua]", "uo" and "üe" are pronounced louder than the first ones, with their volume becoming greater gradually but not abruptly. The second elements are full vowels and should be given their full value in pronunciation.

在 ai, ei, ou, ao 等复韵母中，前一元音比后一元音响亮，响度逐渐变小。第二个元音常常不表示终点，只表示方向。

The first elements in such compound finals as "ai", "ei", "ao" and "ou" are pronounced louder than the second ones, with their volume becoming smaller gradually but not abruptly. The second elements indicate the directions towards which the vowels move rather than the limits.

在 iao, iou, uai, uei 等复韵母中，中间的元音最响亮。

In the compound finals "iao", "iou", "uai" and "uei" the medial elements are pronounced loudest.

发复元音时要注意：从前一元音到后一元音是滑行的，而不是跳跃的。

Care must be taken that, in the pronunciation of the compound finals above mentioned, the movement from one vowel to another is one of gliding but not abrupt jumping.

汉字笔顺表 Table of Stroke-order of Chinese Characters

1	还	不		還
		辶		
2	画	一		畫
		田（丨 冂 日 田 田）		
		凵（㇄ 凵）		
3	报	扌（一 十 扌）		報
		艮 阝（㇇ 阝）		
		又		
4	词	讠		詞
		司（𠃌 ヨ 司）		
5	典	曲（丨 冂 日 由 曲 曲）		
		八（丿 八）		
6	现	王（一 二 王 王）		現

109

		见（丨 冂 贝 见）					
7	用	丿	几	月	月	用	
8	下	一	丁	下			
9	再	一	厂	丌	冂	丏	再
10	见						見
11	六	亠（丶 亠）					
		八					
12	七	一	七				
13	八	丿	八				
14	九	丿	九				
15	十						

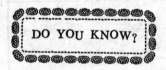

DO YOU KNOW?

Chinese Dictionaries

The most popular current Chinese dictionaries are "新华字典" dealing mainly with individual characters, which contains about 8,000 entries, and "现代汉语词典", a medium-sized dictionary containing more than 56,000 entries. Among the large-sized dictionaries are "辞海" and "辞源".

第十二课 Lesson 12

复习 Revision

一、课文 Text

她们是很好的朋友

Pàlánkǎ shì Gǔbō de nǚ péngyou. Xiànzài
Pàlánkǎ 是 Gǔbō 的 女 朋友。 现在

tāmen dōu xuéxí Hànyǔ. Tāmen lǎoshī xìng Wáng,
他们 都 学习 汉语。 他们 老师 姓 Wáng,

shì Zhōngguó rén. Wáng Xiānsheng shì tāmen de
是 Zhōngguó 人。 Wáng 先生 是 他们 的

lǎoshī, yě shì tāmen de péngyou.
老师，也 是 他们 的 朋友。

Pàlánkǎ rènshi Zhōngguó
Pàlánkǎ 认识 Zhōngguó

liúxuéshēng Dīng Yún. Dīng Yún
留学生 Dīng Yún。Dīng Yún

xuéxí Yīngyǔ, yě xuéxí
学习 英语， 也 学习

Fǎyǔ. Pàlánkǎ cháng qù
法语。Pàlánkǎ 常 去

xuésheng sùshè kàn tā. Tāmen shì hěn hǎo de
学生 宿舍 看 她。她们 是 很 好 的

péngyou.
朋友。

生词 New Words

1. 女　　(名) nǚ　　　　female
2. 先生　(名) xiānsheng　Mr., sir, gentleman
3. 认识　(动) rènshi　　to know, to be familiar
　　　　　　　　　　　with, to recognize
4. 英语　(名) Yīngyǔ　　English

112

5.	法语	（名）	Fǎyǔ	French
6.	常	（副）	cháng	often
7.	去	（动）	qù	to go
8.	她们	（代）	tāmen	they, them (for females)

二、注释 Notes

1. "Pàlánkǎ 常去学生宿舍看她。"

"Palanka often goes to the students' dormitory to see her."

2. "她们是很好的朋友。"

"They are good friends."

3. "Dīng Yún 学习英语，也学习法语。"

汉语里表示"某国语言"，一般在国名的简称（如果有"国"字，须去掉）后面加"语"或"文"，如"英语"、"法语"。

The idea of "the language of a certain nation" is expressed in Chinese by adding the word "语, yǔ" or "文, wén" (both here meaning "language") to the short form of the name of the nation (the word "国", if there is one in the Chinese, should be dropped), as in "英语", "法语".

1. 韵母和声母小结 A brief summary of the finals and initials

韵母 Finals	单韵母 Simple finals a[a]　o[o]　e[ɤ]　ê[ɛ]　i[i]　u[u]　ü[y] -i[ɿ][ʅ]　er[ɚ]
	复韵母 Compound finals ai[ai]　ei[ei]　ao[au]　ou[əu] ia[ia]　ie[iɛ]　iao[iau]　iou(-iu)[iəu] ua[ua]　uo[uo]　uai[uai]　uei(-ui)[uei] üe[yɛ]
	鼻韵母 Nasal finals an[an]　en[ən]　　　ang[aŋ]　eng[əŋ]　ong[uŋ] ian[iɛn]　in[in]　　　iang[iaŋ]　ing[iŋ]　iong[iuŋ] uan[uan]　uen(-un)[uən]　uang[uaŋ]　　　ueng*[uəŋ] üan[yan]　ün[yn]
声母 Initials	唇音 Labials　　　　　b[p]　　p[pʻ]　　m[m]　　f[f] 舌尖音 Alveolars　　　d[t]　　t[tʻ]　　n[n]　　l[l] 舌尖前音 Blade-alveolars　z[ts]　c[tsʻ]　s[s] 舌尖后音 Blade-palatals　zh[tʂ]　ch[tʂʻ]　sh[ʂ] 　　　　　　　　　　　r[ʐ] 舌面音 Alveolars　　　j[tɕ]　q[tɕʻ]　x[ɕ] 舌根音 Velars　　　　　g[k]　　k[kʻ]　　h[x]

---

* 鼻韵母 ueng 在前十一课中尚未出现。它不能跟声母拼合，只能自成音节。

The nasal final "ueng", which has not appeared in any of the preceding 11 lessons, never occurs after an initial but always forms a syllable by itself.

(1) 元音在汉语中占优势。一个音节中最多包含两个辅音，两个辅音不能连在一起，必须用元音隔开。

Vowels predominate in Chinese syllables. A syllable can consist of two consonants at most, which can never follow each other but must always be separated by a vowel.

(2) 现代汉语声母浊音很少，只有 r, m, n, l, 其它声母都是清音，发音时声带不要振动。

Modern Chinese has altogether 21 initials only a few of which are voiced, i.e. "r, m, n" and "l", and the rest are all voiceless.

(3) 在21个声母中，有六组（共12个）相对应的送气音和不送气音。送气音与不送气音有区别词汇意义的作用，发音时必须严格注意。

In the 21 initials there are 6 pairs of corresponding initials (12 in all) in which 6 are aspirated and the other are unaspirated. Since in Chinese aspiration or the lack of it is capable of differenciating meaning, care must be taken to pronounce the sounds correctly and not to confuse the aspirated sounds with the unaspirated ones or vice versa.

(4) 汉语每一个音节都有自己的声调，声调有区别意义的作用。学习每一个生词时必须同时记住它的声调和在一定情况下的变调。

Every syllable in Chinese has its specific tone. Change of tone involves change of meaning. So, in learning a new word, we should bear in mind what tone it has as well as what change in tone there should be under a given condition.

2．拼写规则小结 A brief summary of the rules of phonetic spelling

115

l — y(yi):

l — yi	ian — yan
ia — ya	in — yin
ie — ye	iang — yang
iao — yao	ing — ying
iou — you	iong — yong

u — w(wu):

u — wu	uan — wan
ua — wa	uen — wen
uo — wo	uang — wang
uai — wai	ueng — weng
uei — wei	

ü — yu:

ü — yu	üan — yuan
üe — yue	ün — yun

四、语音练习与会话练习
Pronunciation Drills and Conversation Practice

(一)

1. 辨音 Sound discrimination

(1) 送气音和不送气音 The aspirated and unaspirated sounds

b — p	z — c
d — t	zh — ch
g — k	j — q

*   *   *

b – biǎoyáng (to praise)   d – dàifu

p – piāoyáng (to flutter)   t – tàidu (attitude)

zh – zhīdao (to know)   J – dǎ jiǔ (to buy some
                                       wine)

ch – chídào (to be late)   q – dǎ qiú (to play bas-
                                       ketball)

g – gānjìng (clean, neat)

k – kàn qīng (to see clearly)

z – xǐzǎo (to take a bath)

c – chú cǎo (to weed, weeding)

(2) 舌尖鼻韵母和舌根鼻韵母 Alveolar-finals and velar-
finals

an – dànshì (but, however)

ang – dāngshí (at that time)

Ian – liánxì (contact)

Iang– liángkuai (nice and cool)

uan – zhuānjiā (expert)

uang– zhuāngjia (crops)

en – pénzi (basin)

eng – péngyou (friend)

In – rénmín (people)

Ing – rénmíng (a personal name)

2. 半三声 Half 3rd tone

Nǐ hē chá ma?   Nǐ kàn shénme?

Nǐ xī yān ma?   Nǐ xìng shénme?

Nǐ yòng cídiǎn ma?   Nǐ jiào shénme?

117

Wǒ xuéxí Hànyǔ.

Wǒ rènshi tā.

Wǒ zhù sùshè.

3. 三音节词 Trisyllabic words

túshūguǎn (library)　　　zhàoxiàngjī (camera)

yuèlǎnshì (reading-room)　zìxíngchē (bicycle)

liúxuéshēng　　　　　　　huǒchēzhàn (railway sta-
　　　　　　　　　　　　　　　　　　　tion)

shōuyīnjī (radio)　　　　bàngōngshì (office)

多音节连读 Try to pronounce the following polysyl-
　　　　　　lables in quick succession:

fùxí kèwén (to review the text)

yùxí shēngcí (to preview new words)

zhùyì fāyīn (to pay attention to pronunciation)

zhùyì shēngdiào (to pay attention to tones)

zài niàn yíbiàn (Read it again.)

zài xiě yíbiàn (Write it once more.)

4. 朗读下面一首诗: Read out the following poem:

Jìng Yè Sī

LǏ Bái

Chuáng qián míng yuè guāng,

Yí shì dì shàng shuāng.

Jǔ tóu wàng míng yuè,

Dī tóu sī gùxiāng.

Homesickness On a Quiet Night
by Li Bai

On the ground before my bed
Is spread the bright moonlight,
But I take it for frost
When I wake up at the first sight.
Then I look up at the bright full moon in the sky,
Suddenly homesickness strikes me as I bow my head
With a deep sigh.

(二)

1. 朗读下列对话: Read out the following dialogues:

(1) A: Shéi? Qǐng jìn₁

    B: Nǐ hǎo₁

    A: Nǐ hǎo. Qǐng zuò.

    B: Nǐ máng ma?

    A: Bù máng. Qǐng hē chá.

    B: Xièxie.

(2) A: Nín shì Rìběn rén ma?

    B: Bú shì.

    A: Nín shì nǎ guó rén?

    B: Wǒ shì Zhōngguó rén.

    A: Nín guì xìng?

    B: Wǒ xìng Wáng. Nín ne?

    A: Wǒ shì Yīngguó rén. Wǒ xìng Gélín.

(3) A: Nín hǎo, tàitai₁

    B: Nín hǎo₁

A: Qǐngwèn, Lǐ Xiānsheng zài ma?

B: Zài. Qǐng jìn.

C: À, shì nǐ. Qǐng zuò, qǐng zuò.

B: Nín hē kāfēi ma?

A: Xièxie.

2. 看图说话：Say as much as you can about each of the following pictures:

① 请喝茶。　② 您是哪国人？　③ 请进。

汉字笔顺表 Table of Stroke-order of Chinese Characters

1	女			
2	先	生（ノ　ト　生　生）		
		儿		
3	认	讠		認
		人		
4	识	讠		識
		只	口	

120

			八
5	英	艹	
		央（丶 冂 ⼝ 央 央）	
6	法	氵	
		去	土
			厶（厶 厶）
7	常	尚	丷（丶 丨 丿 ⺌ ⺌ 尚）
			口
		巾	
8	去		

词类简称表
Abbreviations

1.	(名) 名词	míngcí	noun
	(专名)专有名词	zhuānyǒu míngcí	proper name
2.	(代) 代词	dàicí	pronoun
3.	(动) 动词	dòngcí	verb
4.	(能动)能愿动词	néngyuàn dòngcí	optative verb
5.	(形) 形容词	xíngróngcí	adjective
6.	(数) 数词	shùcí	numeral
7.	(量) 量词	liàngcí	measure word
8.	(副) 副词	fùcí	adverb
9.	(介) 介词	jiècí	preposition
10.	(连) 连词	liáncí	conjunction
11.	(助) 助词	zhùcí	particle
	动态助词	dòngtài zhùcí	aspect particle
	结构助词	jiégòu zhùcí	structural particle
	语气助词	yǔqì zhùcí	modal particle
12.	(叹) 叹词	tàncí	interjection
13.	(象声)象声词	xiàngshēngcí	onomatopoeia
	(头) 词头	cítóu	prefix
	(尾) 词尾	cíwěi	suffix

第十三课 Lesson 13

一、课文 Text

你认识不认识她

古波： 你看，她是不是中国人？
Gǔbō： Nǐ kàn, tā shì bu shì Zhōngguó rén?

帕兰卡： 是，她是中国人。
Pàlánkǎ： shì, tā shì Zhōngguó rén.

古波： 你认识不认识她？
Gǔbō： Nǐ rènshi bu rènshi tā?

帕兰卡： 我 认识 她。
Pàlánkǎ:　　Wǒ　rènshi　tā.

古　波： 她 叫 什么 名字？
Gǔbō:　　Tā　jiào　shénme　míngzi?

帕兰卡： 她 叫 丁 云。
Pàlánkǎ:　　Tā　jiào　Dīng　Yún.

喂， 丁 云， 你 去 哪儿？
Wèi,　Dīng　Yún,　nǐ　qù　nǎr?

丁　云： 啊！ 是 你，帕兰卡。 我 去 商店
Dīng Yún:　　À!　shì　nǐ,　Pàlánkǎ.　Wǒ　qù　shāngdiàn

买 笔。
mǎi　bǐ.

帕兰卡： 我们 也 去 商店 买 纸。来， 我
Pàlánkǎ:　　Wǒmen　yě　qù　shāngdiàn mǎi　zhǐ.　Lái,　wǒ

介绍 一下儿。 这 是 我 的
jièshào　　yíxiàr.　　Zhè　shì　wǒ　de

中国 朋友， 丁
Zhōngguó　péngyou,　Dīng

云。他 是 我 的
Yún.　Tā　shì　wǒ　de

男 朋友——
nán péngyou——

古　波：我　叫　古波。你　好！
Gǔbō:　Wǒ　jiào　Gǔbō.　Nǐ　hǎo!

丁　云：你　好！你　也　学习　汉语　吗？
Dīng Yún:　Nǐ　hǎo!　Nǐ　yě　xuéxí　Hànyǔ　ma?

古　波：对　了，我　和　帕兰卡　都　学
Gǔbō:　Duì　le,　wǒ　hé　Pàlánkǎ　dōu　xué

汉语。
Hànyǔ.

帕兰卡：他　常　说　汉语。
Pàlánkǎ:　Tā　cháng shuō　Hànyǔ.

生词　New Words

1. 名字　（名）míngzi　name

2. 喂　（叹）wèi　*an interjection*, hello

3. 啊　（叹）à　*an interjection*, oh

4. 商店　（名）shāngdiàn　shop

5. 买　（动）mǎi　to buy

6. 笔　（名）bǐ　pen

7. 纸　（名）zhǐ　paper

8. 来　（动）lái　to come

9. 介绍　（动）jièshào　to introduce

10. 男　（名）nán　male

125

11. 对	(形)	duì	right, correct
12. 了	(助)	le	*a modal particle*
13. 和	(连、介)	hé	and, with
14. 说	(动)	shuō	to speak, to say

专名 Proper Names

1. 古波	Gǔbō	*a personal name*
2. 中国	Zhōngguó	China
3. 帕兰卡	Pàlánkǎ	*a personal name*
4. 丁云	Dīng Yún	*a personal name*

补充词 Supplementary Words

1. 英国	(专名)	Yīngguó	Britain
2. 法国	(专名)	Fǎguó	France
3. 本子	(名)	běnzi	note-book, exercise-book
4. 邮局	(名)	yóujú	post office
5. 邮票	(名)	yóupiào	stamp
6. 教授	(名)	jiàoshòu	professor

二、注释 Notes

1. "喂, 丁云, 你去哪儿?"

"喂"是叹词, 打招呼的声音。

126

"喂" is an interjection used to express informal greeting, equivalent to "hello" or "hey".

2. "啊，是你，帕兰卡。"

"啊"是叹词。这里读第四声，表示明白过来（原来没有想到）。

"啊" is also an interjection. Here it is pronounced in the 4th tone, expressing unexpectedness or sudden realization.

3. "来，我介绍一下儿。"

"我介绍一下儿"是给别人作介绍时的常用语。"一下儿"在这里表示比较随便的意思。

"我介绍一下儿" is a common expression used while introducing people to each other. "一下儿" here softens the tone, making it sound informal.

4. "对了，我和帕兰卡都学习汉语。"

"对了"用来肯定对方说的话。

"对了" means "right", "all right" or "correct".

连词"和"一般只用来连接名词、代词或名词结构，不能连接分句，例如，不能说"我买书，和他买笔"。在汉语里这两个分句之间不需要用连词连接。"和"也很少连接动词或动词结构。

In Chinese, the conjunction "和" is used to connect nouns, pronouns or nominal constructions only. No "和" is needed between two clauses and it is wrong to say "我买书，和他买笔". Nor is "和" often used to join verbs or verbal constructions.

三、替换与扩展 Substitution and Extension

(一)

1. 他是不是中国人？

他是中国人。

大夫	英国*人
学生	法国*人

2. 你认识不认识他？

我不认识他。

他们	谢老师
丁云	我朋友

3. 你说不说汉语？

我说汉语。

英语	法语
外语	

有＊号的是补充词。Words marked with the asterisk "＊" are supplementary words.

4. 你买不买书？

   我不买书，我买地图。

词典，	书
画报，	地图
笔，	本子

5. 你去哪儿？

   我去商店买笔。

宿舍，	喝茶
学院，	还书
邮局，	买邮票
商店，	买纸

6. 你也学习汉语吗？

   我也学习汉语。

   你们都学习汉语吗？

   对了，我们都学习汉语。

(二)

1. 介绍 Introducing people to each other

A: 你们认识吗？我介绍一下儿。

这是丁教授。

这是我的女朋友谢英。

B: 您好。

C: 您好。

2. 见面 Meeting each other

A: 请问，您叫什么名字？

B: 我叫谢英。

A: 您是哪国人？

B: 我是中国人。

A: 您说英语吗？

130

B: 我说英语。

3. 相遇 Running into each other

A: 喂，谢英！

B: 啊，是你，丁朋！你好。

A: 你好。你去哪儿？

B: 我去商店买本子*，

你去不去？

A: 我也去。

· · ·

名　片

(míngpiàn, card)

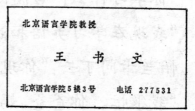

北京语言学院教授

王　书　文

北京语言学院5楼3号　　电话 277531

帕兰卡问古波："你认识丁云吗？"古波说，不认识。帕兰卡说："你看，那是丁云。来，我介绍一下儿。"

"喂，丁云，你来一下儿。"帕兰卡说，"这是古波，这是丁云——我的中国朋友。"

古波说汉语："你好！"

丁云问他："你也学习汉语吗？"

"我和帕兰卡都学习汉语。我们的汉语老师姓 Wáng，你认识吗？"

"认识，"丁云说，"Wáng 老师常去宿舍看我们。"

"你学习什么？"古波问她。

"我现在学习英语和法语。"

帕兰卡问丁云："你现在忙不忙？"

"我很忙。你爸爸、妈妈好吗？"

"谢谢你，他们都很好。"帕兰卡说。

五、语法 Grammar

1. 正反疑问句 Affirmative-negative questions

正反疑问句是又一种提问题的方法，将谓语中主要成分（动词或形容词）的肯定形式和否定形式并列起来，就可以构成正反疑问句。这种正反疑问句跟用"吗"的一般疑问句作用一样。

An affirmative-negative question is another form of question which is made by juxtaposing the affirmative and negative forms of the main element of the predicate (the predicative verb or adjective). Such a question has the same function as a general question with the interrogative particle "吗".

名词或代词 Nouns or pronouns	动词形容词肯定形式 Affirmative forms of the predicative verb or adjective	动词形容词否定形式 Negative forms of the predicative verb or adjective	名词或代词 Nouns or pronouns
他	是	不是	学生？
大夫	来	不来？	
你	喝	不喝	茶？
你哥哥	认识	不认识	她？
老师	忙	不忙？	
你的笔	好	不好？	

133

2. 连动句　Sentences with verbal constructions in series

在动词谓语句里，如果几个连用的动词（或动词结构）共一个主语，这就是连动句。连用的动词结构先后顺序是固定的，不能改动，中间也没有语音上的停顿。

A sentence with verbal constructions in series is a sentence in which the predicate consists of more than one verb (or verbal construction) sharing the same subject. In a sentence of this kind, the verbs or verbal constructions follow a definite and unalterable order and admit no pause between them in actual speech.

在本课所介绍的连动句中，后一动词往往是前一动词所表达的动作的目的，如：

Sentences of this type fall into several kinds. The kind covered in this lesson includes sentences having in their predicate two verbs the second of which denotes the purpose of the action expressed by the first. E.g.

名词或代词 Nouns or pronouns	动词(1) Verbs(1)	名　词 Nouns	动词(2) Verbs(2)	名　词 Nouns	助词 Particles
你	去	外语学院	看	朋友	吗？
我	去	学生宿舍	看	朋友。	
他	来	学院	问	老师。	
你	去		还	书	吗？
我朋友	来		帮助	我。	

134

3. "也"和"都"的位置 Position of the adverbs "也" and "都"

副词"也"和"都"必须放在主语之后、谓语动词或形容词之前。"也"、"都"在句中同时修饰谓语时，"也"必须在"都"的前边。

The adverbs "也" and "都" usually follow the subject but precede the predicative verb or adjective. Used simultaneously in a sentence to qualify the predicate, "也" must precede "都".

名词或代词 Nouns or pronouns	副　词 Adverbs	动词、动词结构或形容词 Verbs, verbal constructions or adjectives
我	也很	好。
我们	都很	好。
他	也不	是学生。
他们	都不	是学生。
我们	不都	是学生。
他	也	说汉语。
她们	也都	说汉语。

注意：在一个句子里，"都"所总括的一般是它前边出现的人或事物，而不是它后面的成分。因此只能说"我们都认识他"，不能说"我都认识他们"。

Note that, in a sentence, what "都" sums up usually refers to all the persons or things that go before it rather than

what comes after it. Thus, we can only say "我们都认识他"
but not "我都认识他们":

练习 Exercises

1. 读下列词组： Read out the following phrases:

(1) 是不是　喝不喝　还不还

在不在　来不来　看不看

问不问　用不用　坐不坐

买不买　去不去　说不说

学习不学习　认识不认识

介绍不介绍　欢迎不欢迎

(2) 中国人　　男人　　女人

中国朋友　男朋友　女朋友

中国学生　男学生　女学生

中国老师　男老师　女老师

中国大夫　男大夫　女大夫

2. 用下列动词作带"吗"的一般疑问句和正反疑问句：
Make a general question with the interrogative particle
"吗" and an affirmative-negative question using each of
the following verbs:

例 Example 看 书

　　→他看书吗？

　　他看不看书？

(1) 在

(2) 来

(3) 是 谢老师

(4) 喝 茶

(5) 用 车

(6) 在 宿舍

(7) 学习 汉语

(8) 说 英语

(9) 买 纸

3. 选择适当的词组填空： Put in an appropriate phrase from the list below in each of the following sentences:

学习汉语　买笔

还书　　　　看朋友

(1) 我去商店_____。

(2) 她去学生宿舍 ＿＿＿＿＿＿。

(3) 丁云来学院＿＿＿＿＿＿。

(4) 他们去中国＿＿＿＿＿＿。

4.用"都"改写下面的句子：　Rewrite the following sentences using "都"：

例　Example　帕兰卡认识丁云，古波也认识丁云。

→帕兰卡和古波都认识丁云。

(1) 他学习汉语，她也学习汉语。

(2) 我爸爸是大夫，我妈妈也是大夫。

(3) 他说英语，他朋友也说英语。

(4) 谢老师是中国人，丁云也是中国人。

(5) 我去商店，我哥哥也去商店。

(6) 他不吸烟，他的女朋友也不吸烟。

(7) 丁云不在宿舍，她朋友也不在宿舍。

(8) 我去外语学院看朋友，古波也去外语学院看朋友。

六、语音语调　Pronunciation and Intonation

1．词的重音(1) Word stress (1)

按普通话发音习惯，汉语的多音节词里，大致可分为"重音"、"中音"、"轻音"三类，在一个多音节词中能够有比较地读出来。双音节词、三音节词、四音节词都清楚地有一个重音节（本书用"·"符号表示）。大多数双音节词末一个音节是重音，它前边的音节常读中音。例如：

Putonghua or the common speech of modern Chinese distinguishes roughly three degrees of stress of polysyllabic words: main (or strong) stress, medium stress and weak stress, which can be distinctly differentiated in the pronunciation of a word of many syllables. Words of two, three or four syllables have a distinct strong stress on one of the syllables (marked with the sign "·" in this book). In most disyllabic words, the strong stress falls on the second syllable, and the first syllable is usually pronounced with a medium stress. E.g.

汉语　英语　词典　地图　画报

学习(名)　老师　丁云　古波

再见　欢迎　商店　学院

小部分双音节词的重音节在前边，它后边的音节即使不是轻声（本身有调号）也要轻读。例如：

A small number of disyllabic words have the main stress falling on the first syllable, and the second syllable is usually pronounced with a weak stress even though it is normally not the neutral tone (with a tone-graph over it). E.g.

朋友　认识　名字　先生　学生

大夫　我们　什么　介绍(动)　学习(动)

2．练习　Exercises

(1) 朗读下列词语,注意"不"的变调：Read out the following phrases, paying attention to the changes of tone of "不"：

不说　不吸烟　不喝茶　不欢迎

不来　不还　不学习

不买　不请

不去　不坐　不住　不看　不问

不用　不介绍　不认识

(2) 朗读下列带 zh、ch、sh、r 的词语,注意发音和词的重音：Read out the following words containing the sounds zh,

140

ch, sh, or r, paying attention to their pronunciation and word stress:

中国　日本　书店　宿舍　商店

介绍　认识　长城　长江　学生

(3) 朗读下面的成语：Read out the proverb:

shú　néng　shēng　qiǎo　(Practice makes perfect.)
熟　能　生　巧

汉字笔顺表　Table of Stroke-order of Chinese Characters

1	名	夕				
		口				
2	字	宀				
		子				
3	喂	口				
		畏	田			
			𧘇 (一　𠃊　𠃊　𧘇)			
4	啊	口				
		阿	阝			
			可			

5	商	、 ㅗ 宀 审 产 产 商 商
6	店	广（、 ㅗ 广）
		占（丨 卜 占）
7	买	一 ··········· 買
		头（、 ˎ 头 头）
8	笔	竹（ノ ˒ ˌ 竹） ·· 筆
		毛（ノ ˴ 三 毛）
9	纸	纟（乚 纟 纟） ·· 紙
		氏（ノ 丿 丆 氏）
10	来	一 ㄱ 丌 五 平 来 来 ·· 來
11	介	人
		川（ノ 川）
12	绍	纟 ·· 紹
	召	刀
		口
13	男	田
		力（丁 力）
14	对	又 ·· 對
		寸（一 十 寸）

142

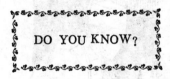

15	了	一 了				
16	和	禾（一 二 千 禾 禾）				
		口				
17	说	讠				说
	丶	兑	⌣			
			兄	口		
			儿			

The name of a Chinese (of the Han nationality or of some of China's minority nationalities) is made up of two elements, the surname and the given name, with the former always preceding the latter. Surnames or family names are usually monosyllabic characters, such as Ding, Wang, Li and Jin. Only a few Chinese surnames, such as Ouyang and Sima are disyllabic. Given names consist sometimes of two characters, such as Shuwen, and sometimes of only one, such as Yun. In present-day China, women retain their own surnames after marriage. Traditionally children have the same surname as their father though there are occasional cases of children using their mother's surname.

第十四课 Lesson 14

一、课文 Text

他 作 什 么 工 作

帕兰卡： 丁 云， 我 问 你， 你 想 不 想
Pàlánkǎ:　Dīng Yún,　wǒ wèn nǐ,　nǐ xiǎng bu xiǎng

家？
jiā?

丁　云： 想。 我 很 想
Dīng Yún:　xiǎng.　Wǒ hěn xiǎng

爸爸， 妈妈。
bàba,　　māma.

帕兰卡： 不 想 你 男
Pàlánkǎ:　Bù xiǎng nǐ nán

朋友 吗？
péngyou ma?

丁　云： 也 想。
Dīng Yún:　Yě xiǎng.

帕兰卡： 他 作 什 么 工 作？
Pàlánkǎ:　Tā zuò shénme gōngzuò?

144

丁　云： 他 是 大夫。
Dīng Yún: Tā shì dàifu.

帕兰卡： 你 有 没 有 妹妹？
Pàlánkǎ: Nǐ yǒu mei yǒu mèimei?

丁　云： 我 没 有 妹妹， 我 有 姐姐。
Dīng Yún: Wǒ mei yǒu mèimei, wǒ yǒu jiějie.

帕兰卡： 你 姐姐 在
Pàlánkǎ: Nǐ jiějie zài

哪儿 工作？
nǎr gōngzuò?

丁　云： 她 在 银行
Dīng Yún: Tā zài yínháng

工作， 她 爱人 在 书店 工作。
gōngzuò, tā àiren zài shūdiàn gōngzuò.

帕兰卡： 她 有 孩子 吗？
Pàlánkǎ: Tā yǒu háizi ma?

丁　云： 有。他们 常常 给 我 写 信，
Dīng Yún: Yǒu. Tāmen chángcháng gěi wǒ xiě xìn,

我 也 常常 给 他们 写 信。
wǒ yě chángcháng gěi tāmen xiě xìn.

帕兰卡： 他们 好 吗？
Pàlánkǎ: Tāmen hǎo ma?

丁　云：　他们　都　很　好。我　告诉　姐姐：
Dīng Yún:　Tāmen dōu hěn hǎo. Wǒ gàosu jiějie:

你　是　我　的　好　朋友。我　姐姐
nǐ shì wǒ de hǎo péngyou. Wǒ jiějie

问　你　好。
wèn nǐ hǎo.

帕兰卡：　谢谢。问　他们　好。
Pàlánkǎ:　Xièxie. Wèn tāmen hǎo.

生词　New Words

1. 作	(动)	zuò	to do
2. 工作	(动、名)	gōngzuò	to work, work
3. 想	(动、能动)	xiǎng	to want, to think, to miss
4. 家	(名)	jiā	family, home, house
5. 有	(动)	yǒu	to have, there be
6. 没	(副)	méi	not, no
7. 妹妹	(名)	mèimei	younger sister
8. 姐姐	(名)	jiějie	elder sister
9. 银行	(名)	yínháng	bank
10. 爱人	(名)	àiren	husband or wife
11. 书店	(名)	shūdiàn	bookstore
12. 孩子	(名)	háizi	child

13.	给	(介、动) gěi	to, for, to give
14.	写	(动) xiě	to write
15.	信	(名) xìn	letter
16.	告诉	(动) gàosu	to tell

补充词　Supplementary Words

1.	职员	(名) zhíyuán	office worker, staff member
2.	工程师	(名) gōngchéngshī	engineer
3.	经理	(名) jīnglǐ	manager, director
4.	公司	(名) gōngsī	company

二、注释　Notes

1. "你想不想家?"

这里的"家"是指家里的人。

The word "家" here refers to members of the family.

2. "想。""也想。"

这两句省略了主语"我"和宾语"家"、"男朋友"。

"想。" and "也想。" are both elliptical sentences in which the subject "我" and the objects "家" and "男朋友" are respectively understood.

3. "不想你男朋友吗?"

"Don't you miss your boy friend?"

用"吗"的疑问句中，动词谓语也可以是否定形式，这样提问常常表示提问者认为答案应该是肯定的。

In a question with the interrogative particle "吗", the

predicative verb may be made negative to imply that an answer in the affirmative is expected.

4．"她爱人在书店工作。"

"Her husband works in a bookstore."

汉语中"爱人"一词既可指丈夫，也可指妻子。

In Chinese, the word "爱人" may refer to either "husband" or "wife".

5．"他们常常给我写信。"

"They often write to me."

"常"在口语中也可以说"常常"。但否定形式仍是"不常"。

In colloquial speech "常" often takes the form of "常常", but the negative form remains "不常".

6．"我姐姐问你好。"

"My elder sister wished to be remembered to you." or "My elder sister sends you her love."

"问他们好。"

"Please remember me to them." or "Give them my love."

"问…好"是转达问候的一种方式。可以是第三者让"我"向对话人问好（"他问你好"）；也可以是第三者请"我"的对话人向别人问好（"他问她好"）。如果是"我"请对话人向第三者问好，主语"我"可以省略，如"（我）问他们好"。

"问…好" is an expression used to ask someone to give one's love or send one's best regards to a third person. "他问你好" is used by the speaker when he gives the regards of a third person to the person spoken to. "他问她好" is used when a third person asks the person spoken to to give his respects to another person. When the speaker asks the person spoken to to say hello to a third person, the subject "I" can be omitted. E.g."(我)问他们好".

三、替换与扩展　Substitution and Extension

(一)

1. 你有汉语词典吗？

   我有汉语词典。

   你现在用不用？

   我现在不用。

中国地图
英语书
车
笔

2. 他有没有妹妹？

   他没有妹妹。

   那是谁？

   那是他姐姐。

姐姐，	妹妹
弟弟，	哥哥
妹妹，	女朋友
爱人，	朋友
孩子，	姐姐的孩子

3. 你爸爸作什么工作？

   他是大夫。

   他好吗？

   谢谢你,他很好。

老师	教授˙
职员˙	经理˙
工程师˙	

149

4. 您在哪儿工作？

我在银行工作。

您忙不忙？

我很忙。

外语学院
书店
商店
公司

5. 你在哪儿学习？

我在外语学院学

习。

住，学生宿舍
看书，家
写信，家

6. 你常常给他写

信吗？

我常常给他写

信。

你朋友	你姐姐
你爸爸	谢先生
你爱人	

(二)

1. 询问职业　Asking about occupation

A: 你好！我们认识一下儿，

我叫_____。

B: 我叫_____。我是职员。

150

请问,你作什么工作?

A: 我是学生。

B: 你在哪儿学习?

A: 我在外语学院学习。

　　　*　　　*　　　*

A: 喂,商先生!

B: 啊,是你,丁先生,你好!

A: 你好。你现在在哪儿工作?

B: 我在银行工作,你呢?

A: 我在公司工作。你忙不忙?

B: 不忙。你孩子好吗?

A: 很好。问你爱人好。

B: 谢谢。再见!

A: 再见!

2. 给别人介绍 Introducing people to each other

A: 我给你们介绍一下儿。

这是我们公司的丁经理，

这是银行的商先生。

B: 您好！

C: 您好！

3. 代问好　Sending someone your love or kind regard

A: 你哥哥常给你写信吗？

B: 他常给我写信。他也问你好。

A: 谢谢。

　　　＊　　　＊　　　＊

A: 你爸爸好吗？

B: 很好，谢谢。

A: 我爸爸问他好。

B: 谢谢。

　　　＊　　　＊　　　＊

A: 问你爱人好。再见！

B: 谢谢，再见！

学　生　登　记　表
Xuésheng　Dēngjì　Biǎo
Registration Form for Students

姓　名 Name	性　别 Sex	年　龄 Age	国　籍 Nation- ality	住　　　址 Address
丁　云	女	22	中　国	学生宿舍 423 号

四、阅读短文　Reading Text

　　帕兰卡家有爸爸、妈妈、哥哥和姐姐。她
爸爸是教授*，在外语学院工作。她妈妈是
大夫。他们都很忙。

　　帕兰卡没有弟弟，也没有妹妹，她有哥哥
和姐姐。他哥哥是公司*的职员*。他不在
家住，我们不认识他。她哥哥的爱人现在没
有工作。他们的孩子叫保尔 (Bǎo'ěr)。

　　帕兰卡的姐姐是学生，现在在法国 (Fǎguó,

France) 学习。帕兰卡很想姐姐，她常给姐姐写信。姐姐常常给她买法语书和画报。

五、语法 Grammar

1. "有"字句 "有" sentences

动词"有"作谓语主要成分的句子常表示领有。它的否定形式是在"有"前加副词"没"（而不是"不"），正反问句则为"…有没有…"。

A "有" sentence is one in which the verb "有", which denotes possession, functions as the main element of the predicate. Such a sentence is made negative by preceding "有" with "没" (and never with "不"). "有没有…" is used to build an affirmative–negative question with "有".

名词或代词 Nouns or pronouns	动　词 Verbs	名　词 Nouns	助词 Particle
老师	有	中国地图。	
我	没有	汉语词典。	
他	有	女朋友	吗?
他家	有没有	车?	

154

2. 介词结构 Prepositional constructions

介词"在"、"给"等跟它的宾语组成介词结构，常用在动词前边作状语。

The preposition "在" or "给" together with its object forms a prepositional construction, which is often placed before verbs as an adverbial adjunct.

名词或代词 Nouns or pronouns	副词 Ad-verbs	介词结构 Prepositional constructions	动词 Verbs	名词 Nouns	助词 Par-ticle
他		在书店	买	书。	
她爱人	不	在银行	工作。		
我朋友	也	在外语学院	学习。		
他们	常	给你	写	信	吗？
她		给我们	介绍	中国。	

注意： Points to be noted:

(1)"在…"、"给…"等介词结构一般不能放在动词之后，不能说"他工作在银行"。

The prepositional construction "在…" or "给…" never comes after the verb it qualifies and it is incorrect to say "他工作在银行".

(2)"在"的宾语一般是表示地点的词或词组。"给"的宾语常常是受动者。

155

· The object of the preposition "在" is usually a word or phrase denoting a place while the object of the preposition "给" is often the receiver of the action expressed by the verb that follows.

(3) 在否定句中，副词"不"放在介词结构的前边。

In a negative sentence, the adverb "不" usually goes before the prepositional construction.

练习 Exercises

1. 读下列词组并造句： Read out the following phrases and make sentences with them:

(1) 在中国学习　　在家写信

　　在学院看书　　在书店买书

(2) 给他们介绍　　给老师写信

　　给谁写信　　给姐姐买画报

　　给留学生还书

(3) 问她好　　问他们好　　问你朋友好

　　问老师好　　问古波好

2. 把下列句子改成正反问句并用否定句回答：
Change the following to affirmative-negative questions and answer them in the negative:

156

例 Example　她有纸。

　　　　→她有没有纸？

　　　　她没有纸。

(1) 你朋友有法语词典。

(2) 他们有中国杂志。

(3) 古波有汉语书。

(4) 他有好笔。

(5) 帕兰卡有中国朋友。

(6) 留学生有外语画报。

3. 在下列句中填入介词"在"或"给"：Put in the preposition "在" or "给" in the following sentences:

(1) 他___书店买书。

(2) 我___朋友买画报。

(3) 她姐姐___中国学习。

(4) 他朋友不___商店工作。

(5) 丁云___他们介绍北京。

(6) 她不常___我写信。

(7) 她常常＿宿舍喝茶。

4. 跟你同学作问答练习：Make up a dialogue with a fellow student of yours, using the hints given:

(1) 你叫什么名字？

(2) 你是哪国人？

(3) 你作什么工作？

(4) 你住哪儿？

(5) 你有没有哥哥？

(6) 他是不是职员？

(7) 他在哪儿工作？

(8) 他有孩子吗？

(9) 孩子在哪儿学习？

(10) 他爱人工作不工作？

(11) 她作什么工作？

(12) 她在不在这儿？

5. 说说你的家庭（仿照阅读短文），然后把它写下来。
   Say something about your family after the fashion of

the Reading Text, and then write it out.

六、语音语调　Pronunciation and Intonation

1．词的重音(2)　Word stress (2)

叠字名词的第一个字重读，第二字读轻声。例如：

When a noun is formed of reduplicated characters the first character receives a strong stress and the second one is pronounced in the neutral tone. E.g.

爸爸　姐姐　哥哥

妈妈　妹妹　弟弟

2．练习　Exercises

(1) 朗读下列双音节词，注意词的轻重音：

Read out the following disyllabic words, paying attention to the main stress and weak stress:

第一声+轻声：the 1st tone ＋ the neutral tone:

妈妈　哥哥　她们　他们

第二声+轻声：the 2nd tone ＋ the neutral tone:

朋友　学生　什么　名字

第三声+轻声：the 3rd tone ＋ the neutral tone:

姐姐　你们　我们

第四声+轻声：the 4th tone + the neutral tone:

妹妹　弟弟　爱人　告诉

(2) 朗读下列词语，注意 j、q、x 的发音：
Read out the following words and expressions, paying attention to the pronunciation of j, q and x:

jiā（家）：他家　谁家　想家　在家

jiě（姐）：姐姐　小姐

qǐng（请）：请问　请进　请坐　请看

xué（学）：学习　学院　学生

朗读下面的短文：Read out the following short passage:

丁云的姐姐在银行工作。她姐姐也学习英语。她很想丁云，常给丁云写信。她问帕兰卡好。

汉字笔顺表 Table of Stroke-order of Chinese Characters

1	作	亻	
		乍 (丿 ⺄ ⺈ 乍 乍)	
2	工	一 丁 工	
3	想	相	木 (一 十 才 木)
		目	
		心	
4	家	宀	
		豕 (一 ⺅ 丁 豖 豖 豖 豕)	
5	有	ナ	
		月	
6	没	氵	
		殳	几 (丿 几)
		又	
7	妹	女	
		未 (一 二 丰 丰 未)	
8	姐	女	
		且 (丨 冂 月 月 且)	

161

9	银	钅（ノ ┗ ┢ ┡ 钅）	銀
		艮	
10	行	彳（ノ ㇗ 彳）	
		亍（一 二 亍）	
11	爱	⺥（ノ ⺊ ⺌ ⺌ ⺍ ⺥）	愛
		友	
12	孩	孑（了 孑）	
		亥（丶 一 亠 岁 亥 亥）	
13	子		
14	给	纟	給
		合（人 亼 合）	
15	写	冖	寫
		与（一 ㇕ 与）	
16	信	亻	
		言（丶 一 亠 言 言）	
17	告	牛	
		口	
18	诉	讠	訴
		斥（ノ 厂 斥 斥 斥）	

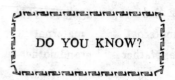

Chinese Forms of Address for Different
Family Relationships

Chinese forms of address for the various family relationships are very complicated. The following diagram will show you how members of a Chinese family call each other.

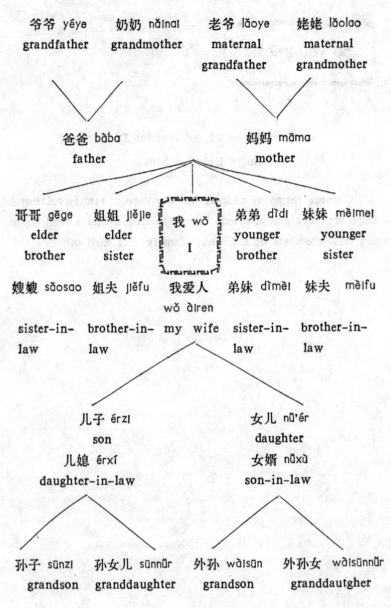

爷爷 yéye
grandfather

奶奶 nǎinai
grandmother

老爷 lǎoye
maternal
grandfather

姥姥 lǎolao
maternal
grandmother

爸爸 bàba
father

妈妈 māma
mother

哥哥 gēge
elder
brother

姐姐 jiějie
elder
sister

我 wǒ
I

弟弟 dìdi
younger
brother

妹妹 mèimei
younger
sister

嫂嫂 sǎosao
sister-in-
law

姐夫 jiěfu
brother-in-
law

我爱人
wǒ àiren
my wife

弟妹 dìmèi
sister-in-
law

妹夫 mèifu
brother-in-
law

儿子 érzi
son

儿媳 érxí
daughter-in-law

女儿 nǚ'ér
daughter

女婿 nǚxù
son-in-law

孙子 sūnzi
grandson

孙女儿 sūnnǚr
granddaughter

外孙 wàisūn
grandson

外孙女 wàisūnnǚr
granddautgher

164

第十五课 Lesson 15

中文系有多少学生

帕兰卡: 这 是 我们 中文 系。
Pàlánkǎ: Zhè shì wǒmen Zhōngwén xì.

丁 云: 中文 系 有 多少 学生?
Dīng Yún: Zhōngwén xì yǒu duōshao xuésheng?

古 波: 我们 系 有 九十八个 学生。
Gǔbō: Wǒmen xì yǒu jiǔshíbāge xuésheng.

165

丁 云： 有 几个 中国 老师？
Dīng Yún: Yǒu jǐge Zhōngguó Lǎoshī?

帕兰卡： 有 三个 中国 老师。王 老师
Pàlánkǎ: Yǒu sānge Zhōngguó lǎoshī. Wáng Lǎoshī

教 我们 语法 和 汉字。
jiāo wǒmen yǔfǎ hé Hànzì.

古 波： 我 和 帕兰卡 还 有 一个 中国
Gǔbō: Wǒ hé Pàlánkǎ hái yǒu yíge Zhōngguó

老师。
lǎoshī.

丁 云： 谁？
Dīng Yún: Shéi?

古 波： 丁 老师，她 教 我们 口语。
Gǔbō: Dīng Lǎoshī, tā jiāo wǒmen kǒuyǔ.

丁 云： 不 敢当。你们 是 我 的 英语
Dīng Yún: Bù gǎndāng. Nǐmen shì wǒ de Yīngyǔ

老师。
lǎoshī.

帕兰卡： 我们 互相 学习。
Pàlánkǎ: Wǒmen hùxiāng xuéxí.

古 波： 这 是 我们 的 新 阅览室。我们
Gǔbō: Zhè shì wǒmen de xīn yuèlǎnshì. Wǒmen

常 在 阅览室 看 画报 和 杂志。
cháng zài yuèlǎnshì kàn huàbào hé zázhì.

丁 云： 阅览室 有 中文 杂志 吗?
Dīng Yún: Yuèlǎnshì yǒu Zhōngwén zázhì ma?

帕兰卡： 有, 阅览室 有 中文 杂志、
Pàlánkǎ: Yǒu, yuèlǎnshì yǒu Zhōngwén zázhì、

中文 报, 还 有 七本 汉语
Zhōngwén bào, hái yǒu qīběn Hànyǔ

词典。
cídiǎn.

丁 云： 图书馆 在 哪儿?
Dīng Yún: Túshūguǎn zài nǎr?

古 波： 在 那儿。
Gǔbō: Zài nàr.

生词 New Words

1. 中文 （名）Zhōngwén Chinese (language)

2. 系 （名）xì department, faculty

3. 个 （量）gè *a measure word*

4. 几 （代）jǐ how many, how much, several

5. 教 （动）jiāo to teach

6. 语法 （名）yǔfǎ grammar

7. 汉字	(名)	Hànzì	Chinese character
字	(名)	zì	character
8. 还	(副)	hái	else, in addition, still
9. 口语	(名)	kǒuyǔ	spoken language
10. 不敢当		bù gǎndāng	I don't really deserve it, you flatter me
11. 互相	(副)	hùxiāng	each other, muturally
12. 新	(形)	xīn	new
13. 阅览室	(名)	yuèlǎnshì	reading-room
14. 杂志	(名)	zázhì	magazine
15. 报	(名)	bào	newspaper
16. 本	(量)	běn	*a measure word*
17. 图书馆	(名)	túshūguǎn	library
18. 那儿	(代)	nàr	there

专名 Proper Names

王	Wáng	*a surname*

补充词 Supplementary Words

1. 班	(名)	bān	class, squad
2. 教室	(名)	jiàoshì	classroom
3. 实验室	(名)	shíyànshì	laboratory

168

4. 借　　　(动) jiè　　　　to borrow, to lend

5. 生词　　(名) shēngcí　　　new word

二、注释　Notes

1. "这是我们中文系。"

"中文系"是中国语言文学系的简称。

"中文系" is the short form for "the Chinese Language and Literature Department".

"汉语"和"中文"都是指中国的主要语言文字——汉族的语言文字。在实际使用中，这两个词的侧重点稍有不同：如果强调汉语语言或汉语的口头形式，常用"汉语"一词；如果指汉语的书面形式或中国汉民族的语言文学，则往往用"中文"一词。如"学习汉语"、"说汉语"、"中文画报"、"中文系"等。

Both "汉语" and "中文" refer to the language of China's Han nationality, the chief language spoken and written in China. In practical use, however, the two terms have slightly different points of emphasis. "汉语" usually refers to Chinese as it is spoken, and "中文", on the other hand, refers to the written language of the Han nationality and its literature. Here are some common expressions that will show you the difference in usage: "学习汉语", "说汉语", "中文画报" and "中文系".

"英语"和"英文"，"法语"和"法文"等，意义上也有同样的差别。

The same is true of "英语" and "英文", "法语" and "法文".

2. "中文系有多少学生？"

"How many students are there in the Chinese Language and Literature Department?"

"阅览室有中文杂志吗?"

"Are there any Chinese language magazines in the reading room?"

动词"有"除了表示领有外，还可以表示存在。在这类句子中，动词"有"前边的表示单位或处所的名词，是句子的主语。否定式用"没有"，如："阅览室没有中文杂志。"

Besides denoting possession, the verb "有" also indicates existence. In a sentence with "有" indicating existence, the noun that precedes the verb, denoting either a collective or a place, is the subject of the sentence. "没有" is used to make the sentence negative, e.g. "阅览室没有中文杂志".

3、"有几个中国老师?"

"几"和"多少"都是用来提问数目的。如果估计数目在"10"以下，一般用"几"提问。"多少"可用来提问任何数目。

"几" and "多少" are both used to ask about numbers. "几" is usually used with respect to a number smaller than ten. "多少" is used for any number.

"几"和名词之间必须用量词。"多少"后边可以加量词，也可以不加量词。如：

There must be a measure word between "几" and the noun it qualifies. "多少" is used with or without a measure word. E.g.

你有多少(本)英文杂志?

她认识几个中国朋友?

4、"我和帕兰卡还有一个中国老师。"

170

副词"还"(1)的用法是表示有所补充。例如：

The use of the adverb "还" (1) is "in addition to" or "besides". E.g.

王老师教语法，还教口语。

我认识那个留学生，还常常去宿舍看他。

5. "谁?"

意思是"那个中国老师是谁"，这是一种简略的问句。其它疑问代词如"什么"、"哪儿"、"多少"等在语言环境清楚时，也可以单独用来提问。

"谁?" here is an elliptical question, meaning "那个中国老师是谁?" Other interrogative pronouns such as "什么", "哪儿" and "多少" can also be used elliptically if the context or situation leaves no room for misunderstanding.

注意："谁"有两个读音：shéi 或 shuí。口语中常用 shéi。

Note that "谁" has two pronunciations: "shéi" and "shuí". The former is preferred in colloquial speech.

6. "不敢当。你们是我的英语老师。"

"不敢当"的意思是承当不起，当对方夸奖自己时用来表示谦虚。

"不敢当", meaning "I don't really deserve it", is used in reply to a complimentary remark from the person spoken to.

7. "我们互相学习。"

"Let's learn from each other."

三、替换与扩展　Substitution and Extension

(一)

1. 你在中文系学习吗？

   我在中文系学习。

   你们系有几个老师？

   我们系有十个老师。

法国学生	教室*
留学生	班*
教授*	

2. 你去哪儿？

   我去外语学院。

   你们学院有几个系？

   我们学院有五个系。

图书馆，	1
阅览室，	6
实验室*，	4

3. 图书馆有多少本

   汉语词典？

   有二十本汉语词典。

   你常去图书馆借*书

   吗？

   我常去图书馆借书。

中文书，	95
语法书，	40
口语书，	37

4. 你有多少<u>中文画报</u>？

我有<u>十二</u>本中文画报，

我还有<u>英文画报</u>。

中文杂志，	18，	英文杂志
英文书，	70，	中文书
法语词典，	3，	汉语词典

5. 谁<u>教</u>你们<u>语法</u>？

王老师教我们语法。

他教不教你们汉字？

他也教我们汉字。

口语
汉语
生词*

6. 你<u>还</u>他什么？

我还他<u>报</u>。

杂志	笔
画报	书

(二)

1. 谈家庭　Talking about your family

　A: 你家有几个人？

B: 我家有五个人：爸爸、妈妈、我爱人，还有一个孩子。

A: 你爱人也工作吗？

B: 她也工作，她在图书馆工作。你有几个孩子？

A: 我有三个孩子。他们都是学生。

2. 谈学习 Talking about your studies

A: 你是不是中文系的学生？

B: 我是中文系的学生。

A: 几个中国老师教你们？

B: 三个中国老师教我们。

A: 中国老师教你们什么？

B: 他们教我们语法和口语。

A: 你常写汉字吗？

B: 我常写汉字。

A: 你现在认识多少汉字？

B: 我现在认识九十个汉字。

3. 回答别人的夸奖 Making a reply to a complimentary remark from the person spoken to

A: 你的英语很好，请多 (duō, many, much, more) 帮助 (bāngzhu, to help) 我。

B: 不敢当，我们互相学习。

4. 买书 Buying books

A: 请问，有汉语语法书吗？

B: 有。你买几本？

A: 我买一本。有没有中文杂志？

B: 没有。

* * *

人民日报

人民画报   光明日报

四、阅读短文　Reading Text

我们学院有八个系。我在中文系学习汉语。我们班有十五个学生——七个男学生，八个女学生。中国老师教我们语法和口语。

我们系有一个阅览室。那儿有英文杂志和英文画报，也有中文杂志和中文报。我们常常在阅览室看书。

我们学院还有一个图书馆。我常常去图书馆借中文书。中国老师常给我们介绍新书。

我们学院没有宿舍，我在学生城 (chéng, city, town) 住。我有一个好朋友，他叫古波。古波也住那儿。他和帕兰卡都在我们班。

五、语法　Grammar

1. 一百以内的称数法　Numeration for numbers under 100

汉语用"十进法"来称数。

In Chinese, the decimal system is used for numeration.

一	二	三	四	五
六	七	八	九	十
十一	十二	十三	十四	十五
十六	十七	十八	十九	二十
二十一	··············		二十九	三十
······················九十九				

2. 数量词作定语 Numeral-measure words as attributives

在现代汉语里，数词一般不能单独作名词的定语，中间必须加量词。如：

In modern Chinese, a numeral alone cannot function as an attributive but must be combined with a measure word inserted between the numeral and the noun it modifies. E.g.

他们有一个孩子。

我买十二本中文书。

他教五十个学生。

名词都有自己特定的量词，不能随便组合。本课先介绍量词"个"和"本"。"个"是用得最广的量词，可以用于指人、物、单位等名词之前；"本"通常用在书籍一类的名词前。

In Chinese, every noun as a rule has its specific measure word and can't go freely with others. In this lesson we only

177

deal with the measure words "个" and "本". Of all the measure words "个" is the most extensively used. It can be placed before a noun denoting a person, thing or unit. "本" is placed before nouns denoting books and suchlike. E.g.

| 一个 | 老师　学生　大夫　人　朋友　哥哥　弟弟　姐姐　妹妹　孩子　学院　系　图书馆　阅览室　宿舍　食堂　书店　银行 |
| 一本 | 书　杂志　画报　词典 |

注意： Points to be noted:

(1) 汉语的名词没有数的区别，同一名词可以指单数，也可以指复数。

Chinese nouns have no number. A noun may be either singular or plural without any change of form.

(2) 名词数量的区别，主要通过句子的其它成分如定语（数量词定语、指示代词定语、形容词定语等）来表示。

Whether a noun denotes one person or thing or more than one is shown mainly by other members of the sentence such as attributives (made of numeral-measure words, demonstrative pronouns or adjectives).

178

3. 双宾语动词谓语句 Sentences with a predicate verb taking two objects

有的动词可以带两个宾语。在双宾语动词谓语句里，间接宾语（一般是指人的）在前，直接宾语（一般是指事物的）在后。

Some verbs can take two objects: an indirect object (usually referring to a person) and a direct object (usually referring to a thing), with the former preceding the latter.

名词或代词 Nouns or pronouns	动词 Verbs	名词或代词 （指人） Nouns or pronouns (referring to persons)	名词（指事物） Nouns (referring to things)
王老师	教	我们	语法。
我	还	丁云	词典。
他	告诉	我	他的名字。
帕兰卡	问	古波	一个汉字。

注意：汉语里能带两个宾语的动词是比较少的，并不是任何一个动词都可以带双宾语。不能说"他买我一本书"或"我介绍他我的朋友"。这两个句子必须用介词"给"引出间接宾语："他给我买一本书"，"我给他介绍我的朋友"。

Note that some but not all Chinese verbs can take two objects; there are only a small number that can. Sentences such as "他买我一本书" and "我介绍他我的朋友" are incorrect. Chi-

179

nese idiom requires that the indirect objects "我" and "他" be preceded by the preposition "给". That is why it is correct to say "他给我买一本书" and "我给他介绍我的朋友"。

练习 Exercises

1. 读下列词组并造句：Read out the following phrases and make sentences with them:

中文系　英文系　法文系　外语系

中文书　英文书　法文书　外文书

中文杂志　中文画报　汉语词典

英文杂志　英文画报　英语词典

法文杂志　法文画报　法语词典

外文杂志　外文画报　外语词典

2. 读下列数目并用汉字写出来：Read the following numbers, then write them out in Chinese characters:

10　54　32　61

40　17　99　82

3. 跟你的同学口头演算下列算术题：Do the following sums orally with a fellow student of yours:

180

例 Example $1+2$

→一加 (jiā, plus) 二是几？

一加二是三。

(1) $4+6$　　(2) $21+18$　　(3) $37+3$

(4) $50+20$　　(5) $68+27$

例 Example $20-3$

→二十减 (jiǎn, minus) 三是多少？

二十减三是十七。

(1) $85-4$　　(2) $48-18$　　(3) $90-32$

(4) $6-1$　　(5) $79-69$

4. 说出乘法口诀：Try to say the following multiplication formulas:

例 Example 一二得 (dé, to get) 二　　$(1 \times 2 = 2)$

二三得六　　　$(2 \times 3 = 6)$

四七二十八　　$(4 \times 7 = 28)$

(1) 一六 _____

(2) 六七 _____

(3) 三八 _____

(4) 四九 _____

(5) 七七 _____

(6) 五八 _____

(7) 八九 _____

(8) 九九 _____

5. 填入量词，然后再用"多少"或"几"提问：Fill in the blanks with measure words, and then ask questions using "多少" or "几"：

例 Example　我有一____中国朋友。

　　　　　→我有一个中国朋友。

　　　　　你有几个中国朋友？

(1) 三____老师教我们。

(2) 他去书店买一____语法书。

(3) 我们医院有五十____大夫。

(4) 阅览室有八十七____画报。

(5) 这儿有一____银行。

6. 回答下列问题：Answer the following questions:

(1) 谁教古波语法？

(2) 丁云是不是老师？她教他们什么？

182

(3) 他们教丁云什么？

(4) 你们班有几个老师？

(5) 谁教你们语法？

(6) 中国老师教你们什么？

(7) 你问老师什么？

(8) 你问谁生词*？

六、语音语调 Pronunciation and Intonation

1. 词的重音(3) Word stress (3)

(1) 数词和量词结合时，一般是数词重读，量词轻读。例如：
When a numeral is combined with a measure word, the numeral generally has a strong stress and the measure word is pronounced with a weak stress. E.g.

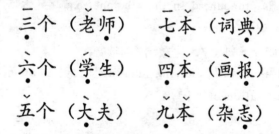

(2) 数词"十"单用时重读。"十"和其他数字结合，"十"在开头时不重读，如"十二"。"十"在末尾重读，如"三十"。但后面有量词时，"十"要轻读，如"三十个"、"四十本"。"十"夹在其他数字中间也轻读，如"九十三个"。

The numeral "十", when standing alone, is uttered with a strong stress. When "十" is combined with other numerals, it is not stressed if it forms the first element, as in "十二", but it is stressed when it is the second element, as in "三十". When "十" is followed by a measure word, it is pronounced with a weak stress, as in "三十个", "四十本". When "十" is sandwiched between other numerals it is also pronounced with a weak stress, as in "九十三个".

2. "一"的变调 The changes of tones of "一":

"一"的原调是第一声。"一"在第四声或由第四声变来的轻声前边读第二声, 如"一个"。如果"一"后边是其他声调, 就读第四声, 如"一本"。

The word "一" is normally pronounced in the 1st tone. When "一" is followed by a syllable in the 4th tone, or by a syllable in the neutral tone transformed from the 4th tone, it is pronounced in the 2nd tone, as in "一个". If "一" is followed by a syllable in tones other than those mentioned above, it is pronounced in the 4th tone, e.g. "一本".

3. 练习 Exercises

(1) 朗读下列数字, 注意"十"的读音:

Read aloud the following numerals, paying attention to the pronunciation of "十":

六 七 八 九 十

十一 十二 十三 十四 十五

二十 三十 四十 五十 六十

七十　八十　二十一　三十二

七十三　八十四　九十五　四十个

五十个　六十个　七十个　八十个

二十二本　七十四本　八十五本

六十三本　九十九本　五十一本

（2）朗读下列带 z, c, s, 的词语，注意发音和声调：

Read aloud the following words and expressions containing the sounds z, c and s, paying attention to their pronunciation and tone:

z: 在　坐　再见　汉字　名字

c: 词典　三层　生词

s: 四个　三千　告诉　宿舍

汉字笔顺表　Table of Stroke-order of Chinese Characters

1	中	丶 ㄇ 口 口 中
2	文	丶 亠 ㄓ 文
3	系	丿

		幺（𠂆 幺 幺）	
		小	
4	个	人	個
		丨	
5	几	丿 几	幾
6	教	孝 耂	
		子	
		攵（丿 乀 𠂉 攵）	
7	口		
8	敢	耳（一 丄 丆 耳 耳 耳 耳）	
		攵	
9	当	业（丨 丷 业）	當
		彐（一 彐 彐）	
10	互	一 工 互 互	
11	相		
12	新	亲 立（丶 丷 亠 立 立）	
		朩	
		斤（丿 厂 斤 斤）	
13	阅	门	閱

186

		兑	
14	览	⺍（丶 丿 ⺍ ⺍）	覽
		见	
15	室	宀	
		至（一 厶 云 至）	
16	杂	九	雜
		朩	
17	志	士（一 十 士）	誌
		心	
18	本	木	
		一	
19	馆	饣（⺈ 饣）	館
		官　宀	
		㠯（丨 𠃌 𠃌 㠯 㠯）	

DO YOU KNOW?

Education in China

China's education is divided into three stages: primary school, secondary or middle school and college or university. According to China's present educational system, the length

187

of schooling is five years for primary school, six years for secondary or middle school (three years for junior middle school and three years for senior middle school), four years for college (five years for certain subjects). There are also secondary vocational or technical schools (usually three years) and technical colleges (usually two or three years). We have universities (大学) such as "Beijing University", "Fudan University". We also have institutions of higher learning specialized in one subject or study known as "学院" (colleges or institutes) such as "Beijing Engineering Institute", "Beijing Foreign Languages Institute".

The various departments in a university or an institute are known in China as "系" each of which consists of a number of specialities.

第十六课 Lesson 16

一、课文 Text

这条裙子是新的

古　波: 帕兰卡，王　老师　给　我们　两
Gǔbō:　　Pàlánkǎ, Wáng Lǎoshī gěi wǒmen liǎng

张　票。
zhāng piào.

帕兰卡: 什么　票?
Pàlánkǎ: Shénme piào?

古　波： 京剧 票。 我们　晚上　去 看
Gǔbō:　　Jīngjù piào. Wǒmen　wǎnshang　qù kàn

京剧。
Jīngjù.

帕兰卡： 太 好 了。
Pàlánkǎ:　Tài hǎo le.

古　波： 我们 从　哪儿 去?
Gǔbō:　　Wǒmen cóng　nǎr　qù?

帕兰卡： 从 我 家 去。
Pàlánkǎ:　Cóng wǒ jiā qù.

妈　妈： 你 找 什么?
Māma:　Nǐ zhǎo shénme?

帕兰卡： 我 找 一条　裙子。 我 和　古波
Pàlánkǎ:　Wǒ zhǎo yìtiáo　qúnzi. Wǒ hé　Gǔbō

190

晚上 看 京剧。
wǎnshang kàn jīngjù.

妈 妈： 你 的 裙子 在 我 这儿。 是 这
Māma: Nǐ de qúnzi zài wǒ zhèr. Shì zhè

条 吗?
tiáo ma?

帕兰卡： 这 条 裙子 不 是 我 的, 这 是
Pàlánkǎ: Zhè tiáo qúnzi bú shì wǒ de, zhè shì

姐姐 的。
jiějie de.

妈 妈： 那儿 还 有 两条。
Māma: Nàr hái yǒu liǎngtiáo.

帕兰卡： 也 不 是。 那 都 是 旧 的。
Pàlánkǎ: Yě bú shì. Nà dōu shì jiù de.

妈 妈： 这 条 裙子 是 新 的, 是 不 是
Māma: Zhè tiáo qúnzi shì xīn de, shì bu shì

这 条?
zhè tiáo?

帕兰卡： 对 了, 是 这 条。 妈妈, 我 穿
Pàlánkǎ: Duì le, shì zhè tiáo. Māma, wǒ chuān

哪 件 衬衫?
nǎ jiàn chènshān?

妈　妈：那件　绿　的　很　好。
Māma:　　Nàjiàn　lǜ　de　hěn　hǎo.

帕兰卡：不，那件　太　大，　我　穿　白
Pàlánkǎ:　Bù,　nàjiàn　tài　dà,　wǒ　chuān　bái

衬衫。
chènshān.

生词　New Words

1. 条	（量）	tiáo	*a measure word*
2. 裙子	（名）	qúnzi	skirt
3. 两	（数）	liǎng	two
4. 张	（量）	zhāng	*a measure word*, piece
5. 票	（名）	piào	ticket
6. 京剧	（名）	jīngjù	Beijing opera
7. 晚上	（名）	wǎnshang	evening
8. 太	（副）	tài	too, too much
9. 从	（介）	cóng	from
10. 找	（动）	zhǎo	to look for, to call on (a person)
11. 这儿	（代）	zhèr	here
12. 旧	（形）	jiù	old
13. 穿	（动）	chuān	to put on, to wear

192

14.	件	（量）	jiàn	*a measure word*
15.	衬衫	（名）	chènshān	shirt, blouse
16.	绿	（形）	lǜ	green
17.	大	（形）	dà	big, large
18.	白	（形）	bái	white

补充词　Supplementary Words

1.	蓝	（形）	lán	blue
2.	上衣	（名）	shàngyī	upper outer garment, jacket
3.	裤子	（名）	kùzi	trousers
4.	大衣	（名）	dàyī	overcoat, topcoat
5.	黑	（形）	hēi	black, dark
6.	剧场	（名）	jùchǎng	theatre
7.	座位	（名）	zuòwèi	seat

二、注释　Notes

1. "王老师给我们两张票。"

这里的"给"是动词。

"给"is here a verb.

"二"和"两"都是表示"2"这个数目。在量词前（或不需要量词的名词前）一般用"两"不用"二"，如"两张票"、"两条裙子"。但10以上数目中的"2"，如12、20、22、32等数目中的"2"，不管后面有没有量词，都仍用"二"，如"十二个老师"。

Both "二" and "两" mean "2". When "2" comes before a measure word (or before a noun which needs no measure word before it), "两" is used instead of "二", as in "两张票", "两条裙子". But in numbers larger than ten (12, 20, 22, 32, etc.), "二" is used irrespective of whether it is followed by a measure word, as in "十二个老师".

量词"张"常用作纸或象纸那样有一个平面的物体的量词。如"一张报"、"一张纸"、"一张桌子"等。

The measure word "张" is used to apply to paper or anything having a smooth surface or top like paper, as in "一张报", "一张纸" or "一张桌子 (zhuōzl, table)".

2. "太好了。"

"太好了"是表示满意、赞叹的用语。"太"在这里表示极高的程度。

"太好了" is an expression used to show satisfaction or admiration. The word "太" signifies a very high degree of such sentiments.

注意：副词"太"在更多的情况下常表示程度过分，如"这条裙子太大"。表示否定的"不太"跟"不很"意思差不多。

Note that the adverb "太" is more often than not used to signify "excess" or something that goes beyond the accepted standard. "这条裙子太大" means "This skirt is much too big for me". "不太", the negative form of "太", means about the same as "不很".

3. "这条裙子不是我的。"

指示代词"这、那"作定语时，名词前也要用量词，如"那张票"、"这件衬衫"。

When the demonstrative pronoun "这" or "那" functions

as an attributive, the noun it qualifies also takes a measure word before it, e.g. "那张票", "这件衬衫":

4. "是这条吗?" "那儿还有两条。"

意思是"你找的是这条裙子吗?" "那儿还有两条裙子"。指示代词和量词或数词和量词作定语时，如果语言环境清楚，它们所修饰的中心语可以省略。例如：

"是这条吗?" means "Is this the skirt you are looking for?" "那儿还有两条" means "There are two more skirts there." When a demonstrative pronoun plus a measure word or a numeral plus a measure word functions as an attributive, the noun it qualifies can be understood if the context leaves no room for doubt. E.g.

我有两本中文书，一本(书)是新的，

一本(书)是旧的。

三、替换与扩展 Substitution and Extension

(一)

1. 这张票是你的吗?

这张票不是我的，是她的。

那张票也是她的吗?

那张票也是她的。

地图	(张)
裙子	(条)
衬衫	(件)
词典	(本)
本子*	(个)

2. 你有几本杂志？

我有一本。

那两本杂志是谁的？

那两本杂志都是<u>古波</u>的。

老师
他们
我哥哥
图书馆

3. 你的衬衫是不是<u>新</u>的？

我的衬衫不是新的，是<u>旧</u>的。

绿，白
白，蓝*

4. 他爸爸给他什么？

他爸爸给他<u>两本书</u>。

十二本杂志	一件上衣*
两件衬衫	两条裤子*

5. 你晚上去不去商店？

我去商店。

你从哪儿去？

我从<u>家</u>去。

宿舍
图书馆
银行
书店

196

6. 你从书店来吗？

不，我从朋友那儿来。

古波的宿舍
谢先生那儿
帕兰卡家

(二)

1. 找东西　Looking for something

A: 喂，你找什么？

B: 我找我的笔。

A: 你的笔是新的吗？

B: 不是新的，是旧的。

A: 是不是黑的？

B: 对了，在哪儿？

A: 在那儿。

B: 谢谢你。

2. 送客人　Seeing a guest off

A: 这是您的大衣。

B: 这不是我的，我的大衣是蓝的。

197

A: 是这件吗？

B: 对了，谢谢您，再见！

A: 再见！

3. 谈书　Talking about books

A: 这是什么书？

B: 这是汉语语法书。

A: 这本书是英文的吗？

B: 不是英文的，是法文的。

A: 你有英文的吗？

B: 我没有。

A: 我去书店买一本英文的。

* * *

京剧票

四、阅读短文　Reading Text

帕兰卡问妈妈："晚上您用不用车？"妈妈
说："不用。你去哪儿？"帕兰卡告诉妈妈，王老师给他们两张京剧票，她和古波晚上去看京剧。

晚上，他们从帕兰卡那儿去剧场。帕兰卡穿一件新衬衫和一条新裙子，衬衫是白的，裙子是绿的。古波穿一件黑上衣，他的上衣也是新的。

这个剧场很大。帕兰卡问古波："我们的座位在哪儿？"古波说："那两个座位是我们的。你看，王老师在那儿。那儿还有两个中国留学生。"

五、语法 Grammar

1. "是"字句(2) "是" sentences type (2)

代词、形容词、名词等后面加上助词"的"所组成的"的"字结构，具有名词的作用，可以单独运用。这种"的"字结构也常出现在"是"字句里。例如：

A pronoun, an adjective or a noun plus the structural particle "的" forms what is called a "的" construction. In a sentence a "的" construction does the same work as a noun and can stand by itself. This type of construction often forms part of a "是" sentence. E.g.

哪本画报是你的？

那条裙子是旧的，你有新的吗？

我们家的车是绿的，他们家的车是蓝的。

我有英文的汉语语法书，我去买一本法文的。

那个老师是你们系的吗？

2．介词"从"的宾语　Object of the preposition "从"

介词"从"的宾语一般是表示地点或时间的词或词组。一个不表示地点的名词或代词，必须在后边加上"这儿"或"那儿"，才能作"从"的宾语，组成介词结构，修饰动词。如：

The object of the preposition "从" is usually a word or phrase denoting place or time. In the case of a noun or pronoun not indicating place, "这儿" or "那儿" must be added to it before it becomes an object of the preposition "从", forming a prepositional construction qualifying the predicative verb. E.g.

我从朋友那儿来。

他从我这儿去书店。

介词"在"以及动词"来"、"去"、"在"的宾语要表示地点时也和"从"的宾语一样。例如：

The same is true of the object of the preposition "在" as well as the objects of the verbs "来", "去" and "在" when they denote places. E.g.

你弟弟在我这儿看杂志。

她去张大夫那儿。

朋友们常常来我这儿。

我的笔在谁那儿？

你的笔在古波那儿。

练习　Exercises

1. 读下列词组并造句：Read out the following phrases and make sentences with them:

新词典　新书　新画报　新地图

新图书馆　旧宿舍　旧笔　旧车

旧杂志　旧衬衫　绿裙子　白纸

大商店　大书店　大词典

2. 把下列数字改成汉字，并填上适当的量词：Write out the following numerals in Chinese characters, and then fill in each blank with an appropriate measure word:

2＿＿书店　　20＿＿裙子

12＿＿衬衫　　2＿＿地图

92＿＿票　　　22＿＿杂志

7＿＿大夫　　　1＿＿孩子

3. 把下列句子改成用"的"字结构做宾语的句子(注意量词的使用)：Change the following to sentences with "的" construction as the object of the verb "是", paying special attention to the use of measure words:

例　Example　这是我的书。

→这本书是我的。

(1) 这是绿衬衫。

(2) 那是中文画报。

(3) 这是阅览室的杂志。

(4) 那是妹妹的裙子。

(5) 这是我们老师的地图。

(6) 那是我们学院的宿舍。

4. 填入适当的介词：Put in an appropriate preposition in each of the following sentences:

(1) 古波____宿舍写汉字。

(2) 她____丁云那儿来。

(3) 我____我朋友买一本书。

(4) 我们____宿舍去商店。

(5) 你____哪儿看京剧？

(6) 他____图书馆来这儿。

5. 根据划线部分将下列句子改为用疑问代词的问句：Change the following to questions with an interrogative pronoun, substituting suitable interrogative pronouns for the underlined words or phrases:

(1) 她给<u>妹妹</u>一条裙子。

(2) 他爱人从<u>银行</u>来。

(3) 王老师教他们<u>汉语</u>。

(4) 我穿<u>绿</u>衬衫。

(5) 他常常在<u>他朋友那儿</u>喝茶。

(6) 那个女学生从图书馆去<u>书店</u>。

(7) <u>他</u>给我一本画报。

(8) 那本书的名字叫《<u>汉语口语</u>》。

6．跟你的同学一起作游戏： Play games with fellow students of yours:

第一个学生念下面两句儿歌，其他学生依次将"一个青蛙"改为"两个青蛙"、"三个青蛙"……。注意：嘴、眼睛和腿的数目也必须跟着变，看谁说得对。

Student A reads aloud the two lines from the nursery rhyme given below, Student B changes "一个青蛙" to "两个青蛙", Student C changes "两个青蛙" to "三个青蛙" and so on. Note that the number of mouths, eyes and legs must increase as the number of frogs increases.

A: 一个青蛙 (qīngwā, frog) 一张嘴 (zuǐ, mouth)
两个眼睛 (yǎnjing, eye) 四条腿 (tuǐ, leg)

B: 两个青蛙……

六、语音语调 Pronunciation and Intonation

1．词的重音(4) Word stress (4)

带词尾"子"的双音节词，前一个音节重读，"子"读轻声。例如：

The first syllable of a dissyllable formed with the suffix "子" is stressed, and "子" is pronounced in the neutral tone. E.g.

裙子　裤子　孩子　本子

结构助词"的"跟名词、代词、形容词等组成"的"字结构时，"的"永远读轻声。例如：

In "的" constructions formed of the structural particle "的" and a noun, a pronoun or an adjective, "的" is always pronounced in the neutral tone. E.g.

新的　旧的　绿的　他的　姐姐的

2. 练习　Exercises

朗读下列双音节词语，注意三声变调和词重音：

Read aloud the following dissyllabic words, paying attention to the changes of the 3rd tone and word stress:

第三声 + 第一声：老师　两张　北京

第三声 + 第二声：两条　五层

第三声 + 第三声：语法　口语　九本

第三声 + 第四声：请问　九号　五件

第三声 + 轻声：晚上　本子　姐姐

朗读下面的成语：　Read aloud the following proverbs:

Zhòng zhì chéng chéng. (Unity of will is an im-
众 志 成 城。 pregnable stronghold.)

Shībài shì chénggōng zhī mǔ. (Failure is the
失 败 是 成 功 之 母。 mother of success.)

汉字笔顺表 Table of Stroke–order of Chinese Characters

1	条	夂						條
		木						
2	裙	衤 (丶 ㇇ 衤 衤 衤)						
		君	尹 (𠃌 ㇇ 彐 尹)					
			口					
3	两	一	一	丙	丙	丙	两	兩
4	张	弓 (𠃌 ㇅ 弓)						張
		长 (丿 ㇅ 长 长)						
5	票	覀 (一 丆 覀 覀 覀 覀)						
		示	二					
			小					
6	京	亠						
			口					
			小					

7	剧	居	尸			劇
			古	十		
				口		
		刂（丨 刂）				
8	晚	日				
		免（ノ ⺈ ⺈ 夕 各 免 免）				
9	上	丨 卜 上				
10	太	大 太				
11	从	人				從
		人				
12	找	扌				
		戈（一 弋 弌 戈）				
13	旧	丨				舊
		日				
14	穿	穴（宀 宂 穴）				
		牙（一 二 于 牙）				
15	件	亻				
		牛（ノ 一 二 牛）				
16	衬	衤				襯

		寸	
17	衫	衤	
		彡 (ノ 彡 彡)	
18	绿	纟	绿
		录 ⺕ (乛 ⺕ ⺕)	
		氺 (丿 氺 氺 氺 氺)	
19	白		

Beijing Opera

Beijing opera is a form of traditional Chinese drama with a history of about 150 years. It took shape in Beijing and became popular throughout the country. It is a comprehensive expression of the traditional Chinese drama, music, dance, boxing and fencing, and it has always been loved by the Chinese people.

Beijing opera is characterized by its symbolic actions, giving full play to the various artistic mediums of singing, acting, recitation and acrobatics accompanied by the rhythmic beats of gongs and drums. It has thus formed a perfect artistic system of its own.

208

第十七课 Lesson 17

一、课文 Text

现在几点

帕兰卡： 你 从 哪儿 来？
Pàlánkǎ: Nǐ cóng nǎr lái?

古 波： 我 从 食堂 来。 现在 几点？
Gǔbō: Wǒ cóng shítáng lái. Xiànzài jǐdiǎn?

帕兰卡： 差 五分 两点。
Pàlánkǎ: Chà wǔfēn liǎngdiǎn.

古 波： 我 两点 一刻 上 课。
Gǔbō: Wǒ liǎngdiǎn yíkè shàng kè.

帕兰卡： 你 几点 下 课？
Pàlánkǎ: Nǐ jǐdiǎn xià kè?

古 波： 四点 二十 下 课。
Gǔbō: Sìdiǎn èrshí xià kè.

帕兰卡： 下 课 以后 你 有 事儿 吗？
Pàlánkǎ: Xià kè yǐhòu nǐ yǒu shìr ma?

古 波： 没 有 事儿。 我 回 宿舍 看
Gǔbō: Méi yǒu shìr. Wǒ huí sùshè kàn

书。 晚上 我 跟 朋友 一起 去
shū. Wǎnshang Wǒ gēn péngyou yìqǐ qù

看 电影。
kàn diànyǐng.

帕兰卡： 你 看 几点 的？
Pàlánkǎ: Nǐ kàn jǐdiǎn de?

古 波： 我 看 八点 的。 你 去 不 去？
Gǔbō: Wǒ kàn bādiǎn de. Nǐ qù bu qù?

帕兰卡： 我 不 去。 下 课 以后， 我们
Pàlánkǎ: Wǒ bú qù. Xià kè yǐhòu, wǒmen

去 咖啡馆， 好 吗？
qù kāfēiguǎn, hǎo ma?

古　波：好 啊。你 四点半 在 那儿 等
Gǔbō:　Hǎo a.　Nǐ　sìdiǎnbàn zài　nàr　děng

我。
wǒ.

帕兰卡：我 跟 丁 云 一起 去。
Pàlánkǎ:　Wǒ gēn Dīng Yún　yìqǐ　qù.

古　波：太 好 了。你们 坐 车 去 吗?
Gǔbō:　Tài hǎo le.　Nǐmen zuò chē qù ma?

帕兰卡：不，我们 走 路 去。
Pàlánkǎ:　Bù,　wǒmen zǒu lù qù.

古　波：好，四点半 再见。
Gǔbō:　Hǎo,　sìdiǎnbàn zàijiàn.

生词 New Words

1. 点　　　(量) diǎn　　*a measure word*, o' clock

2. 食堂　　(名) shítáng　dining-hall

3. 差　　　(动) chà　　to lack, to be short of

4. 分　　　(量) fēn　　*a measure word*, minute

5. 刻　　　(量) kè　　*a measure word*, quarter

　　　　　　　　　　　　(of an hour)

6. 上(课)　(动) shàng(kè)　to attend (a class), to

　　　　　　　　　　　　teach (in a class)

7. 课　　　(名) kè　　class, lesson

8.	下（课）	(动) xià (kè)	class is over or dismissed
9.	以后	(名) yǐhòu	later on, in the future
10.	事儿	(名) shìr	business, thing
11.	回	(动) huí	to return, to go back
12.	跟	(介、动) gēn	with, to follow
13.	一起	(副、名) yìqǐ	together
14.	电影	(名) diànyǐng	film, movie
15.	咖啡馆	(名) kāfēiguǎn	café
	咖啡	(名) kāfēi	coffee
16.	半	(数) bàn	half
17.	啊	(助) a	*a modal particle*
18.	等	(动) děng	to wait
19.	走	(动) zǒu	to go, to walk
20.	路	(名) lù	road, way

补充词 Supplementary Words

1.	上班	shàng bān	to go to work
2.	下班	xià bān	to come or go off work
3.	电影院	(名) diànyǐngyuàn	cinema
4.	表	(名) biǎo	watch
5.	钟	(名) zhōng	clock

212

6. 以前　(名) yǐqián　　　　　before, in the past, ago

二、注释　Notes

1. "下课以后你有事儿吗?"

名词"以后"（及"以前"）除了单用外，还常用在单词或词组之后，表示时间。如"两点以后"、"认识以后"、"来中国以后"。

As well as standing alone, the noun "以后" (or "以前") may be used after a word or phrase denoting time, e.g. "两点以后", "认识以后", "来中国以后".

"有事儿"的意思是"有事儿要作"。

"有事儿" means "to have something to do" or "to be engaged".

2. "好啊。"

这里的"啊"是助词，读轻声，表示肯定、赞同的语气。

"啊" here is a modal particle, showing affirmation, approval or consent, and is pronounced in the neutral tone.

3. "我跟丁云一起去。"

介词"跟"与它的宾语组成的介词结构，常用在动词前作状语。这种结构又常常跟副词"一起"连用（"跟…一起"）。

The prepositional construction "跟…", which is made up of the preposition "跟" and its object, is very often used in front of the verb as an adverbial adjunct. Besides, "跟…" frequently goes with the adverb "一起" to form the construction "跟…一起" which means "together with".

4. "你们坐车去吗?"

这也是连动句。这类连动句中前一个动词往往是后一个动词所表示的动作的方式。如"走路去"、"用笔写"、"用汉语介绍"。

"你们坐车去吗?" is another instance of a sentence with

verbal constructions in series. In sentences of this kind, the first verb usually tells the manner of the action expressed by the second verb, as in "走路去", "用笔写" and "用汉语介绍":

三、替换与扩展　Substitution and Extension

（一）

1. 现在几点？
   现在两点。

3:05	6:30
4:15	10:45
5:20	11:58

2. 你几点上课？
   我两点一刻上课。

下课，	12:10
去食堂，	12:30
上班·，	8:00
下班·，	4:00
去咖啡馆，	4:30

3. 你现在有课吗？

   有课。

   下课以后你作什么？

   我回宿舍看书。

去商店买衬衫
回家写信
去阅览室看报
去咖啡馆喝茶
去电影院 买票

4. 你常常坐车去<u>学院</u>吗?
   我常常坐车去学院。

来学院　回宿舍
去图书馆　回家

5. 你跟谁一起<u>去</u>?
   我跟我朋友一起去。
   他叫什么名字?
   他叫 Jiǎkè。

住
走
工作
学习
看电影

6. 两点一刻你在哪儿等我?
   我在<u>咖啡馆</u>等你。

食堂　书店
家　　宿舍

(二)

1. 问时间　Asking the time

　　A: 请问，您的表*现在几点？

　　B: 差五分九点。我的表*快 (kuài, fast)。

　　你看，那儿是邮局*的

　　钟*，现在八点五十。

　　A: 谢谢。

2. 约会　Making an appointment

　　A: 晚上你有事儿吗？

　　B: 没有事儿。

　　A: 你来我家，好吗？

　　B: 好啊。几点？

　　A: 七点半，好吗？

3. 邀请　Making an invitation

　　A: 喂，晚上我们看电影，好吗？

　　B: 什么电影？

A: 中国电影，是新的。

B: 太好了，你买几点的票？

A: 我去买八点十分的票，好吗？

B: 好。七点五十我在家等你，我们一起
坐车去。

*　　　*　　　*

便　条　(biàntiáo, note)

丁云：你好！

今天下午三点半我来找你，你不在宿舍。
我告诉你，明天晚上八点我们学校有一个中文
电影。我们一起去看好吗，你明天晚上七点来我
家，我在家等你。再见！

帕兰卡
三月三日

四、阅读短文　Reading Text

Jiǎkè 是古波的好朋友，他也学习汉语，他
跟古波在一个班*。他们常常一起去看电
影。

今天 (jīntiān, today) 有一个新电影，是中国的。Jiǎkè 晚上没有事儿，他找古波看电影。十二点，他去电影院买电影票，十二点半他坐车去宿舍找古波，古波不在。

古波今天有课，他很忙。一点半他去食堂，两点一刻还有口语课。帕兰卡差五分两点来找他，她告诉古波，下午四点半她跟丁云一起去咖啡馆。古波说："好，现在我去上课，四点半再见。"

五、语法 Grammar

1. 钟点的读法：Ways of telling the time

2:00	两点
2:05	两点五分
2:12	两点十二分
2:15	两点一刻(两点十五分)
2:30	两点半(两点三十分)

2:45	两点三刻（差一刻三点）
2:55	差五分三点（两点五十五分）
3:00	三点

2. 表时间的名词或数量词作状语 Nouns or numeral-measure words denoting time as adverbial adjuncts

表时间的名词或数量词（如"现在、晚上、以后、两点十分"）可以作主语、谓语、定语等。例如：

A noun or a numeral-measure word such as "现在", "晚上", "以后" or "两点十分" can be used as the subject, predicate or attributive of a sentence. E.g.

现在两点。

今天星期三。

他看晚上的电影。

我去买八点十分的票。

表示时间的名词或数量词还可以直接作状语。作状语时它可以放在主语之后、谓语主要成分之前，也可以放在主语前（放在主语前更强调时间）。例如：

Such a noun or numeral-measure word can be used as an adverbial adjunct as well. When so used, it can be put either between the subject and the main element of the predicate or before the subject (in this case special emphasis is laid on the time). E.g.

名词或代词 Nouns or pro-nouns	时　间　词 Time words	动词和其它成分 Verbs and other elements
我们	晚上	去看电影。
我	两点一刻	上课。
你	下课以后	有事儿吗?
我	三点以前	在家。

时　间　词 Time words	名词或代词 Nouns or pronouns	动词和其它成分 Verbs and other elements
晚上	我们	去看电影。
两点一刻	我	上课。
下课以后	你	有事儿吗?
三点以前	我	在家。

注意: Points to be noted:

(1) 表时间的名词或数量词直接作状语,前边不需要再加介词。不能说"我在两点一刻上课"。

When used adverbially, a noun or a numeral-measure word denoting time does not necessarily take a preposition before it, and it is wrong to say "我在两点一刻上课".

（2）表时间的名词或数量词作状语，决不能放在句末。不能说"我们去看电影晚上"。

Such a noun or numeral-measure word, when used adverbially, can never be put at the end of the sentence. Therefore, you can't say "我们去看电影晚上".

（3）如果作状语的时间词不止一个，表示较大时间单位的词总是在表示较小时间单位的词的前边，如："晚上八点我去看电影"不能说成"八点晚上我去看电影"。

If there is more than one adverbial of time in a sentence, the time word denoting the biggest time unit usually precedes those denoting the smaller time units. That is why "晚上八点我去看电影" is correct and "八点晚上我去看电影" is wrong.

（4）一个句子里既有表示时间的状语，又有表示地点的状语同时修饰动词时，表时间的状语常常放在表地点的状语的前边。

In a sentence, if there are both an adverbial of time and an adverbial of place to simultaneously qualify the verb, the former usually precedes the latter.

名词或代词 Nouns or pronouns	时 间 词 Time words	地 点 词 Position words	动词和其它成分 Verbs and other elements
你们	四点半	在那儿	等我。
我姐姐	现在	在食堂	工作。
他	晚上	从咖啡馆	来我这儿。

时 间 词 Time words	名词或代词 Nouns or pronouns	地 点 词 Position words	动词和其它成分 Verbs and other elements
四点半	你们	在那儿	等我。
现在	我姐姐	在食堂	工作。
晚上	他	从咖啡馆	来我这儿。

3. 用"……，好吗？"来提问　Tag question "…，好吗？"

"……，好吗？"也是一种提问的方法，常用来提出建议，征询对方的意见。这种疑问句的前一部分是陈述句。如：

The tag question "…，好吗？" is often used to make a request or a suggestion and ask for the opinion of the person addressed. The first part of such a tag question is usually a statement. E.g.

晚上你来我这儿，好吗？

我们跟他一起去，好吗？

下课以后我们去咖啡馆，好吗？

你用英语给我们介绍这个京剧，好吗？

答句中常用"好啊"、"好"表示同意。

The usual form of answer to this type of question is "好

啊" or "好", indicating consent or agreement of the person addressed.

1. 读下列词组并造句：Read out the following phrases and make sentences with them:

(1) 下课以后　回家以后　来中国以后

看电影以后　介绍以后　上课以前˙

回宿舍以前˙

(2) 跟老师说中文　跟朋友看电影

跟丁云一起去图书馆

跟他们一起学习　跟谁一起工作

2. 说出下列时间：Say the following time in Chinese:

6：00　　3：30

8：22　　4：55

9：45　　10：35

7：08　　11：57

3. 根据划线部分提出问题：Make up questions asking about the underlined parts of the following sentences, using interrogative pronouns:

223

(1) 现在十二点二十五分。

(2) 我五点半回家。

(3) 晚上他们学习外语。

(4) 他跟他弟弟一起去看电影。

(5) 她坐车去王老师家。

(6) 下课以后他从学院去图书馆。

4. 根据本课阅读短文进行问答练习　Ask each other questions on the Reading Text.

5. 向你的朋友提出建议：Make a suggestion to a friend of yours:

例　Example　去商店

⟶ A: 现在你有事儿吗？

B: 没有事儿。

A: 我们一起去商店好吗？

B: 好。几点去？

A: 现在四点二十，四点半去，好吗？

B: 好。

(1) 看京剧

224

(2) 去图书馆

6. 根据下列内容写一段话。 Write a short passage, using the information given.

7:35 坐车去学院

8:00 上课

11:55 下课

2:15 去阅览室看杂志

4:30 跟朋友一起去咖啡馆

5:50 回宿舍

7:45 看电影

六、语音语调 Pronunciation and Intonation

1. 词的重音(5) Word stress (5)

(1) 大多数三音节词和四音节词的最末一个音节是重音。三音节词常用的重音格式是"中轻重"。例如：

Most words of three or four syllables have a main stress falling on the last syllable. The usual stress pattern of the trisyllables is "medium-weak-strong". E.g.

咖啡馆　图书馆　中文系

留学生　阅览室　实验室

四音节词常用的重音格式是"中轻中重"。例如：

The usual stress pattern of the four syllables is "medium-weak-medium-strong". E.g.

外语学院　汉语词典

中国画报　中文杂志

(2) 语气助词"啊、吗、呢"等不能重读，永远读轻声。例如："好啊!""你呢?""你有事儿吗?"

The modal particles "啊", "吗" and "呢", etc. are never stressed, but pronounced always in the neutral tone. E.g. "好啊!" "你呢?" "你有事儿吗?"

2. 练习　Exercises

朗读下列带 g、k 的词语，注意 g、k 的发音：

Read aloud the following words and expressions containing the sounds g and k, paying special attention to the pronunciation of these two sounds:

g: 个　哥哥　中国　工作　公司

k: 刻　上课　下课　口语　课文

汉字笔顺表　Table of Stroke-order of Chinese Characters

1	点	占		點
		灬（丶 丶 灬 灬）		

2	食	人	
		良（丶 ㇉ ㇋ ㇌ 自 自 良）	
3	堂	峃	
		土	
4	差	羊（丶 丷 ㇍ ㇎ 兰 羊）	
		工	
5	分	八	
		刀	
6	刻	亥	
		刂	
7	课	讠	課
		果（丶 冂 口 曰 旦 甲 早 果）	
8	以	㇄ ㇋ 以	
9	后	一 厂 ㇋ 后	後
10	事	一 ㇌ ㇍ 曰 ㇎ 写 写 事	
11	回	口	
		口	
12	跟	𧿹	口
		止（丨 ㇂ 止 止）	

		艮					
13	起	走	土				
			此（㇝ 丨 丬 此）				
		己（乛 コ 己）					
14	电	丨 冂 冂 日 电						電
15	影	景	日					
			京					
		彡					
16	咖	口						
		加	力					
			口					
17	啡	口						
		非	㇒（丨 ㇒ 丰 丰）					
			丰（丨 丨 丨 丰）					
18	半	丶 丷 半 半 半						
19	等	竹						
		寺	土					
			寸					
20	走							

第十八课 Lesson 18

复习 Revision

一、课文 Text

丁 云 的 一 天

丁　云　是　英语　系　的　学生。她　从

Dīng Yún shì Yīngyǔ xì de xuésheng. Tā cóng

北京 来 这儿 学习。英语 系 有 五个
Běijīng lái zhèr xuéxí. Yīngyǔ xì yǒu wǔge

中国 留学生。他们 都 在 学生 宿舍
Zhōngguó liúxuéshēng. Tāmen dōu zài xuésheng sùshè

住。
zhù.

丁 云 每天 六点 一刻 起 床。起
Dīng Yún měi tiān liùdiǎn yíkè qǐ chuáng. Qǐ

床 以后，她 学习 英语 和 法语。七点
chuáng yǐhòu, tā xuéxí Yīngyǔ hé Fǎyǔ. Qīdiǎn

半 她 坐 车 去 学院。每天 上午 她 都
bàn tā zuò chē qù xuéyuàn. Měi tiān shàngwǔ tā dōu

有 课。他们 八点 上 课，十一点 五十分
yǒu kè. Tāmen bādiǎn shàng kè, shíyīdiǎn wǔshífēn

下 课。
xià kè.

下 课 以后，丁 云
Xià kè yǐhòu, Dīng Yún

去 食堂 吃 饭。那 是
qù shítáng chī fàn. Nà shì

学生 食堂，她 在 那儿
xuésheng shítáng, tā zài nàr

认识 很 多 朋友。
rènshi hěn duō péngyou.

下午 丁 云 没 有 课， 她 回 宿舍 休
Xiàwǔ Dīng Yún méi yǒu kè, tā huí sùshè xiū-

息。 三 点 她 去 阅览室 看 画报 和 杂志。
xi. Sāndiǎn tā qù yuèlǎnshì kàn huàbào hé zázhì.

有 时候 她 去 朋友 家， 跟 朋友 说
Yǒu shíhou tā qù péngyou jiā, gēn péngyou shuō

英语， 有 时候 她 去 老师 那儿 问 问题。
Yīngyǔ, yǒu shíhou tā qù lǎoshī nàr wèn wèntí.

朋友们 也 常常 来 看 她。
Péngyoumen yě chángcháng lái kàn tā.

晚上 丁 云 在 宿舍 学习。有 时候
Wǎnshang Dīng Yún zài sùshè xuéxí. Yǒu shíhou

她 跟 朋友们 去 看 电影， 有 时候 给
tā gēn péngyoumen qù kàn diànyǐng, Yǒu shíhou gěi

爸爸、 妈妈 和 朋友 写 信。她 十一点
bàba, māma hé péngyou xiě xìn. Tā shíyīdiǎn

睡 觉。
shuì jiào.

生词 New Words

1. 天 　　(名) tiān 　　　　 day

2.	每	(代)	měi	every, each
3.	起床		qǐ chuáng	to get up
	起	(动)	qǐ	to get up, to rise
	床	(名)	chuáng	bed
4.	上午	(名)	shàngwǔ	morning
5.	吃	(动)	chī	to eat
6.	饭	(名)	fàn	meal, cooked rice, food
7.	多	(形)	duō	many, much, a lot of
8.	下午	(名)	xiàwǔ	afternoon
9.	休息	(动)	xiūxi	to rest, to take a rest
10.	有时候		yǒu shíhou	sometimes
	时候	(名)	shíhou	time
11.	问题	(名)	wèntí	question, problem
12.	睡觉		shuì jiào	to go to bed, to sleep

专名 Proper Names

北京　　　　Běijīng　　　Beijing

二、注释 Notes

1. "丁云每天六点一刻起床。"

指示代词"每"修饰名词时，也要在名词前用量词，如"每个学生"、"每本书"。"天"是一个特殊的名词，不需要用量词，所以可以说"每天"。

When qualified by the demonstrative pronoun "每", a noun usually takes a measure word before it, as in "每个学生" or "每本书". But the noun "天", when preceded by "每", doesn't need a measure word inserted in between, as in "每天".

用"每"的句子，谓语中常有表示数量的词语或副词"都"，如"每天上午她都有课"。

The word "每" is often accompanied in the predicate of the sentence by a word or phrase denoting quantity or by the adverb "都", as in "每天上午她都有课".

2."她在那儿认识很多新朋友。"

形容词"多"（及"少"）作定语时，前面要加上副词，如"很"等。不能说"多朋友"，要说"很多（的）朋友"。"很多"后边可以省略"的"。

When used attributively, the adjective "多" or "少" (shǎo, few, little) is usually preceded by such an adverb as "很", Instead of "多朋友" we practically always say "很多（的）朋友". "的" after "很多" may be omitted.

三、看图会话 **Talk About These Pictures**

1．介绍与了解 Getting acquainted with each other

我介绍一下儿，　　你叫什么名字？

这是……　　　　　你是哪国人？

　　　　　　　　　你在哪儿工作？

2. 谈家庭　Talking about your family

这是谁？

他是不是你哥哥？

他作什么工作？

你家有几个人？

你有没有孩子？

你有几个孩子？

3. 问好　Sending regards

你忙不忙？

问……好

……问你好

4. 谈学校　Talking about the institute

你们学院有几个系？

你们系有多少学生？

谁教你们语法？

你们下午有课吗？

5. 问去哪儿　Asking where someone is going

你从哪儿来？

你去哪儿？

你坐车去吗？

你跟谁一起去？

6. 描述一件东西　Talking about an article

这件衬衫是你的吗？

哪件衬衫是你的？

你的衬衫是不是绿的？

你的衬衫是新的吗？

7. 问时间、提建议　Asking the time, and making a suggestion

现在几点？

你几点吃饭？

下午你有事儿吗？

我们去书店，好吗？

太好了。

四、语法小结　A Brief Summary of Grammar

1. 主语、谓语、宾语、定语和状语　The subject, predicate, object, attributive and adverbial adjunct

汉语的句子一般可分为主语和谓语两大部分。

主语的主要成分常常是名词或代词，谓语的主要成分常常是动词或形容词等。主语一般在谓语的前边。例如：

A Chinese sentence is made up of two parts: the subject and the predicate.

The main element of the subject is usually a noun or a pronoun while the main element of the predicate is a verb or an adjective etc. The subject normally precedes the predicate. E.g.

这本书是新的。

丁云去商店。

你好！

在对话中，主语常常省略，如：
In a conversation, the subject is often omitted. E.g.

你几点下课？

（我）四点一刻下课。

如果语言环境清楚，谓语也可以省略。如：
The predicate can also be omitted if the context or situation leaves no room for misunderstanding. E.g.

你好吗？

我很好，你呢？

宾语是谓语的一部分，通常在动词的后边。宾语一般是名词或代词，有的动词还可以有两个宾语。例如：

The object, which may be either a noun or a pronoun, forms part of the predicate and usually follows the predicative verb. A number of verbs may have two objects. E.g.

他有一个哥哥。

我认识他。

王老师教我们汉语。

定语主要是修饰名词的，必须放在它所修饰的名词之前。名词、代词、形容词、数量词以及一些其它词类和结构都可以作定语。

An attributive is mainly used to qualify a noun and is placed before the noun it qualifies. Nouns, pronouns, adjectives, numeral-measure words etc. may all function as attributives.

状语主要是修饰动词或形容词的。副词、形容词、名词及介词结构等都可以作状语。状语必须放在它所修饰的动词或形容词的前边。例如：

An adverbial adjunct is mainly used to qualify a verb or an adjective. Adverbs, adjectives, nouns and prepositional constructions etc. may all function as adverbial adjuncts. Adverbial adjuncts regularly precede the words they qualify instead of coming after them. E.g.

我很好。

他们都学习汉语。

上午我们没有课。

我朋友从北京来。

2. 定语和结构助词"的" (1) Attributives and the structural particle "的" (1)

(1) 名词作定语表示领属关系，后边一般都要用"的"，如：

When used attributively to show possession, a noun usually takes "的" after it. E.g.

妈妈的车

图书馆的书

如果名词定语是说明中心语的性质，一般不用"的"，如：

When a noun is used attributively to indicate the characteristic or quality of the object denoted by the word it qualifies, it usually doesn't take "的" after it. E.g.

中国人　中国地图　外语学院

京剧票　学生宿舍　法文电影

英语系　汉语词典　中文杂志

(2) 人称代词作定语，表示领属关系，后边一般用"的"，如：

When used attributively to show possession, a personal pronoun usually takes "的" after it. E.g.

她的笔　我们的阅览室

他们的问题

如果它所修饰的词是指亲属或所属单位时一般不用"的"，如：

But if the word that the personal pronoun modifies refers to a family relation or a unit to which the person denoted by the pronoun belongs, the personal pronoun usually does not take "的" after it. E.g.

你哥哥　我家　你们系

(3) 数量词（或指示代词和量词）作定语，后边不用"的"，如：

When used attributively, a numeral-measure word (or a demonstrative pronoun together with a measure word) usually takes no "的" after it. E.g.

两张票　九十八个学生　这条裙子

(4) 单音节形容词作定语，后面不用"的"，如：

When used attributively a monosyllabic adjective usually takes no "的" after it. E.g.

男朋友　白衬衫　新地图

(5) 形容词结构作定语必须加"的"，如"很好的朋友"。形容词"多"（或"少"）作定语时，前边要加上副词，后边一般不加"的"，如"很多朋友"。

An adjective construction, when used attributively, must take "的" after it, e.g. "很好的朋友". The adjective "多" or "少", when used attributively, usually has an adverb before it but doesn't take a "的" after it, e.g. "很多朋友".

练习　Exercises

1. 写出下列动词的宾语（或双宾语），然后用每个动词作一个

240

句子： Supply each of the following verbs with one or two (direct and indirect) objects, then make a sentence with the verb:

(1)

等	说	写	看	认识
在	买	有	找	学习
穿	回	去	用	介绍

(2) 问　还　教　给　告诉

2. 回答下列问题： Answer the following questions:

(1) 你每天几点起床？

(2) 起床以后你作什么？

(3) 你每天上午都有课吗？

(4) 你每天上午几点上课？

(5) 你每天都坐车去学院吗？

(6) 你每天都在食堂吃饭吗？

(7) 你每天下午都在宿舍吗？

(8) 你每天都去图书馆吗？

(9) 你常常去咖啡馆吗？

(10) 每天晚上你都看电影吗?

(11) 晚上你常常作什么?

(12) 你每天几点睡觉?

3. 用括号里的三个词分别填空，作三个不同的句子，注意结构助词"的"的使用：
Fill in each blank with all the three words or phrases given in brackets in turn, adding the structural particle "的" where necessary:

(1) 这是＿＿＿＿杂志。(我　中文　阅览室)

(2) 我有＿＿＿＿朋友。(一个　很多　中国)

(3) 她穿＿＿＿＿裙子吗?(蓝　她姐姐　旧)

(4) 我哥哥下午去买＿＿＿＿＿票。(四张　京剧　八点钟)

(5) 我常常看＿＿＿＿＿书。(语法　新　我们老师)

4. 填入适当的量词： Put in an appropriate measure word in each of the following sentences:

(1) 我哥哥给我一＿＿语法书。

(2) 那＿＿孩子是他姐姐的。

(3) 我朋友不常去这___食堂吃饭。

(4) 这___衬衫不是新的。

(5) 你去哪___银行?

(6) 每___学生都有词典吗?

(7) 那是一___北京地图。

(8) 我问王老师两___问题。

(9) 她不穿那___绿裙子。

(10) 这课有几___新汉字?

5. 选择适当的词语完成下列对话: Complete the following dialogues with the appropriate phrases from the list given:

对了　好啊　问…好　谢谢你

我们认识一下儿　太好了

(1) A: 他给你这本书。

　　B: _____。

(2) A: 王先生问你好。

　　B: _____。

(3) A: 我们走去, 好吗?

243

B: _____。

(4) A: _____。

B: 我叫谢明，我是留学生。

(5) A: 你是法国人吗？

B: _____。

(6) A: 晚上我们去看中国电影，这是两张票。

B: _____。

6. 改正下列错句： Correct the following erroneous sentences:

(1) 我朋友不学习汉语在北京。

(2) 谁教你语法吗？

(3) 她从古波来。

(4) 你常常写他信吗？

(5) 帕兰卡学习汉语从丁云。

(6) 你有几汉语词典？

(7) 你认识不认识那大夫？

(8) 她们是很好朋友们。

244

(9) 我们班有多中国留学生。

(10) 她的车是新。

(11) 在图书馆不有中文杂志。

(12) 他每天上课在八点。

(13) 她常常写信用中文。

(14) 我去宿舍和看我朋友。

汉字笔顺表　Table of Stroke-order of Chinese Characters

1	天	一
		大
2	每	⺈ (′ ⺈)
		母 (乚 乙 母 母 母)
3	床	广
		木
4	午	′ ⺊ ⺁ 午
5	吃	口
		乞 ⺈
		乙

6	饭	饣								飯
		反（丿 厂 反）								
7	休	亻								
		木								
8	息	自（丿 亻 竹 白 自 自）								
		心								
9	时	日								時
		寸								
10	候	亻								
		丨								
		矣	丄（丶 丄）							
			矢（丿 矢）							
11	题	是								題
		页（一 丆 厂 万 页 页）								
12	睡	目								
		垂（丿 二 三 千 千 乖 垂 垂）								
13	觉	丷								覺
		见								

第十九课　Lesson 19

一、课文　Text

您要什么

（在 咖啡馆）
(Zài　kāfēiguǎn)

服务员：　您　要　什么？
Fúwùyuán:　Nín　yào　shénme?

帕兰卡：　我　要　一杯　咖啡。
Pàlánkǎ:　Wǒ　yào　yìbēi　kāfēi.

服务员：　小姐，　您　也　要　咖啡　吗？
Fúwùyuán:　Xiǎojie,　nín　yě　yào　kāfēi　ma?

古　波： 中国　人喜欢　喝茶，是吗？
Gǔbō: Zhōngguó rén xǐhuan hē chá, shì ma?

丁　云： 是啊，有花茶吗？
Dīng Yún: Shì a, yǒu huāchá ma?

服务员： 没有花茶，有红茶。您要
Fúwùyuán: Méi yǒu huāchá, yǒu hóngchá. Nín yào

红茶还是要咖啡？
hóngchá háishì yào kāfēi?

丁　云： 不，我要一杯桔子水。
Dīng Yún: Bù, wǒ yào yìbēi júzishuǐ.

古　波： 我要一瓶啤酒。
Gǔbō: Wǒ yào yìpíng píjiǔ.

服务员： 好，一杯咖啡、一杯桔子水、
Fúwùyuán: Hǎo, yìbēi kāfēi, yìbēi júzishuǐ,

一瓶啤酒。
yìpíng píjiǔ.

帕兰卡： 听，这是我
Pàlánkǎ: Tīng, zhè shì wǒ-

们的民歌。
men de míngē.

你喜欢古典音乐还是喜欢
Nǐ xǐhuan gǔdiǎn yīnyuè háishì xǐhuan

现代 音乐？
xiàndài yīnyuè?

丁 云： 我 喜欢 你们 的 古典 音乐。
Dīng Yún: Wǒ xǐhuan nǐmen de gǔdiǎn yīnyuè.

帕兰卡： 我 也 很 喜欢 听 中国 音乐。
Pàlánkǎ: Wǒ yě hěn xǐhuan tīng Zhōngguó yīnyuè.

以后 请 你 给 我们 介绍 一下儿
Yǐhòu qǐng nǐ gěi wǒmen jièshào yíxiàr

中国 音乐。
Zhōngguó yīnyuè.

古 波： 帕兰卡 还 喜欢 唱 歌儿。 丁 云，
Gǔbō: Pàlánkǎ hái xǐhuan chàng gēr. Dīng Yún,

你 让 她 唱 一个 歌儿。
nǐ ràng tā chàng yíge gēr.

帕兰卡： 别 听 他 的。 你 教 我们 中国
Pàlánkǎ: Bié tīng tā de. Nǐ jiāo wǒmen Zhōngguó

歌儿， 好 吗？
gēr, hǎo ma?

丁 云： 好 啊。 晚上 八点 以后 我
Dīng Yún: Hǎo a. Wǎnshang bādiǎn yǐhòu wǒ

常常 在 宿舍， 欢迎 你们 去。
chángcháng zài sùshè, huānyíng nǐmen qù.

249

生词 New Words

1. 要 (动、能动) yào to want, to be going to, must

2. 服务员 (名) fúwùyuán waiter, waitress, attendant

3. 杯 (量) bēi *a measure word*, cup

4. 小姐 (名) xiǎojie miss, young lady

5. 喜欢 (动) xǐhuan to like, to be fond of

6. 花茶 (名) huāchá scented tea

7. 红茶 (名) hóngchá black tea

   红 (形) hóng red

8. 还是 (连) háishì or

9. 桔子水 (名) júzishuǐ orangeade, orange juice

   桔子 (名) júzi orange

   水 (名) shuǐ water

10. 瓶 (量) píng *a measure word*, bottle

11. 啤酒 (名) píjiǔ beer

12. 听 (动) tīng to listen

13. 民歌 (名) míngē folk song

14. 古典 (名) gǔdiǎn classical, classic

15. 音乐 (名) yīnyuè music

16.	现代	(名)	xiàndài	modern
17.	唱	(动)	chàng	to sing
18.	歌儿	(名)	gēr	song
19.	让	(动)	ràng	to let, to ask
20.	别	(副)	bié	don't

补充词 Supplementary Words

1.	枝	(量)	zhī	*a measure word*, branch
2.	苹果	(名)	píngguǒ	apple
3.	香蕉	(名)	xiāngjiāo	banana
4.	葡萄	(名)	pútao	grape
5.	唱片	(名)	chàngpiàn	gramophone record
6.	糖	(名)	táng	sugar, sweets, candy
7.	绿茶	(名)	lüchá	green tea

二、注释　Notes

1. "你要什么?"

这里是问别人的需求。商店售货员和饭店服务员常用来询问顾客。

"你要什么?" is an expression used to ask what someone wants, an expression employed mostly by shop assistants or restaurant waiters.

2. "中国人喜欢喝茶，是吗?"

"……，是吗?"（或"……，是不是?" "……，对吗?"）这种

格式常用来表达一种不太有把握的估计，向对方询问。回答的时候，如果同意对方的估计，就用"是啊"（或"对"），如果不同意对方的估计，就用"不"。

"…，是吗？"（"…，是不是？" or "…，对吗？"）is a tag question. It is used to ask the person addressed to confirm one's own estimate of which he is not very sure. In answering it, "是啊"（or "对"）is used if the person addressed agrees to him, and "不" is used if the contrary is the case.

3. "有花茶吗？"

"有……吗？"是顾客问售货员或服务员的用语，主语常常省略。

"有…吗？" is an expression that a customer uses to ask a shop assistant or a restaurant waiter if they have the thing he wishes to buy. The subject is more often than not omitted.

4. "我也很喜欢听中国音乐。"

动词或动宾结构可以作动词的宾语。动词"喜欢"的宾语可以是名词，也可以是动词或动宾结构。

A verb or a verb-object construction can function as the object of the predicative verb. The object of the verb "喜欢" may be either a noun or a verb or a verb-object construction.

"听音乐"的意思就是欣赏音乐。

"听音乐" means "to appreciate music".

5. "别听他的。"

"Don't listen to him."

三、替换与扩展　Substitution and Extension

（一）

1. 你要什么？

252

我要一杯咖啡。

> 两,啤酒(瓶)
> 三,红茶(杯)
> 四,桔子水(瓶)
> 一,水(杯)

2. 你要多少电影票?
   我要两张电影票。

> 词典(本),五
> 地图(张),十二
> 画报(本),两
> 笔(枝), 三

3. 你要英文报还是
   要中文报?
   我要中文报。
   他也要中文报。

> 上语法课,上口语课
> 喝茶, 喝咖啡
> 找古波, 找帕兰卡
> 回家, 去咖啡馆
> 买桔子, 买苹果'

4. 她喜欢古典音乐还是喜欢现代音乐?

她喜欢现代音乐，有时候她也听古典音乐。

用新笔，用旧笔
穿裙子，穿裤子.
吃香蕉.，吃葡萄.

5. 你请谁<u>介绍中国音乐</u>?
   我请我朋友介绍中国音乐。

唱中国歌	看电影
教你汉语	听现代音乐
吃饭	买唱片.

6. 他让你作什么?
   他让我<u>唱一个歌</u>。

写汉字	给他写信
问问题	还他的杂志
看语法	在他家吃饭

（二）

1. 买苹果　Buying some apples

A: 您要什么？

B: 有好苹果˙吗？

A: 有。您要多少？

B: 我要两公斤 (gōngjīn, kilogram) 。

A: 还要什么？

B: 还要一公斤葡萄˙。

2. 招待　Serving a customer

A: 你要咖啡还是要茶？

B: 我要咖啡。

A: 加 (jiā, to add) 糖˙吗？

B: 不加糖˙。

3. 邀请　Making an invitation

A: 现在你有事儿吗？

B: 没有。

A: 我们去咖啡馆，我请你喝咖啡，好吗？

B: 好啊，谢谢你。

4. 问看法 Asking someone's opinions about something

A: 你喜欢不喜欢

这本书？

B: 我不太喜欢。

A: 我很喜欢这本

书。

四、阅读短文 Reading Text

听中国唱片

古波和帕兰卡都喜欢中国音乐。晚上八点半，他们去丁云的宿舍听唱片*。丁云有很多中国唱片*，有现代音乐的，也有古典音乐的。

丁云请他们喝中国茶。她有花茶和绿茶*。古波要花茶，帕兰卡要绿茶*。

古波和帕兰卡都很喜欢那个歌儿，他们

问丁云："这是一个民歌，对吗？"丁云说："对了，这是一个民歌。"古波问："这个歌儿叫什么名字？"丁云说："这个歌儿的名字是《茉莉花》(Mòlìhuā, Jasmine Flowers)。"

帕兰卡请丁云教他们这个歌儿。丁云说："好。"

五、语法 Grammar

1. 选择疑问句 Alternative questions

用连词"还是"连接两种可能的答案，由回答的人选择其一。这种疑问句叫选择疑问句。例如：

An alternative question is one formed of two statements joined by "还是" suggesting two different alternatives for the person addressed to choose from. E.g.

你去还是不去？

——我去。

你喜欢古典音乐还是喜欢现代音乐？

——我喜欢现代音乐。

你回家还是去咖啡馆？

——我回家。

他下午去图书馆还是晚上去图书馆？

——他晚上去图书馆。

"是"字句的选择疑问形式如下：

Here are two forms of how a "是" sentence is turned into an alternative question:

这杯茶是你的还是他的？

——这杯茶是他的。

他是老师还是学生？

——他是学生。

2. 兼语句 Pivotal sentences

有一种动词谓语句，谓语是由两个动词结构构成的，前一个动词的宾语又是后一个动词的主语，这种句子叫兼语句。兼语句的前一个动词常常是"请"、"让"一类的带有使令意义的动词。

In Chinese, there is a kind of sentence with a verbal predicate composed of two verbal constructions in which the object of the first verb is at the same time the subject of the following verb. Such a sentence is known as a pivotal sentence. In a pivotal sentence the first verb is often such a causative verb as "请" or "让" etc.

名词或代词 Nouns or pronouns	动词 Verbs	名词或代词 Nouns or pronouns	动 词 Verbs	名词或代词 Nouns or pronouns
帕兰卡	请	丁云	教	中国歌儿。

她	请	我们	去	她家。
老师	让	他	写	什么？
爸爸	不让	这个孩子	喝	啤酒。

"请"和"让"都有要求别人作某事的意思，"请"用于比较客气的场合。"请"还有邀请的意思，如"他请我吃饭"。

Both "请" and "让" mean to ask someone to do something. "请" is much more polite and may also be used to mean "to invite", as in "他请我吃饭".

练习 Exercises

1. 读下列词组并造句：Read out the following phrases and make sentences with them:

   (1) 现代音乐　现代英语　现代语法

   　　现代口语　现代汉语词典

   (2) 喜欢看　喜欢学习　喜欢作

   　　喜欢用　喜欢吃　喜欢喝　喜欢穿

2. 造选择式疑问句并回答：Make alternative questions in the same way as the examples given, using the following groups of words, and then answer them:

例 Example 桔子水　你的　他的

　　　→这杯桔子水是你的还是他的？

　　　　这杯桔子水是我的。

(1) 杂志　图书馆的　阅览室的

(2) 书　英文的　法文的

(3) 衬衫　新的　旧的

(4) 裙子　红的　绿的

例 Example 去咖啡馆　上午　下午

　　　→你上午去咖啡馆还是下午去

　　　　咖啡馆？

　　　　我下午去咖啡馆。

(1) 起床　6:15　6:30

(2) 上课　8:00　8:20

(3) 看朋友　下午　晚上

(4) 睡觉　10:30　11:00

(5) 给他写信　现在　以后

例 Example 下午　去书店　去商店

→他下午去书店还是去商店？

他下午去书店。

(1) 现在　教汉语　教外语

(2) 以后　学习英语　学习法语

(3) 下课以后　休息　复习课文

(4) 每天晚上　在宿舍　在学院

3. 根据阅读短文回答问题：Answer the following questions on the Reading Text:

(1) 古波和帕兰卡喜欢不喜欢中国音乐？

(2) 他们去哪儿听中国唱片？

(3) 丁云请他们喝什么？

(4) 他们喜欢喝什么茶？

(5) 古波和帕兰卡喜欢哪一个歌儿？

(6) 那是什么歌儿？

(7) 他们请丁云作什么？

4. 根据划线部分用疑问代词提问：Make up questions asking about the underlined parts of the following sentences, using suitable interrogative pronouns:

(1) 王先生让他们写汉学。

(2) 帕兰卡请丁云教她汉语。

(3) 我们请她朋友在北京买两本语法书。

(4) 古波请我去看电影。

(5) 我朋友请我去他家吃饭。

5. 仿照例子进行会话练习：Make up dialogues in the same way as the following examples, using the information given:

例 Example 中文杂志 两本

→A: 您要什么？

B: 我要中文杂志。

A: 您要几本？

B: 我要两本。

(1) 啤酒 五瓶

(2) 《中国民歌》 一本

(3) 七点五十的电影票 两张

例 Example 咖啡 红茶

→A: 你要咖啡吗？

B: 谢谢，我不要咖啡。

请(你)给我一杯红茶。

(1) 啤酒　桔子水

(2) 红茶　花茶

(3) 中文画报　英文画报

六、语音语调　Pronunciation and Intonation

1. 意群重音 (1)　Sense group stress (1)

　　意群就是一口气能说出来有比较完整意义的几个音节。一个意群有时是一个短句，有时是句子中的一个成分。每个意群都有它的重音，就是"意群重音"。意群重音只是在词重音上稍微加重。它不会转移词的重音位置，使原来非重读的音节变重。意群的重音和句子的结构有密切关系。可以按句子成分来分析意群重音。(本书用"～～～"表示意群重音。)

A sense group is a series of syllables that express a comparatively complete idea and can be uttered in one breath. A sense group may be a short sentence or part of a sentence. All sense groups have one of its syllables uttered with greater force than the others: this is known as "sense group stress". Sense group stress is given merely by uttering a stressed syllable with slightly greater force, and it does not shift the position of word stress, making originally unstressed syllables stressed ones. Sense group stress is closely related to sentence structure and can be determined by an analysis of the sentence elements (in this book the sense group stress is marked with the sign "⌣⌣⌣").

(1) 主语＋谓语，谓语重读。例如：

In Subject＋Predicate constructions, the predicate is usually stressed. E.g.

你们认识吗？

——我们认识。

你去吗？

——我去。

现在几点？

——现在两点半。

"是"字句中的"是"字一般不重读，后面的词重读。例如：

The word "是" in "是" sentences is usually not stressed, but the words that follow are stressed. E.g.

她是丁云。

这是我们的民歌。

(2) 主语＋动词＋宾语，宾语重读。例如：

In Subject ＋ Verb ＋ Object constructions, the object is stressed. E.g.

我要咖啡。

中国人喜欢茶。

丁云有姐姐，没有妹妹。

(3) 定语一般都重读。例如：
Attributive modifiers are usually stressed. E.g.

你喜欢中国音乐吗？

这是新裙子，那是旧裙子。

注意：Points to be noted:

(1)人称代词作定语一般不重读，后面的名词重读。例如：
Personal pronouns used attributively are usually unstressed,
but the nouns that follow are stressed. E.g.

我喜欢你们的民歌。

(2)数词"一"和量词组成的定语不重读，其他数量词作定语
都重读。例如：
Attributive modifiers formed of the numeral "一"
and a measure word are not stressed. All other numeral-
measure words, when used attributively, are usually stressed.
E.g.

我要一瓶啤酒。

你要两杯咖啡。

(3)几个词连用作定语，距中心语最近的重读。例如：

In attributive modifiers formed of a series of words, the word closest to the head-word is usually stressed. E.g.

他喜欢你们的现代音乐。

帕兰卡喜欢中国的新民歌。

2.练习 Exercises

朗读下面的民歌：Read aloud the following folk rhyme:

Yípiàn   qīng lai   yípiàn   huáng,
一 片　青 来　一 片　黄，

huáng shì màizi qīng shì yāng.
黄　是 麦子 青　是 秧。

Shì shéi xiù chū huā shìjiè,
是　谁 绣 出 花　世界，

láodòng rénmín shǒu yìshuāng.
劳动　人民　手　一双。

汉字笔顺表 **Table of Stroke-order of Chinese Characters**

1	要	西

		女		
2	服	月		
		艮		
3	务	夂		務
		力		
4	员	口		員
		贝（丨 冂 贝 贝）		
5	杯	木（一 十 才 木）		
		不		
6	小	亅 小 小		
7	喜	士		
		口		
		丷（丶 丷 丷）		
		口		
8	花	艹		
		化	亻	
			匕	
9	红	纟		紅
		工		

							橘
10	桔	木					橘
		吉	士				
			口				
11	水	亅	丬	办	水		
12	瓶	并	⸜⸝				
			开（一 二 干 开）				
		瓦（一 厂 瓦 瓦）					
13	啤	口					
		卑（ノ 白 甶 鱼 卑）					
14	酒	氵					
		酉（一 厂 厉 丙 西 西 酉）					
15	听	口					聽
		斤					
16	民	⸗	⸗	尸	巨	民	
17	歌	哥					
		欠					
18	古						
19	音	立					
		日					

20	乐	一	丆	牙	乐	樂
21	代	亻				
		弋（一 弋 弋）				
22	唱	口				
		昌	日			
			日			
23	让	讠				讓
		上				
24	别	另	口			
			力			
		刂				

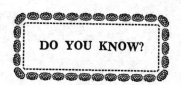

DO YOU KNOW?

Chinese Tea

In many languages the word for "tea" originated from Chinese, for China is the home of tea shrubs and one of the oldest tea growing and producing countries in the world. China is well-known for her great varieties of tea and their fine quality. Chinese tea falls into different kinds because of the different methods by which tea leaves are processed. There are mainly five kinds: black tea (e.g. Keemun black tea, produced in Qiman County, Anhui Province), green tea (e.g. Lung Jing tea, produced in Hangzhou, Zhejiang Province), scented tea, Oolong tea, white tea and other kinds.

Tea is the favourite drink of the Chinese people. Visitors to a Chinese home are invariably served with tea as well as with candies and cookies. The Chinese usually make their tea by pouring boiling hot water into a tea-pot with tea leaves in it, and putting the lid back on, and the tea is ready for drinking in few minutes' time. Then they pour the tea not into a teacup. Most Chinese prefer green tea or scented tea, usually with no sugar or lemon in it.

第 二 十 课　Lesson 20

四月二十八号是我的生日

（下 课 以 后）
(Xià kè yǐhòu)

古 波： 王 老师， 您 今天 还 有 课
Gǔbō: Wáng Lǎoshī, nín jīntiān hái yǒu kè

吗?
ma?

王 ： 有。 十点 一刻 我 给 他们 班
Wáng: Yǒu. Shídiǎn yíkè wǒ gěi tāmen bān

上 课。 今天 的 语法 你们 有
shàng kè. Jīntiān de yǔfǎ nǐmen yǒu

问题 吗?
wèntí ma?

古 波： 我 有 两个 问题。 帕兰卡 也
Gǔbō: Wǒ yǒu liǎngge wèntí. Pàlánkǎ yě

有 问题。
yǒu wèntí.

王 ： 好， 下午 我 来 给 你们 辅导。
Wáng: Hǎo, xiàwǔ wǒ lái gěi nǐmen fǔdǎo.

你们 两点 来 还是 三点 来?
Nǐmen liǎngdiǎn lái háishì sāndiǎn lái?

帕兰卡： 我们 三点 来。 老师， 二十八号
Pàlánkǎ: Wǒmen sāndiǎn lái. Lǎoshī, èrshíbāhào

272

晚上 您 有 空儿 吗？
wǎnshang nín yǒu kòngr ma?

王 ： 你们 有 什么 事儿？
Wáng: Nǐmen yǒu shénme shìr?

帕兰卡： 四月 二十八号 是 我 的 生日。
Pàlánkǎ: Sìyuè èrshíbāhào shì wǒ de shēngrì.

我 今年 二十岁。
Wǒ jīnnián èrshísuì.

王 ： 是 吗？ 祝贺 你！
Wáng: Shì ma? Zhùhè nǐ!

帕兰卡： 谢谢。 我 家 有 一个 舞会， 请
Pàlánkǎ: Xièxie. Wǒ jiā yǒu yíge wǔhuì, qǐng

您 参加， 好 吗？
nín cānjiā, hǎo ma?

古 波： 我们 班 的 同学 都 参加。
Gǔbō: Wǒmen bān de tóngxué dōu cānjiā.

王 ： 那 一定 很 有 意思。 今天 几
Wáng: Nà yídìng hěn yǒu yìsi. Jīntiān jǐ

号？
hào?

古 波： 今天 四月 二十六号， 星期五。
Gǔbō: Jīntiān sìyuè èrshíliùhào, xīngqīwǔ.

四月 二十八号 是 星期日。
Sìyuè èrshíbāhào shì xīngqīrì.

王 ： 好，我 一定 去。
Wáng: Hǎo, wǒ yídìng qù.

帕兰卡： 太 好 了。您 知道 我 家 的
Pàlánkǎ: Tài hǎo le. Nín zhīdao wǒ jiā de

地址 吗?
dìzhǐ ma?

王 ： 我 知道。
Wáng: Wǒ zhīdao.

生词 New Words

1. 月 (名) yuè month

2. 日 (名) rì date, day of the month

3. 生日 (名) shēngrì birthday

4. 今天 (名) jīntiān today

5. 班 (名) bān class, squad

6. 辅导 (动) fǔdǎo to coach

7. 号 (名) hào date, day of the month

8. 空儿 (名) kòngr spare time

9. 今年 (名) jīnnián this year

10. 岁 (量) suì *a measure word,* year (age)

11. 祝贺	(动)	zhùhè	to congratulate, congratulation
12. 舞会	(名)	wǔhuì	dance, ball
13. 参加	(动)	cānjiā	to take part in, to attend
14. 同学	(名)	tóngxué	classmate, schoolmate
15. 一定	(副、形)	yídìng	surely, certainly, certain, given, particular
16. 有意思		yǒu yìsi	interesting
17. 星期	(名)	xīngqī	week
18. 星期日	(名)	xīngqīrì	Sunday
19. 知道	(动)	zhīdao	to know
20. 地址	(名)	dìzhǐ	address
21. 年	(名)	nián	year

补充词 Supplementary Words

1. 去年	(名)	qùnián	last year
2. 明年	(名)	míngnián	next year
3. 音乐会	(名)	yīnyuèhuì	concert
4. 结婚		jié hūn	to get married
5. 对不起		duì bu qǐ	(I'm) sorry
6. 约会	(名)	yuēhuì	appointment
7. 没关系		méi guānxi	it doesn't matter

8. 谈　　　(动) tán　　　　　　to talk, to chat

二、注释　Notes

1. "今天的语法你们有问题吗？"

"Do you have any questions about today's grammar lesson?"

2. "你有空儿吗？"

意思是"你有没有时间"，用于安排约会或请别人做某事。否定的回答是"我没(有)空儿"。

"你有空儿吗？" means "Are you free?" or "Do you have some time to spare?" It is used when one wishes to make an appointment with someone or ask someone to do something. The negative answer to it is "我没(有)空儿".

3. "是吗？祝贺你！"

这里的"是吗"表示对某事原来不知道，有点儿觉得意外(有时还表示不太相信)。

"是吗？" here implies that one is surprised to know something he didn't know before. Sometimes it implies disbelief on the part of the speaker.

"祝贺你"是表示道贺的一般用语。

"祝贺你" is an expression used to offer congratulations.

4. "我们班的同学都参加。"

"同学"一词的意思是指在同班或同一个学校学习的人，如"他是我同学"。这个词也常用作对学生的称呼，如"丁云同学"、"同学们"（不说"丁云学生"、"学生们"）。

The word "同学" means "classmate" or "schoolmate", as in "他是我同学". It is also a form of address for students, e.g. "丁云同学", "同学们". But it is rare to address "丁云学

生" or "学生们".

5. "那一定很有意思。"

"It must be very interesting."

三、替换与扩展 Substitution and Extension

(一)

1. 今年一九八一年。

去年*，一九八〇
明年*，一九八二

2. 今天（几月）几号？

今天四月二十五号。

现在几点？

现在三点一刻。

1981 四月 小	星 期 二 21

1981 七月 大	星 期 三 1

1981 十二月 大	星 期 四 31

3. 今天几号？星期几？

今天十一号，星期四。

你上午有课还是下午有课？

我下午有课。

日	一	二	三	四	五	六
		1	2	3	4	5	6
7	8	9	10	11	12	13
14	15	16	17	18	19	20
21	22	23	24	25	26	27
28	29	30	31			

4. 星期二是几号？

   星期二是八月十五号。

你的生日

舞会

音乐会*

5. 你几号去你朋友家？

   我(六月)二十二号去我朋友家。

去北京　有辅导

| 来 | 去听音乐会 |
| 休息 | 有空儿 |

6. 星期日你作什么？

星期日我<u>去看同学</u>。

每个星期日你都<u>去</u>
<u>看同学</u>吗？

不,有时候我去看电
影。

| 在家写信 |
| 看京剧 |
| 参加舞会 |
| 在宿舍写汉字 |

7. 他今年<u>二十二</u>岁还是
<u>二十三</u>岁？

他今年二十二岁。

| 8, 9 |
| 32, 33 |
| 40, 42 |

(二)

1. 道贺 Offering congratulations

A: 我星期六结婚*。

B: 太好了,祝贺你!

A: 谢谢。

2. 邀请 Making an invitation

A: 五号下午你有空儿吗?

B: 什么事儿?

A: 我请你去听音乐,好吗?——是现代音乐。

B: 那一定很有意思。我喜欢听现代音乐,我一定去。

　　　　*　　　　*　　　　*

A: 星期四晚上你有空儿吗?

B: 什么事儿?

A: 我们去参加舞会,好吗?

B: 对不起*,星期四晚上我有一个约会*。

A: 没关系*。

3. 约会 Making an appointment

A: 你什么时候有空儿?

B: 你有事儿吗?

A: 我跟你谈谈*,好吗?

280

B: 今天晚上七点我在家。

A: 好，我一定去。

B: 这是我家的地址。

* * *

通知　(tōngzhī, notice)

舞　会

　　一九八一年十月十五日（星期四）晚上七点半在俱乐部
举行舞会，欢迎老师和同学们参加。

俱乐部　十月十一日

四、阅读短文　Reading Text

丁云给爸爸的信

亲爱 (qīn'ài, dear) 的爸爸：

　　您好。

　　我现在很忙，每天上午都去学院上课。星
期一、星期三有语法课，星期二、星期四和星
期五有口语课，星期三下午有历史 (lìshǐ, history) 课。我还常常去阅览室看画报和杂志。

今天是星期四,晚上我有空儿,给您写信。

　　这儿的老师和同学们都很好。我现在有很多朋友。帕兰卡是我的新朋友,她今年二十岁,是外语学院的学生。她爸爸教我们历史,她妈妈是大夫,他们常常问您好。星期日是帕兰卡的生日,她家有一个舞会,请我们中国同学参加。

　　妈妈好吗?姐姐工作忙不忙?问她们好,我很想你们。　　　祝您

健康 (jiànkāng, health)

云

1981 年 4 月 25 日

五、语法　Grammar

1. 年、月和星期　"年","月" and "星期"

汉语年份的读法是直接读出每个数字, 如:

In Chinese, the four figures making up the name of a year are read out as four separate numbers, such as:

一九七九年 (yījiǔqījiǔnián)

一九八〇年 (yījiǔbālíngnián)

一九八五年 (yījiǔbāwǔnián)

汉语十二个月的名称是：

In Chinese, the names of the twelve months of the year are:

一月 January	二月 February	三月 March
四月 April	五月 May	六月 June
七月 July	八月 August	九月 September
十月 October	十一月 November	十二月 December

一个星期七天的名称是：

The names of the seven days of the week are:

星期一 Monday	星期二 Tuesday	星期三 Wednesday
星期四 Thursday	星期五 Friday	星期六 Saturday
星期日（星期天）Sunday		

2. 年、月、日、时的顺序 The order of the year, month, day and hour

年、月、日、时连在一起时，顺序是：

When given simultaneously in a date, the year, month, day and hour are arranged in the following order:

年	月	日（星期　）	上（下）午	时

例如： For example:

一九四九年十月一日

一九八一年十月二十六日（星期一）

下午七点

"日"和"号"都表示一个月里的"某一天"。口语中常用"号"，书面用"日"。

To refer to a particular day, both "日" and "号" are used: "号" is used mostly in spoken language, and "日" in written language.

注意：在现代汉语里，表时间的名词"年、月、日、星期"等一般不能单独使用，必须跟数词或其它词连用。

Note that in modern Chinese, nouns denoting time such as "年", "月", "日" and "星期" cannot stand all by themselves but must be preceded by a numeral or other words.

3. 名词谓语句 Sentences with a nominal predicate

由名词或名词结构、数量词等直接作谓语的句子，叫名词谓语句。这种句子一般不用动词"是"。名词谓语句主要用于表达时间、年龄、籍贯及数量等。

A sentence in which the main element of the predicate is a noun, a nominal construction or a numeral-measure word is called a sentence with a nominal predicate. The verb "是" is, as a rule, not used in a sentence of this kind. Such a sentence is mainly used to show time, quantity, one's age or native place etc.

名词或代词 Nouns or pronouns	名词或数量词 Nouns or numeral-measure words
今天	四月二十五号。
现在	几点？
今天	星期三吗？
她	今年二十岁，还是二十一岁？
我	北京人。

要表达否定的意思，必须在名词谓语前加"不是"。例如：
"不是" is added in front of the predicative noun to make the sentence negative. E.g.

今天不是四月二十五号。

现在不是两点三十五分。

她今年不是二十岁。

注意：这种句子一般也可以加"是"，成为动词谓语句。例如：
Note that in a sentence of this kind, however, the verb "是" can also be used in front of the main element of the predicate. Thus, it becomes a sentence with a verbal predicate. E.g.

今天是星期日。

星期二是八月十五号。

现在是两点三十五分吗?

练习 Exercises

1. 读下列词组并造句: Read out the following phrases and make sentences with them:

(1) 我们班　　我们班的同学

他们系　　他们系的老师

你们学院　你们学院的学生

(2) 一年　一个月　一个星期　一天

两年　两个月　两个星期　两天

每年　每个月　每个星期　每天

2. 回答问题: Answer the following questions:

(1) 一年有几个月?

(2) 一个星期有几天?

(3) 这个月有多少天?

(4) 这个月有几个星期天？

(5) 今天几月几号？

(6) 今天星期几？

(7) 星期天是几号？

(8) 星期天你常常作什么？

3. 把下面两段话翻译成英文，然后再根据你的译文，用汉语口头复述：Translate the two passages into English, and then put them orally back into Chinese:

(1) 我哥哥今年三十二岁。今年九月他去中国教英语。现在他是北京外语学院的老师。他每个月都给我写信，他还常常给我买中文杂志和中文书。

(2) 他姐姐在书店工作。她每天都回家。她有两个好朋友。她常常请她们去看电影、听音乐。有时候她跟她们一起去参加舞会。

4. 你同学跟你有一个约会，你根据下面的内容谈谈一周的安

排,告诉他你什么时候有空儿:

Suppose a classmate of yours wants to make an appointment with you, tell him about your activities of the week and what time you will be free, booking yourself on the following time-table:

	上午	下午	晚上
星期一	语法课 (8:00—10:00)		朋友来 (7:30)
星期二	口语课 (8:25—10:25)		听音乐 (8:00)
星期三	口语课 (10:45—12:45)	去图书馆 (3:15)	
星期四	历史课 (8:20—10:20)		看电影 (7:50)
星期五	语法课 (9:15—11:15)		
星期六		参加舞会	朋友结婚*
星期日			(7:00)

288

5. 给你朋友写信，谈谈你的生活。

Write a letter to a friend of yours, telling him (or her) about your everyday life at the Institute.

六、语音语调 Pronunciation and Intonation

1. 意群重音(2) Sense group stress (2)

(1) 名词谓语句中，谓语重读。例如：

In sentences with a nominal predicate, the predicate is stressed. E.g.

今天几号？

今天星期五。

他二十二岁。

(2) 人称代词作宾语则动词重读，宾语反而轻读。例如：

When a personal pronoun is used as an object, the verb is stressed, the personal pronoun receiving a weak stress only. E.g.

祝贺你！

谢谢您！

(3) 状语一般都重读。例如：

Adverbial adjuncts are usually stressed. E.g.

我一定去。

我们班的同学都参加。

(4) 兼语句　Pivotal sentence

A: 兼语＋动词，动词重读。例如：

In Pivotal word＋Verb constructions, the verb is stressed. E.g.

请您参加，好吗？

B: 兼语＋动词＋宾语，宾语重读。例如：

In Pivotal word＋Verb＋Object constructions, the object is stressed. E.g.

以后我请你们听中国音乐。

2. 练习　Exercises

朗读下面的对话，注意 j、q、x 的发音和意群重音：

Read aloud the following dialogue, paying attention to the pronunciation of j, q, x and sense group stress:

A: 谁啊？请进！

B: 你今天去学院吗？

A: 今天星期几？

B: 今天星期二。

A: 我去学院，你有事儿吗？

B: 请你告诉王老师，今天我有事儿，不去上课。

A: 好，我一定告诉他。

B: 谢谢你，再见！

汉字笔顺表 Table of Stroke-order of Chinese Characters

1	月		
2	日		
3	辅	车	辅
		甫（一 厂 丆 丂 甬 甫 甫）	
4	导	巳（⺋ ⺕ 巳）	導
		寸	
5	空	穴（宀 穴）	
		工	
6	今	人 𠆢 今	
7	年	⺈ 𠂉 ⺀ ⺀ 𠃌 年	
8	岁	山（丨 屮 山）	歲
		夕	

291

9	祝	礻			
		兄	口		
			儿		
10	贺	加	力		贺
			口		
		贝			
11	舞	無 (´ ˇ ˋ ˊ ⌒ ⌒ 無 無)			
		舛	夕		
			牛		
12	会	人			會
		云	二		
			厶		
13	参	厶			參
		大			
		彡			
14	加				
15	班	王			
		丿			
		王			

16	同	冂 冂 同
17	定	宀
		疋
18	意	立
		日
		心
19	思	田
		心
20	星	日
		生
21	期	其（一 十 廿 甘 甘 其 其 其）
		月
22	知	矢
		口
23	道	首（丶 丷 丷 丷 丷 首 首 首）
		辶
24	址	土
		止

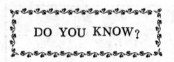

China's Lunar Calendar and Main Holidays

China's lunar or Xia calendar, which is said to have come into existence as early as the Xia Dynasty (about 2,100 —1,600 B.C.), has been in use for several thousand years and is still in common use today. According to the lunar calendar China's main holidays are as follows:

The Spring Festival　This holiday falls on the first day of the first lunar month. It is the most important festival in China, usually celebrated with great pomp, feasting and merry making.

The Clear and Bright Day　This holiday falls on the early days of the 3rd. lunar month. On this day people in China visit the graves of their dead to pay them homage.

The Dragon Boat Festival　This holiday falls on the 5th day of the 5th lunar month, the traditional day set aside to commemorate Qu Yuan, a great poet and patriot of the ancient Chinese State of Chu.

The Mid-autumn Festival　This holiday falls on the 15th day of the 8th lunar month. On the night of this day in China people eat a special kind of pastry called moon-cakes and enjoy looking at the full moon which is particularly clear and bright at the time of the year.

After the founding of the People's Republic of China in 1949, the Gregorian calendar, called the "solar calendar" in China, was adopted. According to the "solar calendar", the main holidays are as follows:

The New Year Day (January 1)

The International Working Women's Day (March 8)

The International Labour Day or May Day (May 1)

The Chinese Youth Day (May 4)

The International Children's Day (June 1)

The Anniversary of the Founding of the Communist Party of China (July 1)

The Army Day (Anniversary of the Founding of the People's Liberation Army) (August 1)

The National Day (October 1)

第二十一课　Lesson 21

一、课文　Text

这束花儿真好看

（帕兰卡 家。丁 云 进。）
(Pàlánkǎ jiā. Dīng Yún jìn.)

丁 云： 祝 你 生日 好！这 是 送 你
Dīng Yún: Zhù nǐ shēngrì hǎo! Zhè shì sòng nǐ

的 花儿。
de huār.

帕兰卡： 啊， 这束 花儿 真 好看， 非常
Pàlánkǎ: À, zhèshù huār zhēn hǎokàn, fēicháng

感谢。 今天 来 的 同学 很 多，
gǎnxiè. Jīntiān lái de tóngxué hěn duō,

我 真 高兴。 请 进。
wǒ zhēn gāoxìng. Qǐng jìn.

丁 云： 布朗 先生、 布朗 太太， 你们
Dīng Yún: Bùlǎng Xiānsheng、 Bùlǎng Tàitai, nǐmen

好！
hǎo!

布 朗： 你 好。 请 坐。
Bùlǎng: Nǐ hǎo. Qǐng zuò.

太 太： 丁云真 年轻。 你 今年 多 大？
Tàitai: Dīng Yún zhēn niánqīng. Nǐ jīnnián duō dà?

丁 云： 我 今年 二十二岁。
Dīng Yún: Wǒ jīnnián èrshíèrsuì.

297

太太: 你 的 生日 是 哪 一天？
Tàitai: Nǐ de shēngrì shì nǎ yìtiān?

丁云: 我 的 生日 是 二月 十六日。
Dīng Yún: Wǒ de shēngrì shì èryuè shíliùrì.

帕兰卡: 丁 云， 他们 都 在 那儿 跳 舞。
Pàlánkǎ: Dīng Yún, tāmen dōu zài nàr tiào wǔ.

你 看， 那个 年轻 的 姑娘 是
Nǐ kàn, nàge niánqīng de gūniang shì

日本 人，我 给 你们 介绍介绍。
Rìběn rén, wǒ gěi nǐmen jièshaojièshao.

丁云: 好。布朗 先生， 您 坐，我们 去
Dīng Yún: Hǎo. Bùlǎng Xiānsheng, nín zuò, Wǒmen qù

看看 她。
kànkan tā.

布朗: 请 吧。
Bùlǎng: Qǐng ba.

太太: 这个 中国 姑娘 很 漂亮。
Tàitai: Zhège Zhōngguó gūniang hěn piàoliang.

布　朗：我 说 帕兰卡 更 漂亮。
Bùlǎng: Wǒ shuō Pàlánkǎ gèng piàoliang.

太　太：是 吗?
Tàitai: Shì ma?

布　朗：她 象 她 妈妈。
Bùlǎng: Tā xiàng tā māma.

*　　　*　　　*

太　太：谁 啊? 我 去 开 门。
Tàitai: Shéi a? Wǒ qù kāi mén.

啊，是 王 老师，请 进。
À, shì Wáng Lǎoshī, qǐng jìn.

生词　New Words

1. 束　（量）shù　　　*a measure word*, bunch
2. 花儿　（名）huār　　flower
3. 真　（形）zhēn　　real, true, genuine
4. 好看　（形）hǎokàn　good-looking
5. 祝　（动）zhù　　　to wish
6. 送　（动）sòng　　to give as a present, to give
7. 非常　（副）fēicháng　extremely

8. 感谢	(动)	gǎnxiè	to thank
9. 高兴	(形)	gāoxìng	glad, happy, delighted
10. 太太	(名)	tàitai	Mrs., madame
11. 年轻	(形)	niánqīng	young
12. 多	(副)	duō	how
13. 跳舞		tiào wǔ	to dance
14. 姑娘	(名)	gūniang	girl
15. 吧	(助)	ba	*a modal particle*
16. 漂亮	(形)	piàoliang	pretty, beautiful
17. 更	(副)	gèng	even, still
18. 象	(动)	xiàng	to be like, to resemble, to take after
19. 开	(动)	kāi	to open
20. 门	(名)	mén	door

专名 Proper Names

1. 布朗	Bùlǎng	*a personal name*
2. 日本	Rìběn	Japan

补充词 Supplementary Words

1. 辆	(量)	liàng	*a measure word*

300

2. 干净	（形）	gānjìng	clean, neat
3. 新年	（名）	xīnnián	New Year
4. 岁数	（名）	suìshu	age
5. 礼物	（名）	lǐwù	present, gift
6. 照片	（名）	zhàopiàn	photograph, picture
7. 儿子	（名）	érzi	son
8. 女儿	（名）	nǚ'ér	daughter

二、注释　Notes

1. "祝你生日好!"

"祝你……"用来向对方表示一种良好的愿望，常有"预祝"的意思。"祝贺你"则常是对已知的或已发生的事情表示道贺。

"祝你…" is used to extend one's good wishes to the person addressed or to offer congratulations in advance. "祝贺你", on the other hand, is used to offer congratulations for something already known or accomplished.

2. "布朗太太"

"太太"以及"夫人、小姐、女士"这类词，现在多用于台湾、港澳及海外华侨社会。在中国大陆，除了外交场合外，一般不用这类称呼，比较通用的称呼是"同志"。

Forms of address such as "太太", "夫人", "小姐" and "女士" are now used mostly in Taiwan Province, Xianggang (Hong Kong), Aomen (Macao) and in Chinese communities overseas. On China's mainland, however, these forms are not used except on diplomatic occasions. The common form of address on the mainland is now "同志" (tóngzhì, comrade).

3. "你今年多大?"

"How old are you?"

汉语询问年龄有几种说法:"你今年多大"用于询问一般成年人或跟自己同辈人的年龄;如果问小孩的年龄则用"你今年几岁";问老人或比自己年长的人,为了表示礼貌,常用"您今年多大岁数"。

In Chinese, in asking about one's age, we can use "你今年多大" for adults or those who belong to the same generation as oneself; "你今年几岁" for children and "您今年多大岁数 (suìshu, age)" for the aged or people older than oneself to show politeness or courtesy.

4. "请吧。"

语气助词 "吧"(1)可以用在表示请求、劝告、命令、商量或同意的句子里,使整个句子的语气比较缓和。如:"坐吧!""休息一下儿吧?""好吧"。

When used at the end of a sentence expressing request, advice, command, consultation or consent or agreement, the modal particle "吧" (1) softens the tone of the sentence, e.g. "坐吧!""休息一下儿吧?""好吧"。

5. "布朗先生,您坐。我们去看看她。"

在跟别人谈话时,如果需要走开,常说"您(你)坐"或"您(你)忙吧"以示礼貌。

"您(你)坐" or "您(你)忙吧" is a polite form used when

302

one wishes to discontinue a conversation or to disengage oneself from some occupation.

6．"我说帕兰卡更漂亮。"

"更"是表示程度的副词，常用在形容词、动词前边作状语。用"更"时有从相同的方面作比较的意思，表示更高的程度。

"更" is an adverb of degree, often used before an adjective or a verb as an adverbial adjunct to imply, in a number of persons or things of the same category, one particular person or thing possesses a higher degree of the quality indicated.

三、替换与扩展 Substitution and Extension

（一）

1．这束花儿好看吗？

这束花儿真好看。

这束花儿是你的吗？

这束花儿是我的。

衬衫	（件）
裙子	（条）
车	（辆）*
照片*	（张）

2. 他们的食堂<u>大</u>不大？

他们的食堂不太大。

中文书，	多
地图，	新
老师，	忙
同学，	年轻
孩子，	漂亮
宿舍，	干净*

3. <u>这本</u>画报好吗？

很好。

那本画报更好，你<u>看看</u>。

啤酒（瓶），	喝
歌儿（个），	唱
词典（本），	用
唱片*（张），	听
大衣*（件），	穿

4. 那条漂亮的裙子是谁的？

是这个姑娘的。

好看，	笔 （枝）*
干净*，	衬衫 （件）
漂亮，	本子*（个）

5. 星期三有没有课？

有课。

来的同学多吗？

来的同学很多。

舞会，	参加舞会的人
电影，	看电影的人
音乐会*，	听音乐会的人
辅导，	参加辅导的同学

6. 你今年多大？

我今年二十二岁。

你的生日是哪一天？

我的生日是<u>五月八日</u>。

19，	2月12日
32，	12月27日
23，	9月29日

7. 祝你<u>生日</u>好！

谢谢你。

工作	新年[*]
学习	

(二)

1. 问年龄 Asking the age

A: 你爸爸好吗？

B: 谢谢你，他很好。

A: 他今年多大岁数[*]？

B: 他今年六十二。

*　　　*　　　*

A: 你有孩子吗？

B: 我有一个男孩子。

306

A: 他今年几岁？

B: 他今年八岁。

*   *

A: 你今年多大？

B: 二十八。

A: 你很年轻，象二十四岁。

B: 是吗？

2. 问看法 Asking for opinions from others

A: 这个电影有没有意思？

B: 很有意思。

A: 以后我也去看看。

3. 送礼 Presenting a gift

A: 这是给你的礼物*。

B: 啊，你太客气了！

A: 你喜欢吗？

B: 我非常喜欢。谢谢你。

贺 年 片

(hènlánplàn, New-year Card)

四、阅读短文 Reading Text

一 张 照 片

星期天,我们去王老师那儿。他让我们

看他一家人的照片*。

王老师是北京语言

(yǔyán, language) 学院的老

师,他教留学生汉语。

他常常在国外 (guówài, abroad) 工作。王老师今

年四十五岁,他爱人今年四十二岁。王老师

的爱人在北京图书馆工作。

王老师的儿子*叫王中。他很年轻，今年十八岁，是北京大学 (dàxué, university) 的学生。他的学习很好。穿裙子的姑娘是他们的女儿*——王英。她今年十岁。王英真漂亮，穿一件白衬衫，红裙子。她很象她妈妈，她妈妈也非常喜欢她。

五月三号是王英的生日。今天，王老师去商店给女儿*买礼物*。

五、语法 Grammar

1. 形容词谓语句 Sentences with an adjectival predicate

汉语形容词谓语句，谓语的主要成分是形容词，不再用动词"是"。例如：

A sentence in which the main element of the predicate is an adjective is known as a sentence with an adjectival predicate. In such a sentence the verb "是" is not necessarily used in the predicate. E.g.

她今天非常高兴。

我的衬衫太大。

这个阅览室很小。

那个服务员很年轻。

在肯定的陈述句里，简单的谓语形容词前如果没有"真、太、非常、更"等副词作状语说明谓语形容词的程度，常常需要加副词"很"。如果不加副词，单用形容词作谓语，往往有比较的意思。例如：

In affirmative sentences of this type, if the simple predicative adjective is not preceded by an adverb of degree such as "真", "太", "非常" or "更", it is usually qualified by the adverb "很". Without adverbial modifiers of any kind, the adjective often implies comparison, as in:

这个阅览室小，那个阅览室大。

那个服务员年轻，这个服务员不年轻。

注意：Points to be noted:

(1) 形容词谓语句里的"很"，表示程度的意义已不明显。"他很忙"跟"他忙"在程度上没有什么区别。

When used in sentences of this type, "很" does not indicate degree as it does elsewhere. "他很忙" and "他忙" have practically the same meaning.

(2) 形容词谓语句的正反疑问句，一般不用"很"等副词修饰形容词，不能说："他很高兴不很高兴?"

But "很" is not used in the affirmative-negative form of sentence of this type and it is incorrect to say "他很高兴不很高兴？"

2．动词重叠 Reduplication of verbs

表示动作的动词可以重叠。动词重叠常表示动作经历的时间短促或表示轻松、随便，有时也表示尝试。双音节动词重叠时，以词为单位（ABAB式）。例如：

Verbs denoting actions can be repeated or reduplicated. This device is usually employed when one wishes to indicate that the action is of very short duration, to soften the tone of a sentence or to make it sound relaxed or informal. Sometimes a verb is reduplicated to imply that what is done is just for the purpose of trying something out. In the case of disyllabic verbs, the reduplication follows the pattern "ABAB". E.g.

老师让我们想想这个问题。

这本画报很好，你看看。

我们去咖啡馆坐坐吧。

请你介绍介绍中国的民歌。

注意：Points to be noted:

(1)不表示动作的动词如"有"、"在"、"是"、"象"等不能重叠。

Verbs such as "有"，"在"，"是" and "象" which do not show actions can never be reduplicated.

(2) 重叠的动词一般不能作定语或状语。

Generally a reduplicated verb can function neither as an

attributive nor as an adverbial adjunct:

3．动词、动词结构及双音节形容词作定语　Verbs, verbal constructions or disyllabic adjectives as attributives

动词、动词结构作定语必须加结构助词"的"，双音节形容词作定语一般也要加"的"。例如：

When used attributively, a verb or a verbal construction must take after it the structural particle "的". So must a disyllabic adjective. E.g.

今天来的同学很多。

这是给她的电影票。

跟他跳舞的姑娘是法国留学生。

教你们口语的老师叫什么名字？

这件漂亮的衬衫是谁的？

练习　Exercises

1．读下列词组：Read out the following phrases:

年轻的大夫　年轻的服务员

年轻的老师　年轻的同学

漂亮的车　　漂亮的咖啡馆

漂亮的裙子　漂亮的姑娘

312

好看的裙子　好看的花儿　好看的笔

有意思的书　有意思的杂志

有意思的电影

2. 回答下列问题（先用肯定式，后用否定式）：
Answer the following questions (first in the affirmative and then in the negative):

(1) 你们学院大不大？

(2) 今天帕兰卡高兴不高兴？

(3) 你现在忙不忙？

(4) 你的中国朋友多不多？

(5) 你的车新不新？

(6) 这个汉字对不对？

(7) 这件衬衫旧不旧？

3. 把陈述句改为选择问句：Change the following to alternative questions:

(1) 他写的汉字很对。

(2) 这个电影没有意思。

(3) 咖啡馆的服务员很年轻。

(4) 那个书店不太大。

(5) 他的笔很好看。

(6) 中国的茶真好。

(7) 他们不太高兴。

4. 选择下列动词的重叠式填空。Fill in the blanks with the reduplicated forms of the verbs given:

找　帮助　介绍　用　休息　问

(1) 他请我_____北京。

(2) 我_____你的车，好吗？

(3) 我回家_____那本书，星期一给你。

(4) 下课以后你回宿舍_____吧。

(5) 我不认识这个汉字，我去学院____老师。

(6) 我朋友的汉语很好，我请他____我。

5. 跟你的同学谈谈你的家庭。

Talk with your classmates about your family:

六、语音语调　Pronunciation and Intonation

1．意群重音(3) Sense group stress (3)

(1) 在形容词谓语句中，谓语重读。例如：

In sentences with an adjectival predicate, the predicate is stressed. E.g.

这束花儿真好看。

丁云很年轻。

注意：在形容词谓语句中，"很"一般要轻读。

Note that in sentences of this type, "很" is usually pronounced with a weak stress.

(2) 指示代词"这"、"那"作主语或定语一般要重读。例如：

The demonstrative pronoun "这" or "那", when used as a subject or an attributive modifier, is usually stressed. E.g.

这是送你的花儿。

那都是旧的。

那个姑娘是日本人。

2．词的重音(5) Word stress (5)

单音节动词重叠后，前一个音节是重音，后一个音节读轻声。例如：

When a monosyllabic verb is reduplicated, the main stress falls on the first syllable, and the syllable that follows is pronounced in the neutral tone. E.g.

看看　说说　听听　想想

穿穿　找找　问问　用用

双音节动词重叠后，第一个音节和第三个音节是重音，其他两个音节读轻声。例如：

When a dissyllabic verb is reduplicated, the main stress falls on the first and the third syllables, the other two syllables are pronounced in the neutral tone. E.g.

辅导辅导　帮助帮助

休息休息　介绍介绍

3. 练习　Exercises

朗读下列双音节词。注意第二声的声调和词的重音。

Read out the following dissyllabic words, paying attention to the 2nd tone and word stress.

第二声 + 第一声：民歌　房间　年轻　结婚

第二声 + 第二声：同学　红茶　食堂　银行

第二声+第三声：词典　苹果　啤酒

第二声+第四声：杂志　邮票　学院

第二声+轻声：裙子　朋友　时候

朗读下面的成语：Read the following proverb:

Zhǐyào　gōngfu　shēn,
只要　功夫　深，

tiěchǔ　móchéng　zhēn.
铁杵　磨成　针。

(Constant grinding can turn an iron rod into a needle; Perseverance spells success.)

汉字笔顺表　Table of Stroke-order of Chinese Characters

1	束	一　丆　甴　甴　東　束　束							
2	真	直（一　十　古　古　肖　肖　直）							
		八							
3	送	关	⺍						
		天（一　二　干　天）							

317

		辶			
4	非				
5	感	咸（一 厂 厂 后 咸 咸 咸）			
		心			
6	高	亠			
		口			
		冋	冂		
			口		
7	兴	⺍（丶 ⺍ ⺍）			興
		一			
		八			
8	轻	车			輕
		圣	又（又 又）		
			工		
9	跳	𧾷			
		兆（丿 丬 丬 兆 兆 兆）			
10	吧	口			
		巴（⁊ 𠃜 𠃌 巴）			
11	姑	女			

318

		古	十								
			口								
12	娘	女									
		良									
13	漂	氵									
		票									
14	亮	亠									
		口									
		冗	冖								
			几								
15	更	一	匚	冂	曱	百	更	更			
16	象	刀	刀	勹	勾	臽	夕	争	象	象	象	像
17	开	一	二	于	开							開
18	门											門

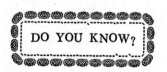

DO YOU KNOW?

The Four Treasures for the Study

The writing brush, inkstick, paper and inkslab have been

traditionally regarded in China as "the four treasures for a study". They have now had a history of more than 2,000 years. Paper was one of the four great inventions of ancient China. Cai Lun, who lived in the Eastern Han Dynasty (A.D. 25—200), improved the method of papermaking and produced paper of much better quality than before.

Of all the "four treasures for a study", Hu brush (produced originally in Huzhou, now the city of Wuxing, Zhejiang Province), Hui inkstick (produced in the city of Huizhou, Anhui Province), Xuan paper (originally made in the city of Xuancheng, Anhui Province) and Duan inkslab (made from stone quarried in Duanxi area, Gaoyao County, Guangdong Province) are well-known for their high quality to the whole country as top-grade writing materials which are indispensable for traditional Chinese calligraphy and painting.

第二十二课 Lesson 22

一、课文 Text

后边有一个小花园

太　太：请　丁　云　看看　我们　的　新
Tàitai:　Qǐng　Dīng　Yún　kànkan　wǒmen　de　xīn

房子　吧。
fángzi　ba.

帕兰卡：好。丁　云，跟　我　来。这　是
Pàlánkǎ:　Hǎo.　Dīng　Yún,　gēn　wǒ　lái.　Zhè　shì

客厅。
kètīng.

丁　云：这个 客厅 很 大，也 很 漂亮。
Dīng Yún: Zhège kètīng hěn dà, yě hěn piàoliang.

太　太：客厅 旁边 是 书房。请 进。
Tàitai: kètīng pángbiān shì shūfáng. Qǐng jìn.

帕兰卡：这儿 有 椅子， 坐 吧。
Pàlánkǎ: Zhèr yǒu yǐzi, zuò ba.

丁　云：谢谢。 你们 的 书 真 不 少。
Dīng Yún: Xièxie. Nǐmen de shū zhēn bù shǎo.

帕兰卡：桌子 上边 的 书 都 是 爸爸
Pàlánkǎ: Zhuōzi shàngbiān de shū dōu shì bàba

　　　　的。 他 总 不 让 我们 整理。
de. Tā zǒng bú ràng wǒmen zhěnglǐ.

太　太：去 看看 我们 的 厨房 吧。厨房
Tàitai: Qù kànkan wǒmen de chúfáng ba. Chúfáng

　　　　在 对面，从 这儿 走。
zài duìmiàn, cóng zhèr zǒu.

帕兰卡：丁 云， 我们 的 厨房 太 小。
Pàlánkǎ: Dīng Yún, wǒmen de chúfáng tài xiǎo.

太　太：不 小——作 饭 的 总是 我 一个
Tàitai: Bù xiǎo——zuò fàn de zǒngshì wǒ yíge

　　　　人。
rén.

322

帕兰卡： 好 了， 妈妈， 以后 我 一定
Pàlánkǎ: Hǎo le, māma, yǐhòu wǒ yídìng

帮助 你 作 饭。
bāngzhu nǐ zuò fàn.

太 太： 谢谢 你。 餐厅 在 厨房 左边，
Tàitai: Xièxie nǐ. Cāntīng zài chúfáng zuǒbiān,

里边 的 房间 是 我们 的 卧室。
lǐbiān de fángjiān shì wǒmen de wòshì.

帕兰卡： 后边 还 有 一个 小 花园。
Pàlánkǎ: Hòubiān hái yǒu yíge xiǎo huāyuán.

丁 云： 帕兰卡， 你 的 卧室 在 哪儿？
Dīng Yún: Pàlánkǎ, nǐ de wòshì zài nǎr?

帕兰卡： 我 的 卧室 在 客厅 左边。 那
Pàlánkǎ: Wǒ de wòshì zài kètīng zuǒbiān. Nà

是 洗澡间。 我们 的 新 房子
shì xǐzǎojiān. Wǒmen de xīn fángzi

怎么样？
zěnmeyàng?

丁 云： 你们 的 新 房子 非常 好。
Dīng Yún: Nǐmen de xīn fángzi fēicháng hǎo.

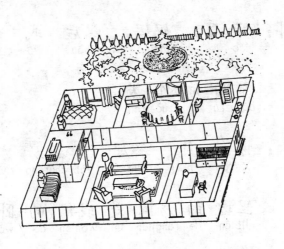

生词 New Words

1. **后边** (名) hòubiān — back, at the back of; behind

2. **小** (形) xiǎo — little, small

3. **花园** (名) huāyuán — garden

4. **房子** (名) fángzi — house

5. **客厅** (名) kètīng — drawing room, parlour

6. **旁边** (名) pángbiān — side

7. **书房** (名) shūfáng — study

8. **椅子** (名) yǐzi — chair

9. **少** (形) shǎo — few, little

10. **桌子** (名) zhuōzi — table

11.	上边	(名) shàngbiān	top, on, over, above
12.	总是	(副) zǒngshì	always
	总	(副) zǒng	always
13.	整理	(动) zhěnglǐ	to put in order, to straighten up, to arrange
14.	厨房	(名) chúfáng	kitchen
15.	对面	(名) duìmiàn	opposite
16.	帮助	(动、名) bāngzhu	to help
	帮	(动) bāng	to help
17.	餐厅	(名) cāntīng	dining-hall
18.	左边	(名) zuǒbiān	left
19.	里边	(名) lǐbiān	inside
20.	房间	(名) fángjiān	room
21.	卧室	(名) wòshì	bedroom
22.	洗澡间	(名) xǐzǎojiān	bath-room
	洗澡	xǐ zǎo	to take a bath
23.	怎么样	(代) zěnmeyàng	how, how is it that...?

补充词 Supplementary Words

1.	外边	(名) wàibiān	outside
2.	下边	(名) xiàbiān	bottom, below, under

3. 前边　(名) qiánbiān　　front, in front of, before

4. 右边　(名) yòubiān　　right

5. 中间　(名) zhōngjiān　　middle

6. 窗户　(名) chuānghu　　window

7. 套　(量) tào　　a measure word a set

8. 把　(量) bǎ　　a measure word for chair & tools

二、注释　Notes

1. "(请)跟我来。"

"(Please) come along with me." or "Come with me, (please)."

"从这儿走。"

"Come this way."

这是给别人带路时的常用语。

Both are everyday expressions used to lead the way for someone.

2. "作饭的总是我一个人。"

"It is always me alone that does the cooking."

"作饭的"是"作饭的人"的意思。这种由动词和它的宾语跟"的"组成的"的"字结构，也是一种名词性结构。如"吃饭的"（吃饭的人）、"学汉语的"（学汉语的人）等。

"作饭的" means the same as "作饭的人". "的" constructions of this kind, composed of a verb and its object plus "的", are also nominal constructions. Here are some more examples: "吃饭的"（吃饭的人），"学汉语的"（学汉语的人）。

326

3. "好了，妈妈，以后我帮助你作饭。"

这里的"好了"表示一种结束的语气，意思是 "妈妈，你不要再说了，以后我帮助你作饭。"

"好了" in "好了，妈妈，以后我帮助你作饭。" is used to express the wish to discontinue an argument, meaning "Oh, mamma, (you) don't complain any more. I'll help you with the cooking."

三、替换与扩展　Substitution and Extension

(一)

1. 餐厅在<u>左边</u>吗？

   餐厅不在左边，在<u>后边</u>。

旁边，	对面
对面，	后边
里边，	外边*
上边，	下边*

2. 阅览室在哪儿？

   阅览室在<u>图书馆里边</u>。

   看书的人多不多？

看书的人很多。

学校里边
食堂后边
实验室*对面
宿舍和食堂中间*

3. 后边有什么?

后边有一个花园。

这个花园大不大?

这个花园不大。

旁边,　书房
左边,　厨房
对面,　洗澡间
前边*,　客厅
右边*,　卧室

4. 食堂里边有什么?

食堂里边有很多桌子和椅子。

图书馆里边，	很多书和杂志
桌子上边，	两瓶啤酒
学院旁边，	一个咖啡馆
学院外边*，	一个银行

5. 桌子后边是什么？

桌子后边是椅子。

书上边，	笔
桌子上边，	一束花儿
书下边*，	两本画报
卧室中间*，	一张床
门旁边，	窗户*

6. 里边的房间是谁的？

里边的房间是我们的。

对面的房子，	白先生的
上边的衬衫，	弟弟的
桌子上边的信，	你的

7. 你们的新房子怎么样？

我们的新房子很小。

那个咖啡馆，	很漂亮
她的裙子，	不好看
今天的电影，	很有意思
这个新餐厅，	不大
这套*房子，	很旧

(二)

1. 问路 Asking the way

A: 请问，新邮局*在哪儿？

B: 对不起*，我不知道。

* * *

A: 请问，这儿有一个新邮局*吗？

C: 有，在对面，咖啡馆旁边。

A: 谢谢你。

C: 不谢。

330

2. 在车上 On a bus

A: 请问,这儿有人吗?

B: 没有人,坐吧。

A: 谢谢。

3. 问看法 Asking for opinions from others

A: 你知道《红楼梦》(《Hónglóumèng》, "The Dream of the Red Chamber") 吗?

B: 我知道,我有一套*英文的。

A: 这本书怎么样?

B: 这本书非常好。

　　　*　　　　*　　　　*

新华书店　　中國人民銀行

四、阅读短文 Reading Text

古 波 的 宿 舍

学生城 (Xuéshengchéng, students' town or university town) 里边有很多宿舍,我们认识的古波和中

国留学生丁云也都在那儿住。现在我们去看
看古波的宿舍。

古波的宿舍在四层 二
十九号。他跟他同学一起
住。这个房间不太大。门对
面是一个很大的窗户*，窗户*旁边有两张
床：左边的床是他的，右边的是他同学的。
他们的桌子在两张床中间*。桌子后边有两
把*椅子。房间里边有很多漂亮的照片*。

古波说："我们的房间不太干净 (gānjing,
clean)。现在我们很忙，每天起床以后去学
院上课，有时候在图书馆看书。晚上常常
十一点回宿舍睡觉。"古波的同学说："古波
常常星期五上午整理房间，那天我们的宿舍
总是很干净——每个星期五下午帕兰卡都
来这儿。"

五、语法　Grammar

1. 方位词 Position words

表示方位的名词叫方位词。如"前边"、"后边"、"上边"、"下边"、"左边"、"右边"、"里边"、"外边"、"中间"、"对面"等。这些方位词跟一般名词一样，可以作主语、宾语、定语，也可以受定语修饰。例如：

Position words are nouns that denote positions and the most commonly used ones are "前边", "后边", "上边", "下边", "左边", "右边", "里边", "外边", "中间" and "对面". Like ordinary nouns, they may serve as the subject of a sentence, as an object, an attributive and be qualified by an attributive. E.g.

里边有什么？

洗澡间在对面。

桌子上边有一束花儿。

下边的报是今天的，你看吧。

左边的绿车是我的。

注意：Points to be noted:

(1) 方位词作定语，后边一般要用"的"，如"里边的房间"。如果方位词被定语修饰，前边一般不用"的"，如"房间里边"。

When used attributively, a position word usually takes "的" after it, as in "里边的房间 (the inner room)". But "的"

333

is not used when the position word is itself preceded by an attributive, as in "房间里边 (inside the room)".

(2) 地理名词后边不用"里边"，如"他在北京学习汉语"。

"里边" is not used after geographical names, as in "他在北京学习汉语".

介词"在"后边如果是有关建筑、组织或地方的名词，表示方位的"里边"也常常省略。如"我姐姐在银行工作"，"他在阅览室看书"。

When the preposition "在" is followed by a noun representing a building, an organization or a place, the position word "里边" is often omitted, as in "我姐姐在银行工作"，"他在阅览室看书".

2．表示存在的句子　Sentences indicating existence

(1) 用"在"表示存在　　"在" indicating existence

动词"在"常表示存在，这种句子的主语通常是存在的人或事物，宾语通常是表示方位与处所的名词。

The verb "在" very often indicates existence, telling that someone or something is in a certain place. In a sentence with "在", the subject is usually the person or thing concerned and the object is usually a noun denoting position or place.

名词或代词(存在的人或事物) Nouns or pronouns (persons or things that exist)	动词"在" Verbs "在"	名词或代词(方位处所) Nouns ro pronouns (positions or locations)
他	在	我左边。
图书馆	不在	书店旁边。
我的书	在	你那儿吗？

334

（2）用"有"表示存在　　　"有" indicating existence

动词"有"除了表示领有外，还可以表示存在。表示存在的"有"作谓语主要成分时，句子的主语通常是表示方位、处所的名词，宾语是存在的人或事物。

Apart from denoting possession, the verb "有" can also indicate existence. In a sentence with "有" as the main element of the predicate, the subject is usually a noun denoting position or place and the object is the person or thing concerned.

名词或代词（方位处所） Nouns or pronouns (positions or locations)	动词"有" Verbs"有"	名词（存在的人或事物） Nouns (persons or things that exist)
后边	有	一个商店。
这儿	没有	人。
那本书里边	有没有	照片？

（3）用"是"表示存在　　　"是" indicating existence

动词"是"也可以表示存在，"是"字句和"有"字句表示存在时，词序是一样的。

The verb "是" can indicate existence as well. The word order of a "是" sentence, when indicating existence, is exactly the same as that of a "有" sentence.

名词或代词（方位处所） Nouns or pronouns (positions or locations)	动词"是" Verbs "是"	名词或代词（存在的人或事物） Nouns or pronouns (persons or things that exist)
图书馆对面	是	我们学院。

客厅旁边	不是	书房。
你前边	是	谁？

注意：用"是"表示存在跟用"有"表示存在的句子有以下两点不同：

Note that there are two points of difference between "是" and "有" when both indicate existence:

(1) 用"有"的句子只是说明某处存在着什么，用"是"的句子是已知某处存在着事物而要进一步说明这事物是什么。

Sentences with "有" merely tell where something is located whereas sentences with "是" tell what something is whose whereabouts is already known.

(2) 用"有"的句子宾语是不确指的，用"是"的句子的宾语可以是确指的也可以是不确指的。因此，不能说"图书馆对面有我们学院"，应该说"图书馆对面是我们学院"或"我们学院在图书馆对面"。

The object of a sentence with "有" is usually indefinite while the object of a sentence with "是" may be either definite or indefinite. So the Chinese for "Our college stands opposite to the library." should be "图书馆对面是我们学院" or "我们学院在图书馆对面" instead of "图书馆对面有我们学院".

练习 Exercises

1. 读下列词组：Read out the following phrases:

卧室后边　　　　　后边的卧室

咖啡馆对面　　　　对面的咖啡馆

银行旁边　　　　　旁边的银行

餐厅左边　　　　　左边的餐厅

桌子上边　　　　　上边的桌子

新房子　　　新地图　　　大花园

旧房子　　　旧地图　　　小花园

大房间　　　很多老师

小房间　　　不少学生

2. 用"有"和"是"分别改写下列句子： Rewrite the following sentences using "有" or "是"：

(1) 那杯茶在桌子上边。

(2) 银行在书店和咖啡馆中间。

(3) 餐厅在厨房外边。

(4) 花园在房子前边。

(5) 图书馆在学院左边。

(6) 客厅在书房旁边。

3. 根据下图用方位词填空： Fill in the blanks with position
words according to the following layout:

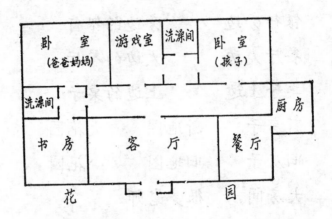

这是我家。我家＿＿＿＿有一个花园，花

园＿＿＿＿有很多好看的花儿。客厅在房子

＿＿＿＿，客厅＿＿＿＿是餐厅。厨房在餐厅

＿＿＿＿。客厅＿＿＿＿是爸爸的书房，＿＿＿＿有

两个卧室：＿＿＿＿的卧室大，是爸爸和妈妈

的，＿＿＿＿的卧室小，是我和弟弟的。两个卧

室＿＿＿＿是我们的游戏室 (yóuxìshì, recreation room)。

338

4. 根据下图进行问答：Ask each other questions about the location of the various places identical in the diagram:

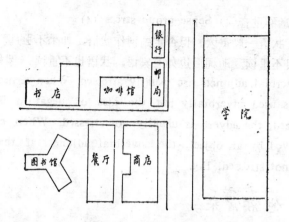

5. 根据下图写一段话：Write a short passage as shown by the following picture:

6. 猜一猜，这是什么？Guess what this is:

上边毛 (máo, hair), 下边毛，

中间一个水葡萄 (shuǐ pútao, watery grape)。

六、语音语调 Pronunciation and Intonation

1. 意群重音(4) Sense group stress（4）

(1) 状语一般重读。但否定副词作状语，如果不强调否定时，一般不重读。动词后边如有宾语，状语也不重读。例如：

Adverbial adjuncts are usually stressed. When a negative adverb is used adverbially but the idea of negation is not emphasized, the adverb is usually not stressed. When a verb is followed by an objcet, the adverbial adjunct, if there is one, is not stressed. E.g.

他常常来。

他不让我们整理。 (The adverbial adjunct"不" is not stressed.)

里边常常有舞会。 (The adverbial adjunct "常常" is not stressed.)

我们晚上去看京剧。 (The adverbial adjunct "晚上" is not stressed.)

(2) 动词"有"和"是"表示存在时都轻读。例如：

When the verbs "有" and "是" indicate existence, they are pronounced with a weak stress. E.g.

后边有一个小花园。

这是客厅。

里边的房间是我们的卧室。

2. 练习 Exercises

朗读下列双音节词语，注意送气音与不送气音的区别：

Read out the following dissyllabic words, paying special attention to the aspirated and unaspirated sounds:

b:	北京	帮助	左边	本子	上班
p:	旁边	啤酒	葡萄	苹果	漂亮
d:	多少	点心	地图	地址	大夫
t:	听课	图书	同学	跳舞	太太
g:	公司	告诉	工作	姑娘	感谢
k:	口语	咖啡	客厅	客气	好看

朗读下面成语：Read out the following proverb:

Lù yáo zhī mǎ lì,
路 遥 知 马 力，

rì jiǔ jiàn rén xīn.
日 久 见 人 心。

(As distance tests a horse's strength, so time reveals a person's heart.)

汉字笔顺表　Table of Stroke-order of Chinese Characters

1	边	力	邊
		辶	
2	园	囗	園
		元（一　二　一　元）	
3	房	户（丶　乛　一　户）	
		方（丶　一　方）	
4	厅	厂（一　厂）	廳
		丁（一　丁）	
5	旁	亠（丶　一　丷　立　立）	
		方	
6	椅	木	
		奇　大	
		可	
7	桌	卜	
		日	
		木	
8	总	丷	總

342

		口	
		心	
9	整	敕	束
			攵
		正（一 丁 下 正 正）	
10	理	王	
		里（丨 口 日 日 甲 甲 里）	
11	厨	厂	
		尌	豆（一 口 戸 豆 豆）
			寸
12	面	一 厂 厂 币 币 而 而 面 面	
13	帮	邦	丰（一 二 三 丰）
			阝
		巾	
14	助	且（丨 刀 月 且 且）	
		力	
15	餐	奴	歹
			卜
			夕
		又	

幫

		食	
16	左	ナ	
		工	
17	里		裏
18	间	门	間
		日	
19	卧	臣（一 丆 丆 臣 臣 臣）	
		卜	
20	洗	氵	
		先	
21	澡	氵	
		喿 品（口 品 品）	
		木	
22	怎	乍	
		心	
23	样	木	樣
		羊（丶 丷 丷 兰 兰 羊）	

344

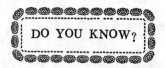

China's Well-known Classical Novels

Most of China's classical novels were produced in the Ming and Qing Dynasties dated from the 14th to 18th centuries. The best-known are "The Romance of the Three Kingdoms" by Luo Guanzhong and "Water Margin" by Shi Naian, both produced in the 14th century, "Pilgrimage to the West" by Wu Chengen and "Jin Ping Mei" by Xiao Xiao Sheng of Lanling, both produced in the 16th century, and "The Scholars" by Wu Jingzhi, produced in the 18th century.

"The Dream of the Red Chamber" written by Cao Xueqin, a great realistic writer of the 18th century, marks the height of China's classical fiction. It occupies an outstanding place in the history of both China's and the world's literature.

第二十三课　Lesson 23

一、课文　Text

我正在看电视呢

帕兰卡：　喂，是学生宿舍吗？
Pàlánkǎ：　Wéi, shì xuésheng sùshè ma?

工　人：　是啊。您找谁？
Gōngrén：　Shì a. Nín zhǎo shéi?

帕兰卡：　我找丁云，请她接电话。
Pàlánkǎ：　Wǒ zhǎo Dīng Yún, qǐng tā jiē diànhuà.

工　人：　好，请等一等。
Gōngrén：　Hǎo, qǐng děngyiděng.

346

丁 云: 喂, 我 是 丁 云。你 是 帕兰卡
Dīng Yún: Wèi, wǒ shì Dīng Yún. Nǐ shì Pàlánkǎ

吧?
ba?

帕兰卡: 对 了, 你 在 休息 吗?
Pàlánkǎ: Duì le, nǐ zài xiūxi ma?

丁 云: 没有, 我 在 复习 课文 呢, 你
Dīng Yún: Méiyou, wǒ zài fùxí kèwén ne, nǐ

呢?
ne?

帕兰卡: 我 在 家里。
Pàlánkǎ: Wǒ zài jiālǐ.

我 正在 看
Wǒ zhèngzài kàn

电视 呢。
diànshì ne.

丁 云: 有 什么 新闻?
Dīng Yún: Yǒu shénme xīnwén?

帕兰卡: 中国 友好 代表团 正在 参观
Pàlánkǎ: Zhōngguó yǒuhǎo dàibiǎotuán zhèngzài cānguān

一个 工厂, 工人们 正 欢迎
yíge gōngchǎng, gōngrénmen zhèng huānyíng

347

他们 呢。
tāmen ne.

丁 云： 你们 的 代表团 也 在 中国
Dīng Yún: Nǐmen de dàibiǎotuán yě zài Zhōngguó

访问 呢， 报上 有 他们 的
fǎngwèn ne, bàoshang yǒu tāmen de

照片。 古波 呢？ 他 怎么样？
zhàopiàn. Gǔbō ne? Tā zěnmeyàng?

帕兰卡： 他 不 在， 他 总是 很 忙。下午
Pàlánkǎ: Tā bú zài, tā zǒngshì hěn máng. Xiàwǔ

我 给 他 打 电话 的 时候， 他
wǒ gěi tā dǎ diànhuà de shíhou, tā

正 上 课 呢。喂， 我 说， 明天
zhèng shàng kè ne. Wèi, wǒ shuō, míngtiān

你 有 空儿 吗？
nǐ yǒu kòngr ma?

丁 云： 什么 事儿？
Dīng Yún: Shénme shìr?

帕兰卡： 我们 去 城外 玩儿玩儿， 好 吗？
Pàlánkǎ: Wǒmen qù chéngwài wánrwanr, hǎo ma?

丁 云： 好 啊。明天 几点 出发？
Dīng Yún: Hǎo a. Míngtiān jǐdiǎn chūfā?

帕兰卡： 七点半 我们 开 车 来 接 你。
Pàlánkǎ: Qīdiǎnbàn wǒmen kāi chē lái jiē nǐ.

丁 云： 好， 再见！
Dīng Yún: Hǎo, zàijiàn!

生词 New Words

1. 正在　　（副）zhèngzài　　an adverb indicating an action in progress

2. 电视　　（名）diànshì　　television, TV

3. 接（电话）

　　　　　　（动）jiē(diànhuà)　　to answer (the phone)

4. 电话　　（名）diànhuà　　telephone call, telephone

5. 没（有）　（副）méi (you)　　not, no

6. 复习　　（动）fùxí　　to review

7. 课文　　（名）kèwén　　text

8. 新闻　　（名）xīnwén　　news

9. 友好　　（形）yǒuhǎo　　friendly

10. 代表团　（名）dàibiǎotuán　　delegation

　　代表　　（名）dàibiǎo　　delegate, representative

11. 参观　　（动）cānguān　　to visit, to pay a visit

12. 工厂　　（名）gōngchǎng　　factory

349

13. 工人	(名) gōngrén	worker
14. 访问	(动) fǎngwèn	to visit, to call on
15. 照片	(名) zhàopiàn	photograph, photo, picture
16. 打(电话)		
	(动) dǎ (diànhuà)	to make (a telephone call)
17. 明天	(名) míngtiān	tomorrow
18. 城	(名) chéng	city, town
19. 外边	(名) wàibiān	outside
20. 玩儿	(动) wánr	to play, to have fun with
21. 出发	(动) chūfā	to start out, to set off
22. 开(车)	(动) kāi (chē)	to drive (a car)
23. 接(人)	(动) jiē (rén)	to meet (a person)

补充词 Supplementary Words

1. 总机	(名) zǒngjī	central exchange, telephone exchange, switchboard
2. 分机	(名) fēnjī	extension
3. 占线	zhàn xiàn	the line is busy (engaged), the number is engaged
4. 打错了	dǎ cuò le	(you have dialled the) wrong number

350

5. 号码　　　(名) hàomǎ　　　　number

6.《人民日报》

　　　　(专名)《Rénmín Rìbào》

　　　　　　　　"the People's Daily"

二、注释　Notes

1."请等一等。"

意思跟"请等等"同。单音节动词重叠，中间可以加"一"，如"听一听"、"走一走"。

"请等一等" has the same meaning as "请等等". When a monosyllabic verb is reduplicated, "一" can be inserted in between, e.g. "听一听", "走一走".

2."你是帕兰卡吧?"

语气助词"吧"(2)常表示不肯定的语气。如果对某事物有了一定的估计，但还不敢肯定时，就在句末用"吧"。例如：

The modal particle "吧"(2) often gives the statement a tone of uncertainty. If one forms an estimate of a thing, and yet is not very sure whether it is true, one can use "吧" at the end of the sentence. E.g.

这个汉字不对吧?

你们现在很忙吧?

她住 423 号吧?

3."我在家里。"

某些方位词如"里边"、"上边"等和前边的名词结合在一起使用时,"边"常常省略,如"城里、家里、桌子上、报上、城外、国外、(工)厂外"等。

When the position word "里边" or "上边" etc. is attached to a noun, "边" is very often omitted, as in "城里", "家里", "桌子上", "报上", "城外", "国外" and "(工)厂外" etc.

4."中国友好代表团正在参观一个工厂。"

"你们的一个代表团现在也在中国访问呢。"

"访问"的对象既可以是某一事物、某个地方, 也可以是某人;"参观"的对象只能是某地方或事物,不能说"参观某人"。"参观"主要是"看",有时有游览的意思。"访问"则常常有交谈的内容。

The object of the verb "访问" may be either a thing or place or a person; the object of the verb "参观" can only be a place or a thing other than a person. That's why you can't say "参观某人". "参观" means chiefly "看" though it is sometimes used in the sense of sightseeing. "访问", on the other hand, is frequently used synonymously with "to interview".

5."他怎么样?"

"How is he?"

"怎么样"也是问候的用语,常用于比较熟悉的人。如:"你怎么样?""我很好。"

"怎么样" is also a conversational greeting used between close acquaintances, e.g. "你怎么样?""我很好".

6."下午我给他打电话的时候,他正上课呢。"

"…的时候"是一种常用的表示时间的结构。跟"以前、以后"

一样，它前边常常是单词（如"休息的时候"）、动词结构（如"参观工厂的时候"）或主谓结构等。

"…的时候" is a common construction denoting time, meaning "when" or "at the time of". Like "以前" or "以后", it is usually preceded by a word (e.g. "休息的时候"), a verbal construction (e.g. "参观工厂的时候") or a subject-predicate construction.

7．"我说，明天你有空儿吗？"

"我说"是打电话或谈话中引起话题的常用语。

"我说" is a common expression used to introduce a new subject in a conversation or a telephone call.

三、替换与扩展 Substitution and Extension

（一）

1．她在作什么呢？

她正在<u>看电视</u>呢。

她跟谁一起看电视？

她跟她妹妹一起看电视。

> 吃饭
> 喝茶
> 看《人民日报》
> 听京剧

2. 他们在<u>跳舞</u>吗？

他们没（有）跳舞，他们<u>唱歌</u>呢。

（没有，他们唱歌呢。）

工作，	玩儿
参观工厂，	参观学校
听音乐，	听新闻
复习课文，	看杂志

3. 他们正在哪儿<u>参观</u>呢？

他们正在<u>城里</u>参观呢。

吃饭，	家里
写字，	桌子上
玩儿，	花园里

4. 下午你给他打电话的时候，他作什么呢？

下午我给他打电话的时候，他正<u>上课</u>呢。

整理房间	给朋友写信
睡觉	复习语法
洗澡	休息

5. 你看书的时候，你同学作什么呢？

他在开车呢。

你去他家，	看电视
你找他，	接电话
你们访问王先生，	学习汉语
你们出发，	穿大衣*
你去邮局*，	打电话

6. 请等一等，好吗？

好。

找	用
看	听

（二）

1. 打电话 Making a telephone call

    （A 打电话）

A: 喂，是外语学院总机*吗？

B: 是啊。

A: 我要 262 分机*。

B: 现在占线*呢，请等一等。

A: 好。

           *   *   *

    （A 接电话）

A: 喂？

B: 是大光吗？我是王中啊。

A: 你找谁啊？

B: 我找谢大光。

A: 这儿没有谢大光，你打错了*。

B: 对不起 (duì bu qǐ, sorry)。

           *   *   *

(A 接电话)

A: 喂？谁啊？

B: 我是王中，请问，谢大光在吗？

A: 他不在，他上课呢。有什么事儿？

B: 请你让他今天晚上给我打个电话，好吗？

A: 好，你的电话号码*是多少？

B: 285742。谢谢你。

A: 不谢。

2. 婉拒 Politely refusing

A: 我用一用这本词典好吗？

B: 对不起，我正用呢。下午给你吧。

A: 好吧。

*   *   *

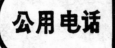

公用电话　　　公共厕所

看　报

帕兰卡去找丁云的时候，丁云正在看报。她问丁云："你在看什么报？"

丁云说："我在看《人民日报》*，你来看，这儿有一条新闻，你们的一个友好代表团正在访问中国。这儿还有他们参观访问的照片。"

帕兰卡说："给我看看。"

这是五月二十七日的新闻，代表团在参观北京的一个小学(xiǎoxué, primary school)。这条新闻旁边有三张照片。左边的这张照片是代表团进教室*的时候，孩子们正在上课。中间这张是他们跟孩子们一起玩儿呢。你看，他们正在唱歌、跳舞。右边的那张是一个老师在给代表团介绍呢。

帕兰卡说："这张报真有意思，给我好吗？我妈妈很喜欢中国的孩子，给她看看中国孩子的照片，她一定很高兴。"

"好，给你吧！"

"谢谢你，丁云。"

五、语法 Grammar

1. 动作的进行 The progressive aspect of an action

(1) 一个动作可以处在进行、持续、完成等不同的阶段。要表示动作处在进行的阶段，可在动词前加副词"正在"、"正"、"在"或在句尾加"呢"。"正在"、"正"、"在"也可以和"呢"同时用。例如：

An action may be represented as being in progress, continuing or completed. To show that an action is in progress, place either one of the adverbs "正在", "正" and "在" bofore the verb or "呢" at the end of the sentence. "正在", "正" or "在" is very often used together with "呢" to express the progressive aspect. E.g.

名词或代词 Nouns or pronouns	副　词 Adverbs	动　词 Verbs	名词或代词 Nouns or pronouns	助　词 Particles
我	正在	看	电视	（呢）。

你	在	作	什么	(呢)?
工人代表	正	欢迎	他们	(呢)。
我		听	新闻	呢。
老师	(正)在	辅导	他们	吗?

否定形式用"没有"。"没有"在动词前边可省略为"没",但在句尾或独立回答问题时,不能省略。例如:

"没有" is used to make up the negative form of the progressive aspect. "没有" may be shortened to "没" if it goes before the verb. But at the end of the sentence or in short answers, "没有" must be used in full. E.g.

他们在跳舞吗?

——他们没有跳舞,他们唱歌呢。

——他们没跳舞,他们唱歌呢。

——没有,他们唱歌呢。

——没有。

(2) 动作所处的阶段与动作发生的时间 (过去、现在或将来) 是两个不同的概念。汉语里动作发生的时间是用时间词语来表示的:

The aspect and the time (past, present or future) of an action are two different concepts. In Chinese the time of an action is expressed by means of time words. E.g.

他以前非常喜欢现代音乐。

我们今天参观工厂。

我朋友明天来看我。

进行的动作可以发生在现在，也可以发生在过去或将来。例如：

An action in progress may take place either in the present or in the past or future. E.g.

喂，你在作什么呢？我在写信呢。
(现在 present)

下午他给我打电话的时候，我正看报呢。(过去 past)

明天晚上你去找他，他一定在看电视呢。(将来 future)

2. 用"呢"的省略式疑问句　Elliptical questions formed
with the modal particle "呢"

在一定的语言环境里，在代词、名词或名词性词组等后面直接加上语气助词"呢"，也可以构成疑问句。这种句子所问的内容，要由上下文来决定。如：

Elliptical questions may be formed by adding merely "呢" to a pronoun, noun or nominal construction. The meaning of this type of question is determined mainly by the context. E.g.

你好吗？

——我很好，你呢？（你好吗？）

你在作什么呢？

——我在复习课文呢，你呢？（你在作什么

呢？）

你现在有空儿吗？

——我没有空儿。

晚上呢？（晚上你有空几吗？）

如果没有上下文，这种句子总是问地点的。如：

When there is no context, elliptical questions of this
type are usually used to ask where someone or something is.
E.g.

古波呢？（古波在哪儿？）

你弟弟呢？（你弟弟在哪儿？）

我的笔呢？（我的笔在哪儿？）

3. 主谓结构作定语 Subject-predicate constructions as the
attributive

主谓结构作定语，定语和中心语之间必须加结构助词"的"。
如：

When a subject-predicate construction is used attribu-

362

tively, there must be the structural particle "的" between the attributive and what it qualifies. E.g.

我给他打电话的时候，他正上课呢。

你看看我们参观访问的照片。

他买的椅子怎么样？

这是谁给你写的信？

我们常去吃饭的餐厅在花园左边。

练习 Exercises

1. 读下列词组：Read out the following phrases:

友好代表团　　工人代表团　　银行代表团

音乐代表团　　参观工厂　　　参观图书馆

参观中文系　　参观食堂　　　访问中国

访问工厂　　　访问留学生　　访问王先生

欢迎新同学　　欢迎你们　　　欢迎中国朋友

欢迎代表团　　打电话　　　　给朋友打电话

接电话

2. 用"正在…呢"和括号里的词语完成下列句子: Complete the answers with sentences formed with "正在…呢" and the words or phrases given in brackets:

(1) A: 帕兰卡在家吗?

　　B: 在,_____。(吃饭)

(2) A: 张先生现在忙不忙?

　　B: 很忙,_____。(上课)

(3) A: 请问,大夫呢?

　　B: 在那儿,_____。(打电话)

(4) A: 你的词典呢?

　　B: 我_____。(用)

(5) A: 古波来不来?

　　B: 他不来,_____。(参观)

3. 用所给的动词(或动宾结构)作带"正在…呢"的句子:
Make sentences with "正在…呢", using the verbs or verb-object constructions given below in the same way as the example:

　　例Example 进食堂

　　　　　　吃饭

　　　　→我进食堂的时候,他正吃饭呢。

364

(1) 去阅览室
　　看杂志

(2) 进商店
　　买东西

(3) 给他打电话
　　复习

(4) 找他
　　起床

(5) 回家
　　喝咖啡

4. 看图说话：Say as much as you can about each of the
　　following pictures:

①

②

③

④

5. 把结构助词"的"填进下列句子的适当的位置：
Insert the structural particle "的" where necessary in the following sentences:

(1) 休息时候他常常听音乐。

(2) 参观工厂人很多。

(3) 这是妈妈给她衬衫。

(4) 我买那本书很好。

(5) 他认识新朋友是中国人。

6. 把下列句子翻译成汉语：Translate the following into Chinese:

(1) When I got to his place, he was watching TV.

(2) When they started out, I was just getting up.

(3) "Liuxuesheng" are students who study in a foreign country.

(4) People who wait on tables in a café are called waiters.

(5) The shop where he bought his clothes is not very large.

(6) Who's the teacher who teaches you Chinese?

六、语音语调 Pronunciation and Intonation

1. 意群重音(5) Sense group stress(5)

(1) 长句一般可先分为几个意群，再按意群分析重音。（本书用"∥"表示意群分节号。）例如：

To determine the sentence stress of a long sentence, divide the sentence into sense groups, then find out which syllable should receive stress. (In this book the sigh "‖" is used to mark out sense group.) E.g.

中国友好代表团‖正在参观一个工厂。

你们的新闻代表团‖现在也在中国访问呢。

（2）介词结构作状语，而动词后又有宾语时，介词的宾语和动词的宾语都重读，介词轻读。例如：

In sentences in which a prepositional construction is used adverbially and the verb is at the same time followed by an object, the objects of both the preposition and the verb are stressed, with the preposition pronounced with a weak stress. E.g.

下午我给古波打电话。

他在家里看电视。

帕兰卡跟丁云一起去咖啡馆。

2．词的重音(6) Word stress (6)

"一"夹在单音节重叠动词中间时，读轻声。重音格式是"重轻轻"。例如：

When "一" is inserted between a pair of reduplicated monosyllabic verbs, it is pronounced in the neutral tone. The stress-pattern of this type of construction is "strong-weak-weak". E.g.

等一等　想一想　坐一坐　找一找

谈一谈　走一走　接一接　玩儿一玩儿

3. 练习　Exercises

朗读下面的成语：Read out the following proverb:

Yìnián zhī jì zàiyú chūn,

一年　之　计　在于　春，

Yírì zhī jì zàiyú chén.

一日　之　计　在于　晨。

(The whole year's work depends on a good start in spring; the work for the day is best begun in the morning.)

汉字笔顺表　Table of Stroke-order of Chinese Characters

1	正			
2	视	礻（丶　㇇　礻　礻）		視
		见		
3	接	扌		
		妾	立	
			女	
4	话	讠		話
		舌（丿　舌）		
5	复	𠂉		復
		日		
		夂		
6	闻	门		聞
		耳（一　㇇　丌　𦥑　耳　耳）		
7	表	一　二　三　丰　主　声　耒　耒　表		
8	团	囗		團
		才（一　十　才）		
9	观	又		觀

		见	
10	厂		廠
11	访	讠	訪
		方	
12	照	昭 日	
		召（刀 召）	
		灬	
13	片	丿 丿' 广 片	
14	打	扌	
		丁	
15	明	日	
		月	
16	城	土	
		成（一 广 厂 成 成 成）	
17	玩	王	
		元	
18	出	凵 凵 屮 出 出	
19	发	一 少 岁 发 发	發

第二十四课　Lesson 24

复习　Revision

一、课文　Text

妈 妈 作 的 点 心

古波　　的　家　在
Gǔbō　　de　jiā　zài

农村，他　爸爸、妈妈
nóngcūn,　tā　bàba、mama

都 是 农民。一天， 他
dōu shì nóngmín. Yìtiān,　tā

妹妹 安娜 坐 火车 来
mèimei Ānnà zuò huǒchē lái

学生　城　看　他。
xuésheng chéng kàn tā.

安娜 不 认识 古波 的　宿舍。这 时候，
Ānnà bú rènshi Gǔbō de　sùshè. Zhè shíhou,

旁边 有 一个 学生，　他 正在 锻炼。
pángbiān yǒu yíge xuésheng,　tā zhèngzài duànliàn.

371

安娜 问 他："请问， 这 是 六号 宿舍
Ānnà wèn tā: "Qǐngwèn, zhè shì liùhào sùshè

吗?" 那个 学生 回答："不， 这 是 二号。
ma?" Nàge xuésheng huídá: "Bù, zhè shì èrhào.

六号 在 后边， 你 跟 我 来。" 安娜 说：
Liùhào zài hòubiān, nǐ gēn wǒ lái." Ānnà shuō:

"谢谢 你， 我 去 找 吧。"
"Xièxie nǐ, wǒ qù zhǎo ba."

安娜 进 宿舍 的 时候， 古波 正在
Ānnà jìn sùshè de shíhou, Gǔbō zhèngzài

复习 汉语 呢。 古波 说："是 你 啊，
fùxí Hànyǔ ne. Gǔbō shuō: "Shì nǐ a,

安娜！ 我 不 知道 你 今天 来。"
Ānnà! Wǒ bù zhīdao nǐ jīntiān lái."

"你 怎么样， 古波?" 妹妹 问。
"Nǐ zěnmeyàng, Gǔbō?" Mèimei wèn.

"我 很 好。 爸爸 妈妈 都 好 吗?"
"Wǒ hěn hǎo. Bàba māma dōu hǎo ma?"

"他们 都 很 好。 看， 这 是 妈妈 给
"Tāmen dōu hěn hǎo. Kàn, zhè shì māma gěi

你们 作 的 点心， 那些 点心 是 给 丁 云
nǐmen zuò de diǎnxin, nàxiē diǎnxin shì gěi Dīng Yún

372

的。"
de."

"太 好 了， 你
"Tài hǎo le, nǐ

回 家 的 时候 谢谢
huí jiā de shíhou xièxie

妈妈。"
māma."

"这 是 汉语 书 吗? 我 看看。"
"Zhè shì Hànyǔ shū ma? Wǒ kànkan."

安娜 说，"汉语 一定 很 难 吧?"
Ānnà shuō, "Hànyǔ yídìng hěn nán ba?"

古波 告诉 她，汉语 语法 不 太 难，
Gǔbō gàosu tā, Hànyǔ yǔfǎ bú tài nán,

汉字 很 难。他 很 喜欢 写 汉字。他
Hànzì hěn nán. Tā hěn xǐhuan xiě Hànzì. Tā

现在 很 忙，每 天 都 学习 生词、念
xiànzài hěn máng, měi tiān dōu xuéxí shēngcí、niàn

课文、写 汉字，晚上 还 作 练习。每 天
kèwén、xiě Hànzì, wǎnshang hái zuò liànxí. Měi tiān

都 十一点 睡 觉。
dōu shíyīdiǎn shuì jiào。

"你们 的 中国 老师 叫 什么?" 安娜
"Nǐmen de Zhōngguó lǎoshī jiào shénme?" Ānnà

问。
wèn.

"我们 的 中国 老师 叫 王 书文。
"Wǒmen de Zhōngguó lǎoshī jiào Wáng Shūwén.

上 课 的 时候 他 很 认真, 常常 问
Shàng kè de shíhou tā hěn rènzhēn, chángcháng wèn

我们 懂 不 懂, 有 没 有 问题。 下 课
wǒmen dǒng bu dǒng, yǒu méi yǒu wèntí. Xià kè

以后 还 跟 我们 一起 说 汉语。我们 也
yǐhòu hái gēn wǒmen yìqǐ shuō Hànyǔ. Wǒmen yě

常常 去 他 那儿 玩儿。"
chángcháng qù tā nàr wánr."

生词 New Words

1. 点心　　(名) diǎnxin　　light refreshments, pastry
2. 农村　　(名) nóngcūn　　countryside, rural areas
3. 农民　　(名) nóngmín　　peasant
4. 火车　　(名) huǒchē　　train
5. 锻炼　　(动) duànliàn　　to do physical training
6. 回答　　(动) huídá　　to reply, to answer

374

7. 些	(量)	xiē	*a measure word*, some
8. 难	(形)	nán	difficult
9. 生词	(名)	shēngcí	new word
词	(名)	cí	word
10. 念	(动)	niàn	to read aloud
11. 练习	(名、动)	liànxí	exercise, to practise
12. 认真	(形)	rènzhēn	conscientious, serious, in earnest
13. 懂	(动)	dǒng	to understand

专名 Proper Names

1. 安娜	Ānnà	*a personal name*
2. 王书文	Wáng Shūwén	*a personal name*

二、注释 Notes

1. "一天，他妹妹安娜坐火车来学生城看他。"

"一天"是某一天的意思，在叙述时常用来指过去的某一无需确切说明的时间。

"一天" means "a certain day", usually used to denote an indefinite time in a past event, that is, not necessary to specify.

2. "我不知道你今天来。"

"I didn't know you would come today."

主谓结构"你今天来"作动词"知道"的宾语。

In "我不知道你今天来", the subject-predicate construction "你今天来" functions as the object of the verb "知道".

3. "那些点心是给丁云的。"

"些"是表示不定数量的量词，常和"这"、"那"、"哪"等连用，修饰名词，如"这些书"、"那些工人"。

"些" is a measure word showing an indefinite quantity and is usually used after "这", "那" or "哪" to qualify nouns, e.g. "这些书", "那些工人".

"些"只能和数词"一"结合，如"一些点心"、"一些报"，不能和其他数词连用。

"些" is used in combination with "一" only, and never with any other numerals, e.g. "一些点心", "一些报".

三、看图会话　Talk about these pictures

1. 邀请与约会 Making an appointment

现在你有事儿吗？

你什么时候有空儿？

……好吗？

2. 招待 Entertaining a guest

请吃……

你要……还是……?

3. 买东西 Shopping

你要什么?

有……吗?

还要什么?

4. 祝贺 Offering congratulations

祝贺你!

5. 问年龄 Asking the age

(1) 他多大岁数?

(2) 你今年几岁?

6. 问路 Asking the way

(1) ……在哪儿？

(2) 哪儿是……？

(3) 这儿有……吗？

7. 问看法 Asking for opinions from others

(1) 喜欢不喜欢……？

(2) ……有没有意思？

(3) ……怎么样？

8. 打电话 Making a telephone call

(1) ……在吗？

(2) 你是……吗？

(3) 请你告诉他……

9. 送礼 Presenting a gift

这是给你的……

四、语法小结 A brief Summary of Grammar

1. 提问的六种方法 The six types of questions

(1) 用"吗"的疑问句 Questions with "吗"

这是最一般、最经常使用的提问方式，用来客观地询问一件事情，对可能的回答不作预先的估计。

Of all the six types of questions, the kind formed with "吗" is the most extensively used to ask about something about which the speaker has no foreknowledge and for which he expects neither an affirmative nor negative answer。

你妈妈是大夫吗？

您忙吗？

(你)不想你的男朋友吗？

(2) 正反疑问句 Affirmative-negative questions

正反疑问句也是用得最多的一种提问方式。用"吗"的疑问句，一般都可改为正反疑问句。

This type of questions is also the most commonly used. Questions formed with "吗" can all be turned into affirmative-negative questions.

他有没有妹妹？

你认识不认识她？

你们的食堂大不大？

（3）用疑问代词的疑问句 Questions with an interrogative
pronoun

这种疑问句用来提问"谁"、"什么"、"哪"、"哪儿"、"怎么样"、"多少"、"几"等，后面不能再用"吗"。

Questions with an interrogative pronoun are used to ask about "谁", "什么", "哪", "哪儿", "怎么样", "多少" and "几". Note that "吗" is never used at the end of this type of question:

今天星期几？

我们的新房子怎么样？

你今年多大？

（4）用"还是"的选择疑问句 Alternative questions with
"还是"

当提问人估计到答案有两种（或更多）可能性的时候，用这个方式提问。

This kind of question is used when two or more different answers may be expected.

你喜欢古典音乐还是喜欢现代音乐？

他是英国人还是法国人？

他下午去图书馆还是晚上去图书馆？

（5）用"是吗"（或"是不是"、"对吗"）的疑问句
Tag questions with "是吗"（or "是不是" or "对吗"）

380

当提问人对某事已有一个估计，但需要进一步明确时，用这个方法提问。

Questions of such kind are used when the speaker forms an estimate of a thing which is necessarily confirmed.

中国人喜欢喝茶，是吗？

这个电影很有意思，是不是？

用"好吗"的疑问句则常常用来提出建议，征求对方的意见。

Tag questions with "好吗" are usually used as a form of polite request when one makes proposals and asks the person thus addressed if he is agreeable or not.

我们去咖啡馆，好吗？

请您参加舞会，好吗？

(6) 用"呢"的省略式疑问句　Elliptical questions with "呢"
这是一种比较简单的提问方式，在口语会话中常用。如：

This is a most simple type of questions, used mainly in colloquial speech. E.g.

我很好，你呢？

我在看电视，你呢？

你的照片呢？

2. 定语和结构助词"的"(2)　Attributives and the structural particle "的" (2)

(1) 双音节形容词作定语，后边一般要用"的"。

Used attributively, a disyllabic adjective as a rule takes "的" after it.

这个年轻的大夫叫什么？

她是一个认真的学生。

(2) 动词作定语，后边要用"的"。

Used attributively, a verb usually takes "的" after it.

参观的人很多。

休息的时候，他常常去锻炼。

(3) 动词结构作定语，后边一定要用"的"。

Used attributively, a verbal construction must take "的" after it.

这是送她的花儿。

给女儿买的裙子真漂亮。

(4) 主谓结构作定语，后边一定要用"的"。

Used attributively, a subject-predicate construction must take "的" after it.

他给我一张他们参观工厂的照片。

帕兰卡给他打电话的时候，他正看报呢。

3．定语的排列次序 Word order of a series of attributives

如果名词前边不止一个定语，表领属关系的名词或代词总是放在最前边，表修饰关系的形容词或名词最靠近中心语。指示代词要放在数量词的前边。例如：

When a noun has more than one attributive, possessive nouns or pronouns are always placed at the head of the series. Adjective or noun modifiers are usually placed closest to the head word. Demonstrative pronouns usually precede numeral–measure words. E.g.

那两本杂志

他的那两本杂志

他的那两本中文杂志

他的那两本新中文杂志

练习　Exercises

1．写出数词和量词：Write out the numerals in Chinese characters and give a measure word for each of the nouns:

（6）	班	（12）	同学
（10）	啤酒	（3）	咖啡
（62）	工人	（85）	农民
（4）	代表团	（7）	问题

（4）	照片	(11)	票
（5）	房间	（8）	衬衫
(32)	字	(26)	词
（1）	图书馆	（1）	花儿
(22)	桌子	（3）	裙子
（9）	工厂	(15)	服务员

2. 把下列句子改成各种疑问句，(2)和(9)不要改成正反问句：
Change the following to different types of questions
(Nos. 2 and 9 are not changed to affirmative-negative
questions):

⑴ 今天二十七号。

⑵ 他从农村来。

⑶ 这是给我朋友的信。

⑷ 图书馆在食堂旁边。

⑸ 我们班星期三去城外。

⑹ 我家有一个小花园。

⑺ 他每天复习课文。

⑻ 这个代表团不大。

（9）她在等我呢。

（10）那本杂志很新。

3．分析下列句子的主语、谓语主要成分、宾语、定语和状语：
Analyze the following sentences, pointing out the subject, main element of the predicate, object, attributive and adverbial adjunct:

（1）老师问的问题不太难。

（2）他在看今天的报呢。

（3）这是他写的汉字吗？

（4）我听他们唱歌。

（5）爸爸给他的衬衫很漂亮。

（6）他知道今天不上课。

（7）那些都是我买的点心。

（8）一个从中国来的代表团在参观这个工厂。

4．填空（不看课文）：Fill in the blanks without referring to the text until! you finish these sentences:

（1）安娜是古波____，她____岁。她____

385

农村来看哥哥。

(2) 古波____学生城住，他现在很____。
他不常常____家看爸爸妈妈，他不知
道安娜____。

(3) 安娜____时候，古波正____汉语呢。
他每天都____生词、____课文、____
练习。

(4) 安娜不____汉语、也不____汉字。她
问古波，汉语____不____？

(5) 王老师是一个____的老师，他教____
课。他非常____，____以后还常常
____学生学习。同学们都____他。

5. 改正下列错句：Correct the following erroneous sentences:

(1) 帕兰卡去古波宿舍在星期五。

(2) 九月四号一九七九年他去中国。

(3) 我们班有十四学生。

386

（4）那个天我跟他一起去看电影。

（5）左边的本画报是我的。

（6）我很喜欢这些五个歌儿。

（7）他复习复习课文的时候，我正锻炼呢。

（8）今天他很高兴不高兴？

（9）这些生词难的。

（10）他写汉字很好。

（11）我回答问题老师问。

（12）他住房间 125 号。

（13）我们问他介绍介绍汉语语法。

（14）他是很认真的一个老师。

（15）晚上我去看一个我朋友。

（16）那件她的衬衫很漂亮。

汉字笔顺表 Table of Stroke-order of Chinese Characters

1	心						農
2	农	一	少	龙	农	农	
3	村	木					
		寸					
4	火	丶	丷	少	火		
5	锻	钅					鍛
		段	阜 (丶 厂 户 阜 阜)				
			殳				
6	炼	火					煉
		东 (一 七 东 东 东)					
7	答	𥫗					
		合					
8	些	此	止				
			匕				
		二					
9	难	又					難

		隹	
10	念	今	
		心	
11	练	纟	練
		东	
12	懂	忄	
		董	艹
			重（一 二 亍 亩 亩 亩 重 重 重）

第二十五课 Lesson 25

一、课文 Text

他作饭作得好不好

帕兰卡： 我们 来 得 太 晚 了， 在 哪儿
Pàlánkǎ: Wǒmen lái de tài wǎn le, zài nǎr

停 车 呢?
tíng chē ne?

古波： 这儿 好。前边 是 条 河，在
Gǔbō: Zhèr hǎo. Qiánbiān shì tiáo hé, zài

这儿 停车 吧？
zhèr tíng chē ba?

帕兰卡： 好。我 和 丁云 去 游 泳，你
Pàlánkǎ: Hǎo. Wǒ hé Dīng Yún qù yóu yǒng, nǐ

准备 吃 的，好 吗？
zhǔnbèi chī de, hǎo ma?

古波： 好 吧。我 去 钓 鱼，请 你们
Gǔbō: Hǎo ba. Wǒ qù diào yú, qǐng nǐmen

喝 鱼 汤。
hē yú tāng.

　　　　　＊　　　　　＊　　　　　＊

古波： 两位 小姐，来 吧。
Gǔbō: Liǎngwèi xiǎojie, lái ba.

帕兰卡： 等一等，我们 在 休息 呢。
Pàlánkǎ: Děngyideng, wǒmen zài xiūxi ne.

古波： 丁云 游泳 游 得 怎么样？
Gǔbō: Dīng Yún yóu yǒng yóu de zěnmeyàng?

帕兰卡： 她 游 得 真 快。
Pàlánkǎ: Tā yóu de zhēn kuài.

丁云： 哪里，我 游 得 很 慢。你 游
Dīng Yún: Nǎli, wǒ yóu de hěn màn. Nǐ yóu

391

得 好。
de hǎo.

帕兰卡： 古波 是 我 的 教练， 他 教 我
Pàlánkǎ: Gǔbō shì wǒ de jiàoliàn, tā jiāo wǒ

教 得 很 好。
jiāo de hěn hǎo.

丁 云： 古波 作 饭 作 得 好 不 好？
Dīng Yún: Gǔbō zuò fàn zuò de hǎo bu hǎo?

帕兰卡： 他 鱼 汤 作 得 不错。 来， 请
Pàlánkǎ: Tā yú tāng zuò de búcuò. Lái, qǐng

吃 吧！
chī baı

古 波： 丁 云， 给 你 面包、 火腿。
Gǔbō: Dīng Yún, gěi nǐ miànbāo、huǒtuǐ.

帕兰卡： 我 要 点儿 奶酪。
Pàlánkǎ: Wǒ yào diǎnr nǎilào.

古 波： 好。丁 云， 再 吃 点儿 吧！
Gǔbō: Hǎo. Dīng Yún, zài chī diǎnr baı

丁 云： 谢谢， 我 吃 得 不 少 了。 我
Dīng Yún: Xièxie, wǒ chī de bù shǎo le. Wǒ

要 点儿 汤。
yào diǎnr tāng.

古 波： 请 你们 喝——
Gǔbō:　Qǐng nǐmen hē ——

帕兰卡： 鱼 汤？
Pàlánkǎ:　Yú tāng?

古 波： 不， 喝 矿泉水。
Gǔbō:　Bù,　hē kuàngquánshuǐ.

生词　New Words

1. 得　　（助）de　　　　a structural particle

2. 晚　　（形）wǎn　　　 late

3. 停　　（动）tíng　　　to stop, to come to a stop

4. 前边　（名）qiánbiān　front

5. 河　　（名）hé　　　　river

6. 游泳　　　yóu yǒng　to swim, swimming

7. 准备　（动）zhǔnbèi　to prepare

8. 钓　　（动）diào　　　to fish with a hook and bait

9. 鱼　　（名）yú　　　　fish

10. 汤　　（名）tāng　　　soup

11. 位　　（量）wèi　　　 a measure word

12. 快　　（形）kuài　　　fast, quick

13. 哪里　（代）nǎli　　　it is nothing

14. 慢	(形)	màn	slow
15. 教练	(名)	jiàoliàn	coach, trainer
16. 不错	(形)	búcuò	correct, right, not bad, pretty good
17. 面包	(名)	miànbāo	bread
18. 火腿	(名)	huǒtuǐ	ham
19. 一点儿		yìdiǎnr	a little, a bit
20. 奶酪	(名)	nǎilào	cheese
21. 再	(副)	zài	again, once more, a second time
22. 矿泉水	(名)	kuàngquánshuǐ	mineral water

补充词 Supplementary Words

1. 清楚	(形)	qīngchu	clear, distinct
2. 流利	(形)	liúlì	fluent
3. 整齐	(形)	zhěngqí	tidy
4. 菜	(名)	cài	dish
5. 饺子	(名)	jiǎozi	Chinese dumpling
6. 鸡蛋	(名)	jīdàn	hen's egg
7. 牛奶	(名)	niúnǎi	(cow's) milk
8. 比较	(副、动)	bǐjiào	comparatively, to compare

二、注释 Notes

1. "来得太晚了。""吃得不少了。"

这里的"了"是语气助词，用来对已经发生的事情表示肯定。

"了" here is a modal particle used to indicate the affir-mative attitude of the speaker towards what has happened.

2. "在哪儿停车呢？"

语气助词"呢"(1)用在用疑问代词的问句、正反问句、用"还是"的问句的句尾，使全句的语气缓和。如：

The modal particle "呢"(1) can be added at the end of a question with an interrogative pronoun, an affirmative-negative question or an alternative question with "还是" to soften the tone. E.g.

我们几点出发呢？

他懂不懂这课语法呢？

你现在去锻炼，还是下午去锻炼呢？

3. "两位小姐，来吧!"

量词"位"是用来指人的。用"位"比用"个"更显得尊敬、有礼貌。这里古波有开玩笑的意思。

The measure word "位" applies to persons only. It is more respectful, courteous or polite than the measure word "个". But Gubo is using the word jocularly here.

4. "哪里，我游得很慢。"

"哪里"本是疑问代词，跟"哪儿"的意思一样。这里的"哪里"表示否定的意思，常用作谦辞，回答别人对自己的夸奖。

"哪里" is an interrogative pronoun having the same meaning as "哪儿". But here it has a negative meaning, used to reply to a complimentary remark, implying that the speaker does not at all deserve the praise.

5. "我要点儿奶酪。"

"一点儿"是表示少量的不定量词（比"一些"要少）。它不在句首时，"一"可以省略。

"一点儿", a measure word, indicates an indefinite small quantity (usually samller than that "一些" indicates). When it appears at any place in a sentence except the beginning, "一" can be omitted.

"一点儿"常用来修饰名词。当语言环境清楚时，它所修饰的名词也可省略。

"一点儿" is more often than not used to qualify a noun. The noun can be omitted if the reference is clear.

6. "再吃点儿吧!"

副词"再"(1)一般用来表示动作将要继续或重复。

The adverb "再" (1) usually indicates that an action is going to be continued or repeated some time in the future.

三、替换与扩展 Substitution and Extension

(一)

1. 他来得晚吗?

他来得不晚。

说,	快
走,	慢
念,	好
起,	晚
学,	认真

2. 你朋友工作得怎么样?

他工作得很好。

休息,	好
回答,	对
复习,	慢
准备,	认真
介绍,	清楚*

3. 丁云在作什么?

她在游泳呢。

她游得怎么样?

她游得不错。

```
白老师，      上课
帕兰卡，      跳舞
古波，        开车
那位小姐，    学汉语
那位太太，    整理房间
```

4. 他<u>作</u>饭作得<u>好</u>不好？

他作饭作得很好。

```
看书，      认真
用纸，      多
写字，      好看
念生词，    对
说汉语，    流利*
念课文，    清楚*
```

5. 你汉字<u>写</u>得<u>快</u>不快？

我汉字写得不太快。

电影票,	买,	多
语法,	学,	好
问题,	回答,	快
生词,	学,	多
汉字,	写,	整齐*
课文,	念,	流利*

6. 老师让谁说英语?

老师让他说英语。

英语他说得怎么样?

英语他说得很慢。

念,	课文
写,	汉字
作,	今天的练习
回答,	这些问题

7. 再吃点儿面包吧!

谢谢,我吃得不少了。

吃，	火腿
吃，	菜*
吃，	饺子*
吃，	鸡蛋*
喝，	汤
喝，	牛奶*

（二）

1. 称赞与回答 Compliment and reply

A: 你是中文系的学生吧？

B: 是啊，我正学习中文呢。

A: 你说汉语说得很流利。

B: 哪里，我说得不太好。

A: 这是你写的汉字吗？写得真漂亮。

B: 我写得很慢，以后请多帮助。

2. 打听情况 Asking for information

A: 你知道哪儿作裙子作得好？

B: 我给你介绍一家，大商店旁边那家

作得好。

A: 谢谢你，我去看一看。

3. 问好 Exchanging amenities

A: 昨天你休息得好吗？

B: 很好，你呢？

A: 昨天晚上我睡得不太好,今天起得很晚。

4. 招待 Entertaining a guest

A: 菜*作得不好,你们都吃得很少。

B: 哪里,太太,您的鱼汤作得真好,我非常喜欢喝。

A: 你再喝点儿吧！

B: 谢谢,我喝得不少了。

*   *   *

四、阅读短文　Reading Text

古波的日记 (rìjì, diary)

七月二十四日　星期六

今天是星期六，下午我跟帕兰卡、比里一起到王老师那儿。王老师正在看书。他看见 (kànjiàn, to see) 我们来，非常高兴。他问我们，现在忙不忙？课文复习得怎么样？他教得快不快？我们告诉他，现在课文比较*难，生词也很多，我们比较*忙。

王老师说，这学期 (xuéqī, term) 我们学习得都很认真，学得很好。帕兰卡汉字写得很清楚*，上课的时候她回答问题回答得很对。比里语法学得很好。我汉语说得比较*流利*。他让我们互相学习，互相帮助。

王老师问我们："你们每天都锻炼吗？"帕兰卡说她不常锻炼。他问我们每天几点睡觉。我告诉他，我十二点半睡觉。比里说他十二点睡。王老师说："你们睡得太晚。"

五点半，王老师还不让我们走。他说："你们在这儿吃饭吧，我们一起包 (bāo, to make) 饺子*。"中国饺子*真不错，我们都吃得不少。

五、语法 Grammar

1. 程度补语 Complement of degree

动词或形容词后边的补充说明成分叫补语。说明动作或事物性质所达到的程度的补语叫程度补语。简单的程度补语一般由形容词担任。动词和程度补语之间要用结构助词"得"来连接。

A verb or an adjective can take after it another word to explain further or complete its meaning, which is known as a complement. Complements that indicate the degree or extent of the quality or character of the action denoted by the verb or of the state denoted by the adjective are called complements of degree. Simple complements of degree are usually made of adjectives and the structural particle "得" is used to connect the verb and its complement of degree.

程度补语所说明的动作常常是已经发生的。程度补语也可以用来说明经常发生的动作。

Complements of degree are usually used to indicate either actions that have already come true or actions that are habitually frequent.

带程度补语的动词谓语句，否定形式是把"不"放在程度补语的前边，不能放在动词的前边。这类句子的正反疑问式是并列程度补语的肯定形式和否定形式。

The negative form of a sentence with a verbal predicate containing a complement of degree is made by adding "不" before the complement and never before the verb. The affirmative-negative form of this type of sentence is made by juxtaposing the affirmative and negative forms of the complement of degree.

名词或代词 Nouns or pronouns	动　词 Verbs	"得" "得"	副　词 Adverbs	形　容　词 Adjectives	助　词 Particle
他	来	得	很	晚。	
她	唱	得	不	好。	
你	休息	得		好	吗?
你	休息	得		怎么样?	
你	休息	得		好不好?	

带宾语的动词如果后边再有程度补语，必须在宾语后先重复动词，再加"得"和程度补语。

When a verb takes an object and is followed at the same time by a complement of degree, the verb must be repeated after the object before "得" and the complement of degree are added to it.

404

名词或代词 Nouns or pronouns	动词 Verbs	名词 Nouns	动词（重复）Verbs (repeated)	"得" "得"	副词 Ad-verbs	形容词 Adjectives	助词 Par-ticle
他	作	饭	作	得	很	好。	
我	写	汉字	写	得	不太	快。	
你	回答	问题	回答	得		对	吗？
你	回答	问题	回答	得		怎么样？	
你	回答	问题	回答	得		对不对？	

2. 前置宾语 Preposed object

为了强调宾语或者当宾语比较复杂时，可以将宾语提到动词的前边或主语的前边。在带程度补语的句子中，如果有前置宾语就不需要重复动词了。例如：

The object may be placed before the verb, or even before the subject to make it emphatic and conspicuous or when the object is long and involved. When a sentence containing a complement of degree has its object placed before the verb or the subject, it will no longer be necessary to repeat the verb. E.g.

他车开得很好。

老师的问题你回答得很对，也很快。

那些生词他用得怎么样？

动词既带宾语又带程度补语时，有三种表达方式：

When the verb takes an object and is followed at the
same time by a complement of degree, the sentence can be
arranged in the following three ways:

他学外语学得很快。

他外语学得很快。

外语他学得很快。

练习　Exercises

1. 读下列词组：Read out the following phrases:

来得很晚　　来得真晚　　走得不快

走得不太晚　写得很快　　写得真慢

穿得不多　　穿得不太好　看得很多

看得真快　　念得不少　　念得不太对

说得很对　　说得真有意思

学得不错　　学得不太快　教得很认真

教得真快　　开得不快　　开得不太慢

介绍得很少　介绍得真多　准备得不好

准备得不太认真　　回答得多

回答得真快　　　　整理得不慢

整理得不太好

2. 用程度补语完成下列句子: Complete the following sentences with complements of degree:

(1) 他玩儿＿＿＿＿＿＿。

(2) 张老师教＿＿＿＿＿。

(3) 古波说汉语＿＿＿＿＿。

(4) 丁云游泳＿＿＿＿＿。

(5) 他们法语＿＿＿＿＿。

(6) 我们问题＿＿＿＿＿。

3. 完成下列对话: Complete the following dialogues:

(1) A: ＿＿＿＿＿＿？

B: 他写汉字写得很好看。

(2) A: ＿＿＿＿＿＿？

B: 我开车开得不快也不慢。

(3) A: ＿＿＿＿＿？

407

B: 他跳舞跳得很好。

(4) A: ＿＿＿＿＿＿？

B: 那个学生来得不晚。

(5) A: 请您再吃点儿。

B: 谢谢，我吃得＿＿＿＿。

4. 模仿下列例子造句：Make sentences in the same way as the example given:

例 Example

作饭　　好

→你作饭作得好不好？

我作饭作得不太好。

谁作饭作得好？

他作饭作得很好。

(1) 睡觉　　晚　　(5) 休息　　好

(2) 作练习　快　　(6) 看书　　多

(3) 念课文　慢　　(7) 写信　　少

(4) 起床　　晚　　(8) 复习语法　认真

408

5. 根据下面的图进行问答（用程度补语）：

Ask each other questions about each of the following pictures, using complements of degree:

(1)　　　　　　(2)　　　　　　(3)

(4)　　　　　　(5)　　　　　　(6)

六、语音语调　Pronunciation and Intonation

1. 句调(1)　Sentence tunes (1)

汉语的基本句调有两种：高句调和低句调。汉语句调的特点是贯穿全句。高句调是全句较均衡地升高；低句调则是全句较均衡地降低。无论升高或降低都必须保持音节原来的声调。

In Chinese, there are two basic sentence tunes: high-pitch and low-pitch. One characteristic of Chinese sentence tunes is that the pitch, whether high or low, is kept up throughout the sentence. In a sentence uttered in high-pitch tune the pitch goes steadily up, while for a low-pitch tune sentence the pitch goes steadily down. But no matter which

tune is used, all syllables forming the sentence must be pronounced in their original tone.

汉语句调尾音的升高或降低，在句尾非轻读音节上表现得很
明显。高句调的句尾除了升高的以外，也有降低的；低句调的句
尾除了降低的以外，也有升高的。

The rise or fall that terminates the two sentence tunes
is most clearly indicated by non-neutral syllables at the end
of the sentence. The high-pitch sentence tune ends in a rising
intonation, but sometimes in a falling intonation as well.
The low-pitch sentence tune ends in a falling intonation,
but sometimes in a rising intonation as well.

(1) 带 "吗" 的疑问句读高句调（本书将调号画在虚线以上
表示），句尾升高(本书用"⌐"符号表示)。例如：

Questions with "吗" are said in the high-pitch tune (in
this book, the tone-graph above the dotted line indicates that
the sentence should be said in the high-pitch sentence tune)
and end in a rising intonation (marked with the sign "⌐"
in this book). E.g.

他来得晚吗？

丁云游得快吗？

她吃得多吗？

(2) 陈述句读低句调（调号画在虚线以下），句尾降低（用
"⌐"符号表示）。例如：

Declarative sentences are said in the low-pitch sentence tune (the tone-graph is placed under the dotted line), and end in a falling intonation (marked with the sigh " ⌐"). E.g.

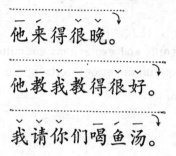

他来得很晚。

他教我教得很好。

我请你们喝鱼汤。

(3) 带程度补语的正反问句，程度补语中的肯定部分要重读，否定部分轻读。结构助词"得"读轻声。"得"字后可以停顿，动词和"得"字之间不能停顿。全句读高句调，句尾降低。例如：

In affirmative-negative questions containing a complement of degree, the affirmative part of the complement is stressed, and the negative is pronounced with a weak-stress. The structural particle "得" is pronounced in the neutral tone. A pause is usually allowed after "得", but there should be no pause between the verb and "得". The whole sentence is said in the high-pitch sentence tune and ends in a falling intonation. E.g.

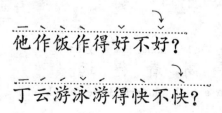

他作饭作得好不好？

丁云游泳游得快不快？

411

她写字写得好看不好看？

2. 练习 Exercises

朗读下列带 s、sh 的词语，注意发音：

Read the following words and expressions containing the sounds s and sh, paying special attentiont to the pronunciation of these two sounds:

送花——老师　　食堂——宿舍

告诉——书房　　卧室——三层

矿泉水——四十四　生词——四十

朗读成语：Read out the following proverbs:

Sāntiān dǎ yú, liǎngtiān shài wǎng.

三天 打 鱼，两天 晒 网。

(Go fishing for three days and dry the nets for two; lack perseverance)

Zhàn de gāo, kàn de yuǎn.

站 得 高，看 得 远。

(Stand on a high plane and see far ahead.)

汉字笔顺表 Table of Stroke-order of Chinese Characters

1.	得	彳		
		록	日	
			一	
			寸	
2	停	亻		
		亭	亠	
			口	
			冖	
			丁	
3	前	丷	（丶 丷 丷）	
		刖	月	
			刂	
4	河	氵		
		可		
5	游	氵		
		方		
		与	㇌	

			子	
6	泳	氵		
		永（丶 ㇀ 沪 沪 永）	
7	准	冫		準
		隹	
9	备	夂		備
		田	
9	钓	钅		釣
		勺	
10	鱼	𠂊		魚
		田	
		一	
11	汤	氵		湯
		𠃓（㇇ 丂 𠃓）	
12	位	亻		
		立	
13	快	忄		
		夬（㇇ ㇕ 尹 夬）	
14	慢	忄		

		曼	日		
			四		
			又		
15	错	钅			錯
		昔	共（一 十 卅 共）		
			日		
16	包	勹			
			巳（宀 口 巳）		
17	腿	月			
		退	艮		
			辶		
18	奶	女			
		乃（乛 乃）			
19	酪	酉			
		各	夂 各		
20	矿	石（一 丆 石）			礦
		广			
21	泉	白			
		水			

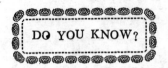

Loanwords in Chinese

There are a great number of loanwords in Chinese one of which in common use is "葡萄". It was introduced into China about two thousand years ago at the same time as the introduction of the grape plant itself. Since the nineteenth century, a great many foreign words, mostly those used in social and natural sciences, have been loaned from other languages, notably English.

Loanwords in modern Chinese fall into two classes: 1, those transliterations of whole words, e.g. "葡萄" and "咖啡", 2, partial transliterations coupled with a Chinese character that indicates the meaning of the loanword, e.g. "啤酒". Loanwords of the latter class conform better to the speech habits of the native speakers of Chinese.

第二十六课　Lesson 26

一、课文　Text

我要研究中国文学

古　波：我们 走 吧。
Gǔbō:　Wǒmen zǒu ba.

帕兰卡：还 早 呢，我 要 再 跟 丁 云
Pàlánkǎ:　Hái zǎo ne,　wǒ yào zài gēn Dīng Yún

谈谈。丁 云，你 会 说 英语 和
tántan.　Dīng Yún,　nǐ huì shuō Yīngyǔ hé

法语，你 以后 想 作 什么
Fǎyǔ,　nǐ yǐhòu xiǎng zuò shénme

417

工作？
gōngzuò?

丁 云： 我 想 当 翻译。 你 呢？
Dīng Yún: Wǒ xiǎng dāng fānyì. Nǐ ne?

帕兰卡： 我 也 想 当 翻译。 翻译 工作
Pàlánkǎ: Wǒ yě xiǎng dāng fānyì. Fānyì gōngzuò

能 加深 两国 人民 的 了解。
néng jiāshēn liǎngguó rénmín de liǎojiě.

丁 云： 你 说 得 真 对。 古波， 你 想
Dīng Yún: Nǐ shuō de zhēn duì. Gǔbō, nǐ xiǎng

作 什么 工作 呢？
zuò shénme gōngzuò ne?

古 波： 我 不 想 当 翻译。 我 要 研究
Gǔbō: Wǒ bù xiǎng dāng fānyì. Wǒ yào yánjiū

中国 文学。 中国
Zhōngguó wénxué. Zhōngguó

有 很 多 有名 的
yǒu hěn duō yǒumíng de

作家。
zuòjiā.

丁 云： 你 要 研究 哪位 作家？
Dīng Yún: Nǐ yào yánjiū nǎwèi zuòjiā?

古波： 鲁迅 或者 郭沫
Gǔbō: Lǔ Xùn huòzhě Guō Mò-

若。
ruò.

帕兰卡： 今年 我们 就 想
Pàlánkǎ: Jīnnián wǒmen jiù xiǎng

去 中国 学习。
qù Zhōngguó, xuéxí.

丁云： 你们 学 得 不错， 应该 去。
Dīng Yún: Nǐmen xué de búcuò, yīnggāi qù.

今年 能 不 能 去?
Jīnnián néng bu néng qù?

帕兰卡： 我们 俩 都 能 去。
Pàlánkǎ: Wǒmen liǎ dōu néng qù.

丁云： 太 好 了， 在 那儿 你们
Dīng Yún: Tài hǎo le, zài nàr nǐmen

能 学 得 更 好。 回 国
néng xué de gèng hǎo. Huí guó

以后， 可以 找 一个 理想
yǐhòu, kěyǐ zhǎo yíge lǐxiǎng

的 工作。
de gōngzuò.

古　波：可是 这 很 不 容易 啊！
Gǔbō:　　Kěshì zhè hěn bù róngyì a!

丁　云："有志者事竟成"， 这 是 中国
Dīng Yún: "Yǒuzhìzhěshìjìngchéng"， zhè shì Zhōngguó

的 成语。
de chéngyǔ。

生词 New Words

1. 研究　（动）yánjiū　　　　to research
2. 文学　（名）wénxué　　　literature
3. 早　　（形）zǎo　　　　　early
4. 谈　　（动）tán　　　　　to talk
5. 会　　（能动、动）huì　　can, to know how to
6. 当　　（动）dāng　　　　to serve as, to act as
7. 翻译　（名、动）fānyì　　interpreter, translator,
　　　　　　　　　　　　　　to interpret, to translate
8. 能　　（能动）néng　　　can, to be able to
9. 加深　（动）jiāshēn　　　to deepen
10. 人民　（名）rénmín　　　people
11. 了解　（动）liǎojiě　　　to understand, to know
12. 有名　（形）yǒumíng　　famous, well-known

420

13. 作家	(名) zuòjiā	writer	
14. 或者	(连) huòzhě	or	*for statements*
15. 就	(副) jiù	at once, right away	
16. 应该	(能动) yīnggāi	should, ought to	
17. 俩	(数量) liǎ	*a numeral-measure word,* two, both	
18. 可以	(能动) kěyǐ	may	
19. 理想	(形、名) lǐxiǎng	ideal	
20. 可是	(连) kěshì	but	
21. 容易	(形) róngyì	easy	

22. 有志者事竟成

yǒuzhìzhě-
shìjìngchéng — where there is a will, there is a way.

23. 成语　(名) chéngyǔ　proverb, idiom

专名　Proper Names

1. 鲁迅　Lǔ Xùn　Lu Xun
2. 郭沫若　Guō Mòruò　Guo Moruo

补充词　Supplementary Words

1. 歌剧　(名) gējù　opera

2. 小说　　（名）xiǎoshuō　　novel

3. 诗歌　　（名）shīgē　　poem

4. 画　　（动）huà　　to paint, to draw

5. 画儿　　（名）huàr　　painting, drawing, picture

6. 晚饭　　（名）wǎnfàn　　supper

7. 进来　　jìn lái　　to come in, to enter

二、注释　Notes

1. "还早呢。"

"It's still early."

副词"还"(2)表示现象的继续存在或动作继续进行。

The adverb "还" (2) indicates the existence of a phenomenon or the continuation of an action.

2. "我要研究鲁迅或者郭沫若。"

连词"或者"和"还是"都是用来连接两种可能性。"或者"一般用在陈述句中，"还是"用在选择疑问句中。

The conjunctions "或者" and "还是" are both used to connect clauses suggesting two alternatives or possibilities. "或者" is mostly used in statements and "还是" in alternative questions.

3. "今年我们就想去中国学习。"

422

副词"就"(1)常表示事情发生得早、快或紧迫。这里表示他们急于想去中国学习。

The adverb "就" (1) very often indicates something happens early, soon, quickly or imminently. Here "就" is used to signify the eagerness of those students to go and study Chinese in China.

4. "我们俩都能去。"

"俩"是口语，就是"两个"的意思，常说"我们俩"、"你们俩"、"他们俩"等。用"俩"时后面不再用量词。

"俩" is a colloquialism used to refer to two persons, as in "我们俩"，"你们俩" and "他们俩". "俩" usually takes no measure word after it.

5. "可是这很不容易啊！"

"可是"是表示转折的连词。"这"指的是前边所说的"找一个理想的工作"。

"可是" is an adversative conjunction used to indicate contrast of ideas. "这" refers to the foregoing statement "找一个理想的工作".

三、替换与扩展 Substitution and Extension

(一)

1. 你想当老师吗？
   我很想当老师。

   学习文学
   参观工厂

> 去锻炼
> 了解那个作家
> 看歌剧*

2. 他要研究中国音乐吗？
   他不想研究中国音乐，
   他要研究中国文学。

> 听京剧，　　听民歌
> 喝啤酒，　　喝矿泉水
> 进城，　　　回家
> 钓鱼，　　　游泳
> 买面包，　　买火腿
> 翻译小说*，翻译诗歌*

3. 他会不会说法语？
   他会说法语。
   他说得怎么样？
   他说得很好。

> 开车
> 游泳
> 写这个汉字
> 念那些生词

> 作今天的练习
> 画*画儿*

4. 你能不能翻译这个成语？
   我不能，他能翻译。

> 翻译这本书
> 看《人民日报》*
> 教他们英语
> 当教练
> 回答他的问题

5. 明天你能来上课吗？
   明天我能来上课。
   你能不能八点来？
   可以。

> 去参观工厂
> 来接你朋友
> 参加舞会
> 去城外玩儿
> 帮助我
> 来吃晚饭*

425

6. 可以问问题吗?

   可以,请吧。

   用一用这个电话
   坐你的车
   从这儿走
   在这儿坐一坐
   吸烟

(二)

1. 谈打算 Talking about plans

   A: 明天你想作什么?

   B: 我想在家休息休息,你想去哪儿?

   A: 我想进城看电影。

2. 约会 Making an appointment

   A: 你好。星期六我想请你吃晚饭*,你
      能来吗?

   B: 谢谢你,我很想来,可是星期六晚
      上我有点事儿。

426

A: 星期天怎么样？

B: 那好，我一定来。几点？

A: 七点。你太太能来吗？

B: 能来，她很想看看你们。

A: 那太好了。

3. 请求允许 Asking permission

A: 可以进来*吗？

B: 请等一等。

·····

好，请进。

  *   *   *

A: 先生，我能听您的课吗？

B: 你是不是这儿的学生？

A: 不是。我是大夫，今年我要去中国
访问。我想听您的汉语课，可以吗？

B: 可以，欢迎你来。

A: 谢谢。

4. 禁止 Prohibitions

A: 先生，阅览室里不能吸烟，您要吸

烟，请在外边吸吧。

B: 好，对不起。

* * *

请 勿 吸 烟 QING WU XI YAN	谢 绝 参 观 XIE JUE CAN GUAN	禁 止 停 车 JIN ZHI TING CHE

四、阅读短文　Reading Text

联　欢

星期六晚上，中文系的同学要跟中国留

学生联欢 (liánhuān, get-together)，同学们都知道帕

兰卡和古波很喜欢中国音乐，让他们准备一

个中国歌儿。他们问帕兰卡能不能用中文

唱，她说她可以跟古波一起唱。

"我们唱什么歌儿呢？"古波问帕兰卡。

"丁云很会唱歌儿。我们去问问她，好

吗？"帕兰卡说。

428

丁云知道他们要参加联欢，还要唱中国歌儿，她非常高兴。她说："你们俩唱一个《洪湖水，浪打浪》(《Hónghú Shuǐ, Làng Dǎ Làng》, The Honghu Lake Waters Surge in Majestic Waves) 吧。"

帕兰卡请丁云介绍这个歌儿。丁云告诉他们，这个歌儿是中国的一个有名的歌剧里边的。古波问丁云有没有这个歌儿的唱片*，丁云说她有，她请他们听这张唱片。

古波和帕兰卡都说这个歌儿很好。帕兰卡问丁云："现在你有空儿吗？你能不能教我们？"

丁云说："可以。我应该帮助你们，我们一起唱吧。这个歌儿不太难，你们一定能唱得很好。"

*   *   *

The Honghu Lake Waters Surge in Majestic Waves
The Honghu Lake waters in majestic waves surge,
And the Honghu Lake is where I was given birth.
At dawn the fishermen cast their nets,
And the boats come back full of fish at sunset.
Wild ducks, catrops and lotus abound everywhere,

During harvest time the fragrance of ripening rice
Fills the air.

The paradise may be beautiful and bright,
But the Honghu Lake is better than paradise
For its abundance of fish and rice.

Hónghú Shuǐ, Làng Dǎ Làng

Zhōngsù

Zhāng Jìng'ān Ōuyáng Shūqiān qǔ

Hóng hú   shuǐ ya,   làngyamalàngdǎ. làng a,

Hóng hú   àn biān   shì yamashì jiā xiāng a.

Qǐng zǎo chuán ér   qù ya qù sā wǎng,

wǎnshang huí lái   yú mǎn cāng.

Sì chù yě yā hé líng ǒu,

qiū shōumǎnfàn dào gǔ xiāng.   Rén rén dōu shuō tiān táng

měi   zěn bǐ wǒ Hóng hú yú mǐ xiāng.

五、语法 Grammar

能愿动词 Optative verbs

能愿动词"想、要、会、能、可以、应该"等常常放在动词前边，表示能力、可能或意愿。除个别情况外，能愿动词只能用"不"否定，这种句子的正反疑问式通常是并列能愿动词的肯定和否定形式。

Optative verbs such as "想", "要", "会", "能", "可以" and "应该" are more often than not used before verbs to express ability, possibility or intention or wishes. Optative verbs are made negative by means of "不" except in a few very special cases. The affirmative-negative form of sentences with optative verbs is usually made by juxtaposing the affirmative and negative forms of the optative verbs.

名词或代词 Nouns or pronouns	副词 Ad- verb	能愿动词 Optative verbs	动词 Verbs	名词或代词 Nouns or pronouns	助词 Par- ticle
古波		要	研究	中国文学。	
你		想	当	老师	
他	不	会	开	车。	吗？
你		能不能	来？		

1. "要"和"想"既是动词（分别见第十九课和第十四课），也是能愿动词。能愿动词的"要"和"想"都表示意愿和要求。"要"更强调作某事的意志（其否定形式常用"不想"）；"想"则侧重于打算、希望。例如：

"要" and "想" are both verbs (See Lessons 19 and 14), and optative verbs as well. As optative verbs, they both indicate volition or intention, but "要" (its negative form is "不想") emphasizes one's strong will or desire to do something while "想" emphasizes one's plan or wish. E.g.

① 同志，我要买那本书。

同志，我想买本字典，你们这儿有吗？

② 星期天你想进城吗？

我不想去，我要回家。

2. "会"是动词，也是能愿动词。能愿动词"会"表示通过学习掌握了某种技巧。例如：

"会" is an optative verb as well as an ordinary verb. As an optative verb, "会" denotes skill acquired or mastered as a result of study. E.g.

你会不会游泳？

他不会说英语。

这个练习我不会作，请你帮助帮助我。

3. 能愿动词"能"和"可以"都表示有能力作某事。例如：

The optative verbs "能" and "可以" are both used to express ability to do something. E.g.

432

他现在能看中文杂志。

每星期你能学几课？

我可以翻译这本书。

"能"和"可以"还表示客观条件允许或禁止。例如：

"能" and "可以" may also be used to express ability or lack of it depending on circumstances. E.g.

你们今年能不能去？

可以进来吗？

阅览室里不能吸烟。

除了在表示禁止时能用"不可以"以外，"能"和"可以"的否定形式一般都是"不能"。

"不可以" usually expresses prohibition. "不能", the negative form of both "能" and "可以", indicates inability to do something.

4. 能愿动词"应该"表示情理上或事实上的需要。例如：

The optative verb "应该" indicates need arising from moral or factual necessity. E.g.

你们学得不错，应该去中国。

你们学习汉语，应该会说、会听、会写。

注意：能愿动词不能重叠，后边不能带动态助词。

Notice that optative verbs can never be reduplicated, nor can they be followed by modal particles.

练习 Exercises

1. 读下列词组：Read out the following phrases:

加深了解　　加深认识　　了解中国

了解他们　　中国人民　　两国人民

《人民日报》　《人民画报》　研究文学

研究音乐　　研究语法　　研究问题

有名的作家　有名的电影　有名的大夫

有名的工厂　理想的工作　理想的房子

理想的朋友　我的理想

2. 用否定式回答下列问题：Answer the following questions in the negative:

(1) 他会不会说汉语？

(2) 她能参加晚上的舞会吗？

(3) 你要不要喝咖啡？

(4) 这儿可以不可以游泳？

(5) 明天你能跟我们一起进城吗？

(6) 这条河能不能钓鱼？

3. 用正反疑问句完成下列对话：Complete the following dialogues with affirmative-negative questions:

(1) A: _____ ？

B: 他不会作这些练习。

(2) A: _____ ？

B: 我能帮助你。

(3) A: _____ ？

B: 我可以教你开车。

(4) A: _____ ？

B: 他不想研究音乐，他要研究文学。

(5) A: _____ ？

B: 我要休息休息。

4. 用"要、想、能、可以、会、应该"填空：
Supply "要"，"想"，"能"，"可以"，"会" or "应该" in the following sentences:

明天我们____去参观图书馆，我____请我朋友跟我们一起去。我给他打电话，问他____去。他说，他很____去，可是他上午有事儿,不＿＿去。我说,这个图书馆很大,很有意思,他＿＿去参观参观,以后＿＿去那儿看书。他问我,明天下午去,好吗? 我说,下午去也＿＿。我哥哥＿＿开车,下午我们一起坐车去。我朋友很高兴,说:"好!"

5. 将下列句子翻译成汉语:Translate the following into Chinese:

(1) He wants to be a doctor.

(2) Do you want to buy a ticket for the Beijing opera?

(3) He is very good at angling.

(4) Singing is prohibited in the reading-rooms.

(5) You should take some exercise every day.

(6) He can teach you English.

(7) Can you watch TV tonight?

(8) You can get to know still more.

(9) I intend to make a study of Chinese proverbs.

六、语音语调 Pronunciation and Intonation

1. 句调(2) Sentence tunes (2)

(1) 用疑问代词的疑问句一般读高句调,疑问代词重读,句尾降低。例如:

Questions formed with interrogative pronouns are usually said in the high-pitch sentence tune. Interrogative pronouns are usually stressed, and the sentence ends in a fall. E.g.

你想作什么工作？

——我想当翻译。

丁云在作什么？

——她在游泳呢。

在哪儿停车？

这是谁的车？

(2) 由能愿动词肯定式与否定式构成的正反问句，一般读高句调，其中肯定式重读，否定式轻读，句尾降低。在答句中，能愿动词要重读。例如：

Affirmative - negative questions formed with affirmative and negative forms of optative verbs are usually said in the high-pitch sentence tune. The affirmative part is stressed, the negative part is pronounced with a weak stress. The sentence ends in a falling intonation. In answers, the optative verbs should be stressed. E.g.

今年能不能去？

437

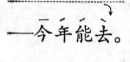

——今年能去。

他会不会说英语？

——他会说英语。

(3) 用语气助词"啊"表示感叹的语气一般读低句调，语速慢，句尾降低，尾音拉长。例如：

Exclamatory sentences containing the modal particle "啊" are usually said rather slowly and in the low-pitch sentence tune, trailing cff to a falling intonation towards the end. E.g.

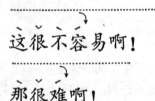

这很不容易啊！

那很难啊！

2. 练习 Exercises

朗读下面的一首诗：Read out the following poem:

Dēng Guàn Què Lóu
登 鹳 雀 楼

Wáng Zhīhuàn
王 之 涣

Bái rì yī shān jìn,
白 日 依 山 尽，

438

Huáng Hé rù hǎi liú:

黄 河 入 海 流。

Yù qióng qiānlǐ mù,

欲 穷 千 里 目,

gèng shàng yìcéng lóu:

更 上 一 层 楼。

汉字笔顺表 Table of Stroke-order of Chinese Characters

1	研	石							
		开							
2	究	穴							
		九							
3	早	日							
		十							
4	谈	讠							谈
		炎	火						
			火						
5	翻	番	釆	(ノ	⺁	⺌	⺅	平	釆)
			田						
		羽	习						

			习	
6	译	讠		譯
		睪	又	
			幸 （一 二 幸）	
7	能	肯	厶	
			月	
		匕	匕	
			匕	
8	深	氵		
		罙	罒 （丶 冖 冖 罒）	
			木	
9	解	角	⺈	
			用	
		𤚩	刀	
			牛	
10	或	一 㦮 㦮 式 或 或		
11	者			
12.	就	京		
		尤 （一 ナ 尢 尤）		

440

13	应	广		應
		业（丶 丷 丷 业）		
14	该	讠		該
		亥		
15	俩	亻		倆
		两		
16	可			
17	容	宀		
		谷	八	
			人	
			口	
18	易	日		
		勿（丿 勹 勹 勿）		
19	成			
20	竟	立		
		曰		
		儿		

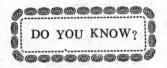

Lu Xun and Guo Moruo

Lu Xun and Guo Moruo were both great modern Chinese writers.

Lu Xun was a great man of letters, thinker and revolutionary, as well as the founder of modern Chinese literature. His real name was Chou Shuren, and Lu Xun was his penname. He was born on Sept. 25, 1881 in Shaoxing County, Zhejiang Province and died on October 19, 1936 in Shanghai. His famous novels "A Madman's Diary" and "The True Story of Ah-Q" laid the foundation of modern Chinese literature and revolutionary realism. His works have been collected in the "Complete Works of Lu Xun", totalling 20 volumes.

Guo Moruo was a great proletarian cultural fighter and an outstanding man of letters, revolutionary, scientist, thinker and social activist. He was born on November 16, 1892 in the town of Shawan, Luoshan County, Sichuan Province and died on June 12, 1978 in Beijing at the age of 86. "Goddess", a famous poem of his, filled with revolutionary romanticism, blazed a trail for modern Chinese poetry. After Lu Xun, Guo Moruo was another brilliant banner on China's cultural front. The "Collected Works of Mo Ruo" total 17 volumes.

第二十七课 Lesson 27

一、课文 Text

电影开始了吗

（在 中国 大使馆）
(Zài Zhōngguó dàshǐguǎn)

王： 你们 都 来 了，请 进！
Wáng: Nǐmen dōu lái le, qǐng jìn!

布 朗：您 好！能 参加 今天 的
Bùlǎng: Nín hǎo! Néng cānjiā jīntiān de

招待会，我 非常 高兴。
zhāodàihuì, wǒ fēicháng gāoxìng.

古 波：丁 云，电影 开始 了 吗？
Gǔbō: Dīng Yún, diànyǐng kāishǐ le ma?

丁 云：还 没有 开始 呢。 你们
Dīng Yún: Hái méiyou kāishǐ ne. Nǐmen

要 喝 点儿 什么 酒？
yào hē diǎnr shénme jiǔ?

布 朗：我 想 尝尝 中国 的
Bùlǎng: Wǒ xiǎng chángchang Zhōngguó de

茅台酒。
máotáijiǔ.

布朗太太：我 不 会 喝 酒，要 一杯
Bùlǎng Tàitai: Wǒ bú huì hē jiǔ, yào yìbēi

桔子水 吧。
júzishuǐ ba.

王：为 布朗 先生 和 布朗 太太
Wáng: Wèi Bùlǎng Xiānsheng hé Bùlǎng Tàitai

的 健康 干 杯！
de jiànkāng gān bēi!

布 朗：谢谢，为 我们 的 友谊 干
Bùlǎng: Xièxie, wèi wǒmen de yǒuyì gān

杯!
bēi!

丁　云： 帕兰卡，　茅台酒　你　喝　了
Dīng Yún: Pàlánkǎ, máotáijiǔ nǐ hē le

没有？
méiyou?

帕兰卡： 没有。我　喝　了　一杯 中国
Pàlánkǎ: Méiyou. Wǒ hē le yìbēi Zhōngguó

葡萄酒。
pútaojiǔ.

丁　云： 请　你们　尝尝　中国　菜。
Dīng Yún: Qǐng nǐmen chángchang Zhōngguó cài.

太　太： 谢谢，我　吃　了。非常　好。
Tàitai: Xièxie, wǒ chī le. Fēicháng hǎo.

古　波： 筷子 我　还 用 得 不 好，我
Gǔbō: Kuàizi wǒ hái yòng de bù hǎo, wǒ

想　再　试一试。
xiǎng zài shìyishi.

*　　　*　　　*

王： 我 给 你们 介绍介绍： 这 是
Wáng: Wǒ gěi nǐmen jièshaojièshao: Zhè shì

大使馆 的 文化 参赞 李
dàshǐguǎn de wénhuà cānzàn Lǐ

先生 和 夫人， 这 是 布朗
Xiānsheng hé fūren, zhè shì Bùlǎng

先生 和 布朗 太太。
Xiānsheng hé Bùlǎng Tàitai.

布 朗： 认识 你们， 我 很 高兴。
Bùlǎng: Rènshi nǐmen, wǒ hěn gāoxìng.

参 赞： 欢迎， 欢迎。
Cānzàn: Huānyíng, huānyíng.

王： 这 两位 是 中文 系 的 学生，
Wáng: Zhè liǎngwèi shì Zhōngwén xì de xuésheng,

古波 和 帕兰卡。 他们 今年
Gǔbō hé Pàlánkǎ. Tāmen jīnnián

九月 就要 去 中国 学习。
jiǔyuè jiù yào qù Zhōngguó xuéxí.

参 赞： 太 好 了， 我们 又 认识 了
Cānzàn: Tài hǎo le, wǒmen yòu rènshi le

两位 年轻 的 朋友。
liǎngwèi niánqīng de péngyou.

446

夫 人： 请 大家 到 楼上 看 电影
Fūren: Qǐng dàjiā dào lóushàng kàn diànyǐng

吧。
ba.

生词 New Words

1. 开始　　（动）kāishǐ　　　　to begin, to start
2. 大使馆　（名）dàshǐguǎn　　embassy
   大使　　（名）dàshǐ　　　　ambassador
3. 招待会　（名）zhāodàihuì　reception
4. 酒　　　（名）jiǔ　　　　　wine, spirit
5. 尝　　　（动）cháng　　　　to taste
6. 茅台酒　（名）máotáijiǔ　Maotai (a Chinese strong drink)
7. 为　　　（介）wèi　　　　　for, to
8. 健康　（名、形）jiànkāng　health, healthy
9. 干杯　　　　　gān bēi　　to drink a toast, to propose a toast, here's to
10. 友谊　　（名）yǒuyì　　　friendship
11. 葡萄酒　（名）pútaojiǔ　grape wine
    葡萄　　（名）pútao　　　grape
12. 菜　　　（名）cài　　　　dish, vegetable

13.	筷子	(名)	kuàizı	chopsticks
14.	试	(动)	shì	to try
15.	文化	(名)	wénhuà	culture
16.	参赞	(名)	cānzàn	counsellor
17.	夫人	(名)	fūren	lady, madame, Mrs.
18.	又	(副)	yòu	again, in addition to, more
19.	大家	(代)	dàjiā	all, everybody
20.	到	(动)	dào	to go, to arrive, to reach,
21.	楼	(名)	lóu	storied building, floor

专名 Proper Names

| 李 | | Lǐ | *a surname* |

补充词 Supplementary Words

1.	白兰地	(名)	báilándì	brandy
2.	香槟酒	(名)	xiāngbīnjiǔ	champagne
3.	武官	(名)	wǔguān	military attaché
4.	一秘	(名)	yīmì	first secretary
5.	病	(动、名)	bìng	to fall ill, illness, disease
6.	小学生	(名)	xiǎoxuéshēng	pupil, schoolboy (schoolgirl)

448

二、注释 Notes

1. "能参加今天的招待会，我非常高兴。"

"I'm very glad that I can attend the reception today."

"认识你们，我很高兴。"

"I'm very glad to make your acquaintance."

这两句都是复合句。前一个分句表示高兴的原因，主语"我"常常省略。

"能参加今天的招待会，我非常高兴。" and "认识你们，我很高兴。" are both compound sentences in which the first clauses tell the reason why the subject "我" is glad. "我" in clauses of this type is more often than not omitted.

2. "为我们的友谊干杯!"

"To our friendship!"

"为…干杯"是祝酒用语。"为"是介词。本课中出现的介词结构"为…"用来说明动作的目的，必须放在动词的前边。

"为…干杯" is an expression used to propose a toast. "为" here is a preposition. The prepositional construction "为…" introduced in this lesson tells the purpose of the action expressed by the verb that is used in this construction and is invariably placed before the verb.

3. "我们又认识了两位年轻的朋友。"

副词"再"(1) 和"又"(1) 都表示动作或情况的重复。"再"(1) 用于尚未重复的动作或情况；"又"(1) 一般用于已重复的动作 或情况。例如：

The adverbs "再"(1) and "又"(1) both indicate the repetition of an action, but they are different in usage: "再"(1) is used to denote an action or a state of affairs which has not been repeated yet while "又"(1) is used when the repetition has already occured.

他今天去图书馆了，他说明天再去。

他昨天上午来了，下午没有再来。

他昨天来了，今天又来了。

他昨天没有来，今天又没有来。

4. "请大家到楼上看电影吧。"

"Well, everyone, please go upstairs and see the film."

代词"大家"指一定范围内所有的人。

The pronoun "大家" refers to all the persons concerned.

"楼上"泛指楼里第二层以上的地方。如果说话人在楼里，也可以指他所在的那层以上的地方。"楼下"则泛指楼房的第一层或说话人所在那层以下的地方。

"楼上" refers to all the upper part of a building from the first floor up. If the speaker is inside the building, "楼上" can also refer to any storey above the storey where he is. "楼下" refers to the ground floor or any floor below where the speaker is.

450

三、替换与扩展 Substitution and Extension

(一)

1. <u>他们来</u>了吗？
   他们都来了。

你们，	锻炼
朋友们，	到
同学们，	走
学生们，	懂
服务员，	休息

2. <u>电影</u>开始了吗？

   (电影)还没有开始呢。

   电影几点开始？

   七点一刻开始。

电视	京剧
舞会	文学课
招待会	音乐会*

3. 中国菜你尝了没有？

我没有尝。
你想尝吗？
我想尝。

面包，	吃
那个问题，	谈
新笔，	试
今天的新闻，	听
饭，	作
电话，	打
桌子，	整理

4. 你喝了茅台酒没有？

我喝了，我喝了一杯茅台酒。
茅台酒怎么样？
不错。

葡萄酒	矿泉水
啤酒	白兰地*
花茶	香槟酒*
桔子水	

5. 他<u>杂志看</u>得多不多?

不多。

他看了几本杂志?

他看了两本杂志。

成语(个),	翻译
杂志(本),	买
朋友(位),	请
菜(个),	要
电影票(张),	给
花儿(束),	送
同学(个),	辅导

6. 昨天代表团参观了什么地方?

代表团参观了<u>那个工厂</u>。

一些图书馆
我们学院
学生城的宿舍楼
中文系和英文系
农村

7. （请大家）为<u>我们的友谊</u>干杯！

干杯！

> 我们两国人民的友谊
> 参赞先生和夫人的健康
> 大使先生和夫人的健康
> 武官*先生和夫人的健康
> 朋友们的健康

（二）

1. 迎接 Welcoming a guest

A: 教授*先生，您来了我们很高兴。

B: 能参加你们的招待会，真太好了。

A: 我来给你们介绍介绍：

这是我们的一秘*和夫人，这是布朗教授*。

B: 认识您很高兴。

C: 欢迎，欢迎。

2. 祝酒 Drinking a toast

A: 请尝尝这个菜。

B: 谢谢，来一点儿。非常好。

A: 来，为我们的友谊再干一杯！

B: 干杯！

3. 在公共汽车站 At a bus stop

A: 请问，这趟 (tàng, a mea-
sure word) 车可以到
日本大使馆吗？

B: 可以。你看，车来
了。

4. 等人 Waiting for somebody

老师：同学们都来了吗？

学生：还没有呢。

老师：谁还没有来？

学生：古波和帕兰卡没有来。
啊，古波来了。古波，快，大家都在
等你呢。

古波：对不起*，我来得太晚了。

学生：帕兰卡呢？

古波：她不能来，她病*了。

　＊　　　　＊　　　　＊

请　柬 (qǐngjiǎn, invitation card)

谨订于一九八〇年十二月二十日星期六晚七点在中国大使馆举行电影招待会，请出席。

中国大使馆文化参赞　李志民

四、阅读短文 Reading Text

学　写　字

一位老师在教小学生*写字。他写了一个"一"字，问小学生认识不认识。小学生说："我认识，这是'一'字。"

老师说："对，你写吧。"

小学生也写了一个"一"字，问老师："您看，我写得对不对？"

"你写得很好。"老师说，"你会写'二'

字吗？"

小学生回答得很快："我会写，'一'字是一横(héng, horizontal stroke in Chinese characters)，'二'字是两横。"他又写了一个"二"字。

老师说："对了。'三'字呢？"

"'三'字是三横。"

老师还想教他写"四"、"五"……小学生说："您不用教我，我都会写。"

老师让他写一个"万 (wàn, ten thousand)"字。

小学生想："万"字一定是一万横。他回家准备了十张纸，开始写"万"字。

下午上课的时候，老师问他："你写的'万'字呢？"

小学生回答："这九张纸都是我写的'万'字，还差八十二横。"

五、语法 Grammar

动作的完成 The perfect aspect of an action

(1) 加在动词之后表示动作所处的阶段的助词叫动态 助 词。

Particles added to verbs to tell in what stage an action is are called aspect particles.

动态助词"了"加在动词后边，表示动作的完成。例如：

The perfect aspect of an action is shown by adding the aspect particle "了" to the verb. E.g

① 他们都来吗？

Are all of them coming?

他们都来。

Yes, they are (all coming).

你看几本杂志？

How many copies of magazines are you going to read?

我看三本杂志。

I am going to read three (copies of magazines).

② 他们都来了吗？

Have they all come?

他们都来了。

Yes, they have (all come).

你看了几本杂志？

How many copies of magazines have you read?

我看了三本杂志。

I have read three (copies of magazines).

458

动作的完成只表明动作本身所处的阶段，它与动作发生的时间（过去、现在或将来）无关。完成的动作常常发生在过去，但过去时间的动作并不一定都用动态助词"了"。如果是过去经常性的动作，或者只是一般地叙述过去的动作并不强调它是否完成时，都不用动态助词"了"。例如：

The completion of an action only tells in what stage the action itself is and has nothing to do with the time (past, present or future) when it takes place. Very often a completed action took place in the past. Nevertheless, a past action is not always followed by the aspect particle "了". For example, if a past action is a habitual one or when it is a simple statement and there is no need to emphasize its completion, the aspect particle "了" is not used. E.g.

以前他常常来看我。

去年 (qùnián, last year) 他在学生宿舍住。

完成的动作不仅发生在过去，也可以发生在未来。例如：

A completed action may take place either in the past or in the future. E.g.

明天晚上我吃了饭看电影。

（2）带助词"了"的动词如果后边有宾语，这个宾语一般要带数量词或其他定语。

When a verb with the aspect particle "了" takes after it an object, the object is usually qualified by a numeral-measure word or other attributive.

名词或代词 Nouns or pronouns	动词 Verbs	"了" "了"	数量词或代词、形容词 Numeral-measure words or pronouns or adjectives	名词或代词 Nouns or pronouns
他	认识	了	两个	朋友。
同学们	访问	了	那位	教练。
我	买	了	新	地图。
她	回答	了	老师的	问题。

　　如果宾语是不带定语的简单宾语（如"他看了杂志"或"代表团参观了工厂"），就显得句子的意思还没有完，需要增加一些附加成分，才能构成完整的句子。

The sentence will sometimes sound incomplete when its object is a simple one and does not have any attributive (e.g."他看了杂志" or "代表团参观了工厂") and it is necessary to add a number of complementary elements to make the meaning complete.

　　(3) 动作完成的否定，是在动词前用上副词"没(有)"，动词后不用"了"，例如：

The negative form of the perfect aspect of an action is made by putting the adverb "没(有)" before the verb after which no "了" is allowed. E.g.

　　　　他们没有来。

　　　　我没看杂志。

如果一个动作必然发生或一定会完成，但是现在还未发生或尚未完成，就用"还没(有)…呢"，例如：

For an action that is bound to happen or be completed, but has as yet not happened or been completed, the construction "还没(有)…呢" is used. E.g.

电影还没(有)开始呢。

他还没(有)来呢。

答句中可以单用"没有"或"还没有呢"来否定动作的完成，例如：

To answer questions of this type, either "没有" or "还没有呢" may be used to indicate that the action hasn't as yet completed. E.g.

你作了练习没有？

没有。

（还没有呢。）

(4) 动作完成的正反疑问式 Affirmative-negative form of the perfect aspect of an action

动作完成的正反疑问式常用"…了没有"。

The affirmative-negative form of the perfect aspect of an action is usually "…了没有".

名词或代词 Nouns or pronouns	动 词 Verbs	"了" "了"	名词或代词 Nouns or pronouns	"没有" "没有"
电影	开始	了		没有？
你	喝	了	茅台酒	没有？
你们	都看	了	今天的报	没有？

也可以并列动词的肯定、否定形式（"…没…"），如"来没来"、"喝没喝"。

The affirmative-negative form of the perfect aspect of an action can also be made by juxtaposing the affirmative and negative forms of the verb (i.e. "…没…"), e.g. "来没来", "喝没喝".

名词或代词 Nouns or pronouns	动 词 Verbs	"没" "没"	动 词 Verbs	名词或代词 Nouns or pronouns
他	来	没	来？	
你	写	没	写？	信？
你们	谈	没	谈？	这个问题？

练习　Exercises

1．读下列词组：Read out the following phrases:

开始工作　　开始学习　　开始研究

开始了解　　　开始访问　　　开始参观

开始跳舞　　　开始锻炼　　　身体健康

祝你健康　　　非常健康　　　不太健康

研究了这本语法　　　访问了这位作家

翻译了他的书　　　认识了很多朋友

参加了那个舞会　　　了解了一些问题

听了这张唱片　　　问了两个问题

穿了新裙子　　　钓了五条鱼

接了不少电话　　　看了中国电影

2. 用表示动作完成的"了"，改写下列各句： Rewrite the following sentences using "了" to indicate the completion of an action:

(1) 我买一本汉语词典。

(2) 他要两杯咖啡。

(3) 王老师给我们两张京剧票。

(4) 今天他们参观我们的学校。

(5) 他跟我们一起访问那位有名的作家。

3. 用否定式回答下列各组问题: Answer the following groups
of questions in the negative:

(1) 你哥哥走吗？

你哥哥走了吗？

(2) 他姐姐来吗？

他姐姐来了吗？

(3) 你们锻炼吗？

你们锻炼了吗？

(4) 古波研究不研究中国音乐？

古波研究没研究中国音乐？

(5) 他们吃不吃饭？

他们吃饭了没有？

(6) 你了解不了解那个问题？

你了解没了解那个问题？

4. 用所给的词根据下列例句造句: Make sentences using the
following words and phrases in the same way as the
example given:

例 Example 喝　　葡萄酒

464

→你们喝了葡萄酒没有？

我喝了两杯，他没喝。

(1) 买　　电影票

(2) 写　　汉字

(3) 参观　工厂

(4) 问　　问题

(5) 学习　生词

(6) 访问　作家

5. 将下列句子改成正反疑问句：Change the following to affirmative-negative questions:

(1) 我们懂了。

(2) 她试了中国筷子。

(3) 我们都参加了大使馆的招待会。

(4) 他看了这个电影。

(5) 我用了那本词典。

(6) 我们谈了那个问题。

6. 用"再"和"又"填空：Supply "再" or "又" in the following
sentences:

(1) 他复习了今天的课文，_____复习了昨天的课文。

(2) 这个商店的面包很好，我买了两个，下午我想____买两个。

(3) 古波下午给帕兰卡打了电话，晚上____给她打了电话。

(4) 这本小说很好，我要____看看。

(5) 那个电影我看了，今天不想____看。

(6) 他星期二没有上课，今天____没有上课。

7. 根据下图复述本课的阅读短文：Retell the Reading Text with the help of the following pictures:

六、语音语调　Pronunciation and Intonation

1．句调(3) Sentence tunes (3)

用"…了没有"格式的正反问句，全句的句调比较高。"没有"轻读，句尾降低。例如：

Affirmative‒negative questions built on the pattern "…了没有" are usually uttered in a rather high pitch. "没有" is pronounced with a weak stress and the sentence ends in a falling intonation. E.g.

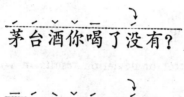

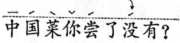

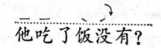

2．练习：Exercises

朗读下列带 c、ch 的词语，注意发音：

Read out the following words or phrases containing c and ch, paying special attention to the pronunciation of these two sounds:

词——吃　词典——吃饭

吃菜——生词

层——成　　千层——成语

三层——长城

朗读下面的成语：Read out the following proverbs:

Chā yǐ háo lí,
差 以 毫 厘，

shī zhī qiānlǐ.
失 之 千里。

(A minimal error or deviation results in wide divergence.)

汉字笔顺表　Table of Stroke-order of Chinese Characters

1	始	女		
		台	ㄥ	
			口	
2	使	亻		
		吏（一　口　旦　吏）		
3	招	扌		

		召		
4	待	彳		
		寺		
5	尝	屵		嘗
		云		
6	茅	艹		
		矛 (丶 乛 彑 予 矛)		
7	台			
8	为	丶 丿 为 为		為
9	健	亻		
		建	聿 (乛 彐 彐 聿 聿 聿)	
			廴 (㇋ 廴)	
10	康	广		
		隶 (乛 彐 彐 肀 肀 肀 隶)		
11	干	一 二 干		乾
12	谊	讠		誼
		宜	宀	
		且 (丨 冂 冃 月 且)		
13	葡	艹		

		甪	勹 (′ 勹)		
			甫		
14	萄	艹			
		匋	勹		
			缶 (′ ⺊ ⺊ 午 缶 缶)		
15	菜	艹			
		采	⺥ (′ ⺊ ⺊ ⺥)		
			木		
16	筷	⺮			
		快			
17	试	讠			試
		式	弋		
			工		
18	化	亻			
		匕			
19	赞	兟	先		贊
			先 、		
		贝			
20	又				

470

21	到	至						
		刂						
22	楼	木						楼
		娄	米	（ 丶	丶	丷	半	半 米 ）
			女					

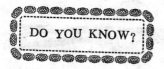

The Chinese Strong Drink--Mao Tai

Mao Tai is a famous alcoholic drink, produced in China in the town of Maotai, Renhuai County, Guizhou Province. It ranks first in China's eight famous drinks. It is of an exquisite flavour, transparent and clear like crystal. Containing 53 percent alcohol, it nevertheless tastes mild and mellow, not going to the head. Maotai enjoys a high reputation throughout the world.

Among China's famous traditional alcoholic drinks are also Fen Wine of Shanxi Province, Daqu Wine of Sichuan Province and Shaoxing Wine of Zhejiang Province.

第二十八课 Lesson 28

一、课文 Text

我去看足球赛了

帕兰卡： 古波， 昨天 上午 我 给 你
Pàlánkǎ:　Gǔbō,　zuótiān shàngwǔ wǒ gěi nǐ

打 电话 了，你 不 在。你 去
dǎ diànhuà le, nǐ bú zài. Nǐ qù

哪儿 了？
nǎr le?

472

古 波： 我 去 中国 大使馆 办 签证
Gǔbō: Wǒ qù Zhōngguó dàshǐguǎn bàn qiānzhèng

了。
le.

帕兰卡： 下午 呢？ 你 又 不 在。
Pàlánkǎ: Xiàwǔ ne? Nǐ yòu bú zài.

古 波： 我 吃 了 午饭 就 去 看 足球
Gǔbō: Wǒ chī le wǔfàn jiù qù kàn zúqiú

赛 了。
sài le.

帕兰卡： 谁 跟 谁 赛？
Pàlánkǎ: Shéi gēn shéi sài?

古 波： 大学生 队 跟 银行 队 赛。
Gǔbō: Dàxuéshēng duì gēn yínháng duì sài.

帕兰卡： 大学生 队 赢 他们 了 吗？
Pàlánkǎ: Dàxuéshēng duì yíng tāmen le ma?

古 波： 没有，大学生 队 输 了，一 比
Gǔbō: Méiyou, dàxuéshēng duì shū le, yī bǐ

二。 裁判 不 公平。
èr. Cáipàn bù gōngping.

帕兰卡： 你 总 说 裁判 不 公平。
Pàlánkǎ: Nǐ zǒng shuō cáipàn bù gōngping.

古　波：你　没　去　看，昨天　　大学生　　队
Gǔbō:　　Nǐ　méi　qù　kàn,　zuótiān　dàxuéshēng　duì

踢　得　很　好。真　气　人。
tī　de　hěn　hǎo. Zhēn　qì　rén.

帕兰卡：好　了，我　问　你，你　的　行李
Pàlánkǎ:　Hǎo　le,　wǒ　wèn　nǐ,　nǐ　de　xíngli

准备　　得　怎么样？
zhǔnbèi　de　zěnmeyàng?

古　波：我　正　整理　箱子　呢。我　还　差
Gǔbō:　Wǒ zhèng zhěnglǐ xiāngzi ne. Wǒ hái chà

一顶　帽子。你　呢？
yìdǐng　màozi. Nǐ　ne?

帕兰卡：我　想　买　一双　冰鞋。北京
Pàlánkǎ:　Wǒ xiǎng mǎi　yìshuāng bīngxié. Běijīng

冬天　可以　滑　冰。
dōngtiān　kěyǐ　huá　bīng.

古　波：我　送　你　一双　冰鞋　吧。
Gǔbō:　Wǒ sòng nǐ　yìshuāng bīngxié ba.

帕兰卡：非常　感谢。我　给　你　买　帽子，
Pàlánkǎ:　Fēicháng gǎnxiè. Wǒ gěi nǐ mǎi màozi,

好　吗？
hǎo　ma?

474

古　波：　我 也 要 谢谢 你。 明天 吃 了
Gǔbō:　　Wǒ yě yào xièxie nǐ. Míngtiān chī le

早饭 我们 就 去 商店。
zǎofàn wǒmen jiù qù shāngdiàn。

生词　New Words

1. 足球　（名）zúqiú　football
   球　　（名）qiú　　ball

2. 赛　　（动）sài　　to compete, competition, match

3. 昨天　（名）zuótiān　yesterday

4. 办　　（动）bàn　　to do, to handle, to attend to, to tackle

5. 签证　（名）qiānzhèng　visa, visé

6. 午饭　（名）wǔfàn　lunch

7. 队　　（名）duì　　team, line

8. 赢　　（动）yíng　　to win, to beat

9. 输　　（动）shū　　to lose

10. 比　　（介、动）bǐ　　*a preposition showing comparison*, than, to (in a score)

11. 裁判　（名、动）cáipàn　referee, umpire, to act as a referee, to judge

475

12.	公平	(形)	gōngpíng	fair
13.	踢	(动)	tī	to kick
14.	气人		qì rén	to get someone angry; to get someone annoyed
15.	行李	(名)	xíngli	luggage, baggage
16.	箱子	(名)	xiāngzi	suitcase
17.	顶	(量)	dǐng	*a measure word*
18.	帽子	(名)	màozi	hat, cap
19.	双	(量)	shuāng	*a measure word*, pair
20.	冰鞋	(名)	bīngxié	skating boots, skates
	鞋	(名)	xié	shoes
21.	冬天	(名)	dōngtiān	winter
22.	滑冰		huá bīng	to skate, skating
23.	早饭	(名)	zǎofàn	breakfast

补充词 Supplementary Words

1.	体育场	(名)	tǐyùchǎng	stadium
2.	公园	(名)	gōngyuán	park
3.	乒乓球	(名)	pīngpāngqiú	table tennis
4.	运动	(名、动)	yùndòng	sports, to sport
5.	网球	(名)	wǎngqiú	~~badminton~~ tennis

476

6. 篮球　　(名) lánqiú　　　basketball

7. 排球　　(名) páiqiú　　　volleyball

8. 滑雪　　　　huá xuě　　　to ski, skiing

二、注释　Notes

1. "我吃了午饭就去看足球赛了。"

"I went to see the football match right after lunch."

"明天吃了早饭我们就去商店。"

"We shall go to the shop right after breakfast tomorrow."

两个动作连续发生，第一个动作完成之后立即发生第二个动作，必须在第一个动词后用动态助词"了"。第二个动词前往往用副词"就"(2)表示两个动作接得很紧。

To indicate that two actions take place one immediately after the other, that is, the second action is to take place just after the completion of the first one, the aspect particle "了" must be added to the verb indicating the first action and the adverb "就"(2) is usually used before the verb indicating the second action.

2. "一比二。"

体育比赛中的比分 "1：2" 读作 "一比二"。提问可说："几比几?"

"1：2" as a record of points gained in sport is read as "一比二". "几比几" is an expression used to ask what the score is.

三、替换与扩展 Substitution and Extension

（一）

1. 上午你去哪儿了？
   我去中国大使馆了。

回，	家
进，	城
去，	城外玩儿
去，	公园*
去，	体育场*

2. 昨天晚上你看电影了没有？
   没有。我看足球赛了。
   你看足球赛的时候，你朋友作什么呢？
   他复习课文呢。

听新闻，	看电视
去咖啡馆，	看朋友
看京剧，	准备行李
跳舞，	打乒乓球*

3. 你<u>买</u>没买<u>冰鞋</u>?

   我没买(冰鞋)。

吃，	午饭
尝，	鱼汤
办，	签证
去，	楼上
当，	裁判

4. 昨天他<u>下</u>了<u>课</u>作什么了?

   昨天他下了课就<u>去滑冰</u>了。

吃，	早饭，	去买箱子
参观，	工厂，	去接朋友
欢迎，	代表团，	参加招待会
看，	电影，	去打网球*
买，	帽子，	去看篮球*赛

5. 明天你<u>吃</u>了<u>午饭</u>去哪儿?

   明天我吃了午饭就<u>进城</u>。

   我想跟你一起去，好吗?

   好，我们一起去。

```
吃，早饭，    去大使馆
下，课，      去工厂
吃，晚饭，    去王老师家
看，排球*赛，去古波那儿
```

6. 大学生队赢他们了吗？

   没有，大学生队输了。

   大学生队踢得怎么样？

   踢得不太好。

```
工人队
留学生代表队
你们队
北京队
男队
```

(二)

1. 肯定已经发生的事 Confirming that something has already taken place

   A: 星期天你休息得怎么样？

B: 我们一家人都去公园*了。

A: 你们玩儿得很好吧?

B: 玩儿得不错。你作什么了?

A: 下午我去商店了。

B: 你买没买东西?

A: 我给孩子买了一双冰鞋和一个小足球。

*　　　　*　　　　*

A: 昨天你去哪儿了? 我下午到宿舍找你了,你不在。

B: 我去看朋友了。真对不起*。

A: 没关系*,我没有给你打电话,你不知道我要来。

B: 你在宿舍等我了吗?

A: 没有, 我留 (liú, to leave) 了一个条子 (tiáozi, note) 就走了。

2. 谈体育运动 Talking about sports

A: 你打篮球*了吗？

B: 没有，我踢足球了。

A: 你每天都锻炼吗？

B: 是啊。你喜欢什么

运动？

A: 我喜欢打网球*，也常常打乒乓球*。

冬天我喜欢滑雪*。

B: 我不太会滑雪*，今年冬天你教我，好

吗？

A: 可以，我也滑得不太好。

*　　　　*　　　　*

看 足 球 赛

今天是八月二十七号，星期四。下午帕兰卡来找我，我不在，我去看足球赛了。

上午我去中国大使馆办了签证就回宿舍了。吃午饭的时候，我的朋友比里问我："古波，一点半体育场*有足球赛，你想去看吗?"他知道我很喜欢看足球赛，以前体育场*有足球赛的时候，我们总是一起去看。我说："我很想去，可是*我正准备行李呢，没有空儿去买票。"他说："我哥哥给了我两张票，我们一起去吧!"我说："太好了，谢谢你。"

吃了午饭，我们就坐车去体育场*了。我们到了那儿的时候，很多人正在外边等票呢。我们从东边的门进体育场。五分钟以后，比赛就开始了。

今天大学生队跟银行队赛，这是两个有名的足球队。比里问我："你说今天哪个队能赢？"我说："大学生队一定赢。"他说："不一定。我想银行队能赢。"

这两个队都踢得很好。今天，大学生队踢得更好，两点三刻，他们进了一个球。这个球踢得很漂亮。我说："比里，怎么样？大学生队能赢吧？"比里没有回答。忽然 (hūrán, suddenly) 他说："好球！银行队进了一个球！"

这时候，两个队是一比一。十分钟以后，大学生队又进了一个球，可是裁判说这个球不算 (suàn, to count)。还有三分钟了，银行队又进了一个球。

二比一，大学生队输了，真气人！

五、语法　Grammar

语气助词"了"(1) Modal particle "了" (1)

1. 除了动态助词"了"以外，还有个语气助词"了"。动态助词"了"在动词后边，语气助词"了"则总是在句尾。语气助词"了"可以表示几种不同的语气。这里介绍的语气助词"了"（1）是肯定某件事或某个情况已经发生。试比较下面两组对话：

Apart from indicating aspect, "了" may also function as a modal particle employed to denote the attitude of speaker. As an aspect particle, "了" usually comes after the verb, but it is always found at the end of the sentence when serving as a modal particle. The modal particle "了" may be used to express various different shades of meaning. "了" introduced in this lesson (Use 1) is used to modify the whole sentence to indicate that the event referred to has already taken place. Compare these two dialogues:

① 你去哪儿？

Where are you going?

我去商店。

I'm going to the shop.

你买什么？

What are you going to buy?

我买面包。

I'm going to buy some bread.

② 你去哪儿了？

Where have you been?
(or Where did you go?)

我去商店了。

I have been to the shop.
(or I went to the shop.)

你买什么了？

What have you bought?
(or What did you buy?)

我买面包了。

I have bought some bread.
(or I bought some bread.)

在第一组对话中，"去商店"和"买面包"这两件事尚未成为过去的事实。第二组对话中，这两件事则肯定已经发生了。

In the first dialogue, "去商店" and "买面包" are represented as not having taken place as yet; in the second dialogue, they are represented as already accomplished.

语气助词"了"(1) 总是表示动作或事情发生在过去的时间。然而，发生在过去的事情不一定都用语气助词"了"。如果只是一般地叙述过去的事情，特别是连续发生的几件事，或描写当时的情景但并不强调已肯定发生的语气，也可以不用"了"。例如：

The modal particle "了" (1) is usually used to indicate that the action or event referred to is something that took place at some time in the past, but past happenings are not always indicated with the help of the modal particle "了". It is not used, for instance, in simple statements of certain events, especially a succession of events in the past, nor is "了" used in mere description of the background against which something took place, that is, there is no need to stress the completion of what happened. E.g.

昨天他上午去中国大使馆，下午去看足球赛。

我去看他的时候，他在家休息呢。

2. 带语气助词"了"的句子，其否定形式也是在动词前加副词"没(有)"，去掉句尾"了"。正反疑问句式是在句尾加上 "…了没有"或者并列动词的肯定和否定形式 "…没…"。

The negative form of the sentence with the modal particle "了" is also made by putting the adverb "没(有)" in front of the verb and at the same time dropping the "了" at the end of the sentence. The affirmative–negative form of such a sentence is made by either adding "…了没有" at the end of the sentence or by juxtaposing the affirmative and negative forms of the verb, (i.e. "…没…").

名词或代词 Nouns or pronouns	副　词 Adverb	动　词 Verbs	名词或代词 Nouns or pronouns	助　词 Particles
我 他 妹妹 你	没(有)	看 买 吃 吃没吃	电影 冰鞋。 午饭 午饭?	了。 了没有?

3. "了"用在动词后，又在句尾，就兼有动态助词"了"和语气助词"了"的作用。例如：

When "了" comes after the verb and at the end of the sentence as well, it functions both as an aspect particle and a modal particle. E.g.

他来了。

我们懂了。

学生队赢了。

练习 Exercises

1. 读下列词组：Read out the following phrases:

昨天上午　昨天下午　昨天晚上

今天上午　今天下午　今天晚上

明天上午　明天下午　明天晚上

吃早饭　吃午饭　吃晚饭　吃点心　　吃菜

打电话　打乒乓球　打篮球　打网球　打球

看球赛　看电视　看电影　看京剧　看信

看杂志　看报　　看书　　看照片　看画报

听音乐　听民歌　听唱片　听新闻

作练习　作饭　　作菜　　作点心　作裙子

2. 将下列各句改为正反疑问句：Change the following to affirmative-negative questions:

(1) 昨天下午我看足球赛了。

(2) 代表团到北京了。

(3) 她跟丁云打乒乓球了。

(4) 古波办签证了。

(5)大学生队赢工人队了。

(6)他当裁判了。

(7)我朋友参加昨天晚上的舞会了。

(8)王老师请布朗先生和布朗太太了。

(9)他们研究这个问题了。

(10)我们都喝咖啡了。

3. 完成下列对话：Complete the following dialogues:

(1) A: 昨天下午你去看比里了没有？

B: _____。

A: 他在宿舍作什么了？

B: _____。

(2) A: _____？

B: 星期日我们去城外玩儿了。

A: 丁云去没去？

B: _____。

(3) A: 你参观农村了没有？

B: _____。

A: 你访问没访问农民？

B: _____。

(4) A: 你接电话了吗？

B: _____。

A: _____？

B: 我同学给我打电话了。

(5) A: 今天下午你去商店了没有？

B: _____。

A: _____？

B: 我在商店买了一双鞋。

(6) A: _____？

B: 我没有给他们买足球票。

A: _____？

B: 他们都不去看足球赛。

4. 用所给的词造句，注意用动态助词"了"和副词"就"表示两个动作连续发生：Make sentences after the example with the words and phrases given, using "了" and the adverb "就" to show that two actions follow closely one after another:

例 Example

吃午饭

490

滑冰

→我吃了午饭就去滑冰了。

(1) 到工厂

开始参观

(2) 复习课文

写汉字

(3) 下课

写信

(4) 作练习

看电视

(5) 听今天的新闻

睡觉

5. 根据本课的阅读短文回答问题：Answer the following questions on the Reading Text:

(1) 上午古波作什么了？

(2) 谁给古波足球赛的票了？

(3) 今天谁跟谁赛？

(4) 古波想哪个队能赢？

(5) 这两个队踢得怎么样？

(6) 哪个队赢了？

6. 根据下面八张图写一篇短文：Write a short passage according to what the following eight pictures indicate.

他昨天作什么了？

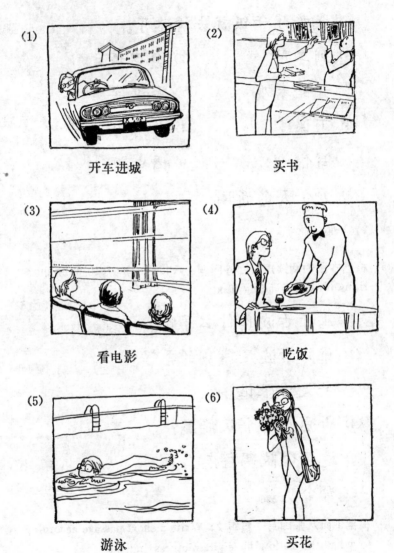

(1) 开车进城

(2) 买书

(3) 看电影

(4) 吃饭

(5) 游泳

(6) 买花

(7)	(8)
到朋友家	跳舞

六、语音语调 Pronunciation and Intonation

1. 句调（4）Sentence tunes (4)

（1）用语气助词"呢"构成的简单问句，如果"呢"前是一个单音节词，这个词要重读，尾音拉长，稍微降低，与"呢"构成句尾下降的高句调。例如：

In simple questions formed with the modal particle "呢", if a monosyllabic word precedes "呢", the monosyllabic word is stressed, with the voice drawing out a bit towards the end and the pitch slightly lower. This word, together with "呢", forms a sentence uttered in the high-pitch sentence tune with a fall at the end. E.g.

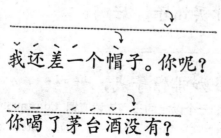

我还差一个帽子。你呢？

你喝了茅台酒没有？

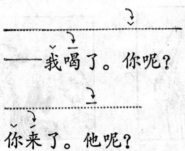

——我喝了。你呢？

你来了。他呢？

(2) 句尾用"好吗"的问句全句句调可分为两个部分。"好"字前读低句调，但这一部分的最后不是下降而是稍稍升高。在"好"前稍有停顿。"好"字重读，尾音拉长稍升，与"吗"构成句尾上升的高句调。例如：

The sentence tune for this type of questions can be divided at the word "好" into two parts. The first part or the part before "好" is uttered in the low-pitch sentence tune, but the voice does not fall but rises slightly at the end. A short pause comes before "好". The word "好" is stressed with the voice drawing out a bit. The word "好", together with "吗", forms the second part uttered in the high-pitch sentence tune with a rise at the end. E.g.

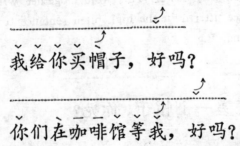

我给你买帽子，好吗？

你们在咖啡馆等我，好吗？

2. 三个三声和三个以上的三声连读变调 Continuous changes of tones of three or more than three 3rd tone

494

syllables

(1) 三个三声字相连，一般情况下，前两个三声字读第二声，第三个读第三声（或半三声）。如果强调第一个三声字或它后面有停顿，这个三声字就读半三声。例如：

When three words in the 3rd tone come together in close succession, the first two words usually change to the 2nd tone with the third one retaining the 3rd tone (or changing to the half 3rd tone). When the first word is emphasized or when it is followed by a pause, then it is pronounced in the half third-tone. E.g.

你好吗？

我很好，你呢？

（"我"、"很"读第二声，"好"读半三声。）

也很好。 （"也"、"很"读第二声。）

(2) 三个以上的三声字相连，可按语法关系划分音段（本书用"/"符号表示），先分成一个、两个或三个音节一组、然后再根据三声变调规律来念。紧连在一起的，前一个或前两个读第二声。稍有停顿的读半三声。例如：

When more than three words in the 3rd tone come together in close succession, they can be divided into tone-groups (marked with a slant stroke "/" in this book) according to their grammatical relationships. Each tone-group may consist of one, two or three syllables and is pronounced according to the rules concerning changes of words in the 3rd tone. For words following closely on one another, the first or the first two words are pronounced in the 2nd tone.

495

Words followed by a slight pause are pronounced in the half 3rd tone. E.g.

我给你 / 买帽子。

（"我"、"给"读第二声，"你"、"买"读半三声。）

我 / 也想买 / 一双冰鞋。

（"我"读半三声，"也"、"想"读第二声，"买"读半三声。）

汉字笔顺表　Table of Stroke-order of Chinese Characters

1	足	口		賽
		火		
2	球	王		
		求（一 十 十 才 才 求 求）		
3	赛	宀		赛
		共（一 一 ヒ 卅 共 共 共）		
		贝		
4	昨	日		
		乍		
5	办	乛 力 办 办		辨
6	签	竹		签

		金	人			
			亚 (一 ㇒ ㇒ 亚 亚)			
7	证	讠				證
		正				
8	队	阝				隊
		人				
9	赢	亡 (丶 亠 亡)				赢
		口				
		朋	月			
			贝			
			凡 (几 凡)			
10	输	车				輸
		俞	人			
			一			
			刖	月		
				刂		
11	比	㇏				
		匕				
12	裁	十				

		戈（一 弋 戈 戈）			
		衣（丶 亠 亠 衤 衣 衣）			
13	判	半（丶 丷 丷 半 半）			
		刂			
14	公	八			
		厶			
15	平	一 丷 丷 平 平			
16	踢	𧾷			
		易	日		
			勿		
17	气	丿 丿 气 气			氣
18	李	木			
		子			
19	箱	⺮			
		相			
20	顶	丁			頂
		页（一 丆 丆 页 页 页）			
21	帽	巾			
		冒	曰		

			目	
22	双	又		雙
		又		
23	冰	冫		
		水		
24	鞋	革(一 十 卄 卝 芇 苗 苩 莒 革)		
		圭	土	
			土	
25	冬	夂		
		冫		
26	滑	氵		
		骨	冎(丶 冂 冃 冎 冎)	
			月	

第二十九课　Lesson 29

一、课文　Text

飞机就要起飞了

（在　机场）
(Zài　jīchǎng)

古波： 你 看， 同学们 都 来 了，王
Gǔbō: Nǐ kàn, tóngxuémen dōu lái le, Wáng

老师 和 丁 云 也 来 了。
Lǎoshī hé Dīng Yún yě lái le.

帕兰卡： 丁 云， 我们 快 要 分别 了，我
Pàlánkǎ: Dīng Yún, wǒmen kuài yào fēnbié le, wǒ

真 不 愿意 离开 你。
zhēn bú yuànyì líkāi nǐ.

丁 云： 帕兰卡， 我 也 不 愿意 离开
Dīng Yún: Pàlánkǎ, wǒ yě bú yuànyì líkāi

你。我 想 我们 很 快 会 在
nǐ. Wǒ xiǎng wǒmen hěn kuài huì zài

中国 见 面。
Zhōngguó jiàn miàn.

古 波： 王 老师， 我们 非常 感谢 您。
Gǔbō: Wáng Lǎoshī, wǒmen fēicháng gǎnxiè nín.

布 朗： 我 太太 和 我 也 要 谢谢 您。
Bùlǎng: Wǒ tàitai hé wǒ yě yào xièxie nín.

您 工作 非常 认真， 教 得
Nín gōngzuò fēicháng rènzhēn, jiāo de

很 好，所以 他们 进步 很 快。
hěn hǎo, suǒyǐ tāmen jìnbù hěn kuài.

501

王： 哪里， 这 是 我 应该 作 的。
Wáng: Nǎli, zhè shì wǒ yīnggāi zuò de.

他们 学习 都 很 努力， 所以
Tāmen xuéxí dōu hěn nǔlì, suóyǐ

能 学 得 很 好。
néng xué de hěn hǎo.

帕兰卡： 爸爸 要 给 我们 照相 了。
Pàlánkǎ: Bàba yào gěi wǒmen zhàoxiàng le.

布 朗： 请 大家 站 得 紧 一点儿！ 好。
Bùlǎng: Qǐng dàjiā zhàn de jǐn yìdiǎnr! Hǎo.

古波， 你们 准备准备 就 上
Gǔbō, nǐmen zhǔnbeizhǔnbei jiù shàng

飞机 吧。
fēijī ba.

太 太： 帕兰卡， 你们 要 注意 身体。
Tàitai: Pàlánkǎ, nǐmen yào zhùyì shēntǐ.

帕兰卡： 妈妈 您 放 心， 我们 身体 都
Pàlánkǎ: Māma, nín fàng xīn, wǒmen shēntǐ dōu

很 好。
hěn hǎo.

太 太： 你们 到 了 北京 就 给 我 来
Tàitai: Nǐmen dào le Běijīng jiù gěi wǒ lái

502

信。别 忘 了，一定 要 来 信。
xìn. Bié wàng le, yídìng yào lái xìn.

布 朗：好 了，别 难过 了。明年　我们
Bùlǎng: Hǎo le, bié nánguò le. Míngnián wǒmen

去 中国 看 他们。
qù Zhōngguó kàn tāmen.

古 波：你们 明年 什么 时候 去 北京？
Gǔbō: Nǐmen míngnián shénme shíhou qù Běijīng?

我们 一定 到 机场 接 你们。
Wǒmen yídìng dào jīchǎng jiē nǐmen.

布 朗：明年 夏天 或者 秋天 去。
Bùlǎng: Míngnián xiàtiān huòzhě qiūtiān qù.

飞机 就 要 起飞 了，你们 快
Fēijī jiù yào qǐfēi le, nǐmen kuài

走 吧。
zǒu ba.

王 ：祝 你们 身体 好，学习 好!
Wáng: Zhù nǐmen shēntǐ hǎo, xuéxí hǎo!

丁 云：祝 你们 一路平安!
Dīng Yún: Zhù nǐmen yílùpíng'ān!

帕兰卡、古波：谢谢 大家。再见!
Pàlánkǎ、Gǔbō: Xièxie dàjiā. Zàijiàn!

生词　New Words

1. 飞机　　（名）fēijī　　　　aeroplane, plane, aircraft

2. 要　　　（副）yào　　　　will, to be going to

3. 起飞　　（动）qǐfēi　　　　to take off

4. 机场　　（名）jīchǎng　　　airfield, airport

5. 分别　　（动）fēnbié　　　to part

6. 愿意　　（能愿）yuànyì　　to be willing

7. 离开　　（动）líkāi　　　　to leave

8. 见面　　　　jiàn miàn　　to meet (to see) each other

　　见　　（动）jiàn　　　　to meet, to see

9. 所以　　（连）suǒyǐ　　　so, therefore, as a result

10. 进步　　（名、动）jìnbù　　progress, advance, to pro-
　　　　　　　　　　　　　gress, to make progress

11. 努力　　（形）nǔlì　　　　hard-working, studious

12. 照相　　　　zhào xiàng　to take a picture, to have
　　　　　　　　　　　　　one's photo taken

13. 站　　　（动）zhàn　　　　to stand

14. 紧　　　（形）jǐn　　　　close, tight, taut

15. 上　　　（动）shàng　　　to get on, to get into, to
　　　　　　　　　　　　　board

504

16. 注意	(动)	zhùyì	to pay attention to
17. 身体	(名)	shēntǐ	body, health
18. 放心		fàng xīn	to set one's mind at rest, to be at ease, to rest assured
19. 忘	(动)	wàng	to forget
20. 难过	(形)	nánguò	sad
21. 明年	(名)	míngnián	next year
22. 夏天	(名)	xiàtiān	summer
23. 秋天	(名)	qiūtiān	autumn
24. 一路平安		yílùpíng'ān	to have a pleasant journey, to have a good trip, bon voyage

补充词 Supplementary Words

1. 汽车	(名)	qìchē	car
2. 船	(名)	chuán	ship
3. 叫	(动)	jiào	to hire, to call (a taxi etc.)
4. 送行	(动)	sòngxíng	to see someone off
5. 旅行	(动)	lǚxíng	to travel, to tour

6. 中国民航

Zhōngguó Mínháng　General Administration of Civil Aviation of China (CAAC)

二、注释　Notes

1. "我真不愿意离开你。"

"愿意"也是能愿动词，表示因符合自己的心愿而同意作某事或希望发生某种情况。

"愿意" is also an optative verb, indicating that one is willing or agrees to do something, or wishes something good would happen.

2. "我想我们很快会在中国见面。"

"I think we'll soon see each other in China."

能愿动词"会"除了表示通过学习掌握的技能外，还表示可能性。例如：

The optative verb "会" also indicates probability besides ability acquired or mastered as a result of study. E.g.

他还没有来。今天他会来吗？

他不会来。

3. "您工作非常认真，教得很好，所以他们进步很快。"

"所以"是表示因果关系的连词，用在复合句的后半句，表示结果。

"所以" is a conjunction showing cause and effect. It

506

usually occurs in the second clause of a compound sentence to tell result.

4. "这是我应该作的。"

回答别人对自己所作事情的夸奖时，这样说有谦虚的意思。

"这是我应该作的" is a polite expression used in reply to the praise someone sings of one for what he has done.

5. "请大家站得紧一点儿!"

"Please stand a bit closer, (you all.)"

"一点儿"用在形容词或某些动词的后边有比较的意思，表示很小的差别，如"快一点儿"、"早一点儿"、"好一点儿"等。

When used after adjectives or some verbs, "一点儿" implies comparison and indicates that the difference is very slight, e.g. "快一点儿", "早一点儿", "好一点儿" etc.

6. "你们要注意身体。"

"You must take care of yourself."

能愿动词"要"除了表示主观的意愿和要求外，还能表示事实上的需要。否定形式是"不用"。例如：

As well as indicating wish and request, the optative verb "要" can also indicate necessity. Its negative form is "不用". E.g.

这个练习要作吗？

这个练习不用作。

7. "你们到了北京就给我来信。"

"来信"是口语，即"写信"的意思。

"来信" is a colloquialism, meaning the same as "写信".

8. "祝你们一路平安!"

"一路平安"是对旅行的人送行或告别时的祝愿语。

"一路平安" means "Have a pleasant journey," "Have a good trip" or "Bon voyage". It is used when one sees somebody off or says good-bye to somebody on departure.

三、替换与扩展 Substitution and Extension

(一)

1. <u>飞机</u>就要<u>起飞</u>了吗？

   <u>飞机</u>就要<u>起飞</u>了。快上吧。

火车，	开
汽车*，	开
船*，	开

2. <u>代表团</u>什么时候<u>来</u>？

   快要<u>来</u>了。

球赛，	开始
你们，	锻炼
飞机，	到
(汽)车，	来

508

3. 现在几点?

   <u>七点五十</u>。

   要<u>上课</u>了,请快一点儿。

9:45,	下课
2:30,	比赛
11:55,	吃饭
7:05,	开车
8:15,	照相

4. 别<u>难过</u>了。

忘	找
说	走
玩儿	喝酒

5. 昨天你去看张大明了吗?

   我去看他了。

   他<u>工作</u>怎么样?

   他工作很<u>忙</u>。

学习，	努力
身体，	好
工作，	认真
身体，	健康

6. 请大家<u>站</u>得<u>紧</u>一点儿。

来，	早
走，	快
说，	慢
翻译，	好
起，	早

(二)

1. 在机场接朋友 Meeting a friend at the airport

   A: 请问，从北京来的飞机到了没有？

   B: 快要到了，还有五分钟。

   A: 谢谢。

   *　　　　*　　　　*

A: 啊,李先生,您来了。

B: 你们好!谢谢你们来接我。

A: 你的行李都到了吗?

B: 还差一个箱子。

A: 你在这儿等一等,我去叫*车。

B: 太感谢你了。

2. 送行 Seeing someone off

A: 火车两点十分就要开了,请上车吧。

B: 谢谢你,再见。

A: 你到了那儿就给我来信。

B: 好,一定给你写信。

A: 祝你一路平安,再见!

B: 再见!

3. 去旅行 Traveling

A: 我快要去中国旅行*了。

B: 你什么时候走?

A: 这个星期六就走。

B: 你坐火车去还是坐飞机去?

A: 我参加了一个旅行*团,我们坐中国民航*的飞机去。

B: 你们旅行*团有多少人?

A: 有二十二个。

B: 真不少。明年我也想去中国看看。

A: 对。你教中国文学,应该去看看。

4. 买飞机票 Buying plane tickets

A: 先生,我要买两张去北京的飞机票。

B: 你要哪一天的?

A: 我要四月十二日中国民航* 612 次 (cì, No., number)的, 还有票吗?

B: 还有。

A: 请问飞机什么时候起飞?

B: 上午七点十分。

A: 谢谢你。

四、阅读短文　Reading Text

在中国民航的飞机上

"女士(nǚshì, lady)们，先生们，你们好！您乘坐(chéngzuò, to sit)的是中国民航*开往(kāi wǎng, to leave for)北京的班机(bānjī, airliner)。飞机就要起飞了，请大家坐好(zuòhǎo, to take one's seat)，请不要吸烟……"

广播(guǎnbō, broadcast)里，汉语说得很清楚*，古波和帕兰卡都懂了，他们非常高兴。

飞机上人真多，很多人都是去中国的。两个穿得很漂亮的中国姑娘请大家吃糖(táng, sweets)、喝茶，她们是飞机上的服务员。

服务员都很年轻，工作非常认真。她们会说英语和法语。古波、帕兰卡跟她们说汉语，她们很高兴。

快十二点了，服务员说："请大家注意，

就要吃午饭了。"午饭有面包和点心，还有四个中国菜。菜作得很好，古波和帕兰卡都很喜欢吃。

帕兰卡吃了饭想喝咖啡。服务员问古波要咖啡还是要茶。古波说："我们快要到中国了，我要喝中国茶。"服务员给了他们一杯花茶、一杯咖啡，说："你们汉语说得真流利*。"帕兰卡说："哪里，我们说得不太好。我们俩都是去中国学习的留学生。"

服务员说："欢迎你们到中国学习。"

五、语法　Grammar

1. "要……了"表示动作很快要发生　"要…了" indicating an action is going to take place in a short time

　　如果要表示动作或情况很快就发生，可以在动词（或形容词）前加上副词"要"，句尾加语气助词"了"（"要……了"）。在"要"的前边还可以用"就"或"快"作状语，表示时间紧迫。例如：

If we want to indicate that an action or a situation is going to take place soon, we can put the adverb "要" in front of the verb (or adjective) and the modal particle "了"

at the end of the sentence to form the construction "要…了". When preceded by "就" or "快" as an adverbial adjunct, "要" shows the imminence. E.g.

爸爸要给我们照相了。

飞机就要起飞了。

我们快要分别了。

这种句子通常用带"吗"的疑问句提问。表示否定的回答，只用否定副词"没有"。例如：

Sentences of this kind are turned into questions by having "吗" added to them at the end. The negative adverb "没有" is used to form negative answers. E.g.

飞机要起飞了吗？

没有。

注意：Points to be noted:

(1) "就要……了" 前边可以加时间状语，如"他们明天就要走了"。但"快要……了"前边不能加时间状语。

"就要…了" may be preceded by an adverbial of time, as in "他们明天就要走了"；"快要…了" cannot be used in this way.

(2) "要……了"也可以改为 "快……了"，意思一样，如"车快开了"。

"要…了" can be changed to "快…了" with its meaning unchanged, e.g. "车快开了"。

515

2. 语气助词"了"(2) Modal particle "了"(2)

语气助词"了"跟"别"、"不要"等否定词一起用于祈使句中，可以表示劝告或禁止的语气。例如：

When combined with the negative word "别" or "不要", the modal particle "了" can be used in imperative sentences to indicate that one asks someone to or not to do something. E.g.

别忘了，一定要常来信。

别难过了。

别说了，大家在看书呢。

别找了，你的帽子在这儿。

3. 主谓谓语句 Sentences with a subject-predicate construction as its predicate

由主谓结构作谓语主要成分的句子叫主谓谓语句。在很大一部分主谓谓语句中，主谓结构的主语所指的人或事物常常属于全句主语所代表的人或事物。例如：

A sentence in which a subject-predicate construction serves as the main element of its predicate is known as a sentence with a subject-predicate construction as its predicate. In a great number of sentences of this kind, the person or thing indicated by the subject of the subject-predicate construction is closely related to or forms a component part of the person or thing indicated by the subject of the whole sentence. E.g.

你身体好吗？

他工作怎么样？

练习 Exercises

1. 读下列词组：Read out the following phrases:

坐飞机　　坐火车　坐汽车*　坐船*

离开朋友　　离开家　　离开图书馆

离开中国

跟朋友分别　　分别以后　分别的时候

忘了那个生词　忘了他的名字　忘了来

忘了吃饭

愿意去　愿意参加　愿意了解　愿意听音乐

注意身体　注意学习　注意锻炼

请(大家)注意

请放心　您放心　不放心　很放心

2. 用"就要……了"完成下列对话：Complete the following dialogues with "就要…了"：

(1) A: 今天的报什么时候来？

B: _____。

(2) A: 电影开始了没有？

B: 没有，_____。

(3) A: 我们_____。

B: 我真不愿意你离开我。

(4) A: 车_____，我该走了。

B: 祝你一路平安！再见！

(5) A: 他们_____。

B: 我们快去欢迎他们。

3．将下列各组词语，按照例句写成对话：Write dialogues using the following groups of words and phrases in the same way as the example given:

例 Example 飞机 起飞 十点 差五分十点

　→A: 飞机几点起飞？

　　B: 十点起飞。

　　A: 现在几点？

　　B: 差五分十点。

　　A: 飞机就要起飞了。

518

(1) 飞机　到　八点　七点五十

(2) 火车　到　九点半　九点二十五

(3) 船　　开　四点一刻　四点十分

(4) 代表团　来　五号　三号

(5) 比赛　开始　星期三　星期二

4. 用"别……了"填空：Supply "别…了" in the following sentences:

(1) A: 昨天我忘了，我没有去上课。

　　B: ＿＿＿＿＿＿＿＿＿＿，你明天上午九点半还有课。

(2) A: 你们就要走了，我很难过。

　　B: ＿＿＿＿＿＿＿＿＿＿，以后我们常给你写信。

(3) A: 我们再跳一个舞，好吗？

　　B: ＿＿＿＿＿＿＿＿＿＿，大家都休息了。

(4) A: 我在找我的鞋呢。

　　B: ＿＿＿＿＿＿＿＿＿＿，你的鞋在这儿。

(5) A: 我们再玩儿玩儿吧？

B: ＿＿＿＿＿＿＿＿＿＿，他们在等我们呢。

5. 将下列句子翻译成汉语（注意用主谓谓语句）：
Translate the following into Chinese, but use sentences with subject-predicate constructions as their predicates:

(1) How are your father and mother?

(2) Is that man a good referee?

(3) There are not many foreign students studying in our institute.

(4) The kitchen in her house is very small, but the dining-hall is quite big.

(5) Are the shirts in this shop good or not?

6. 根据本课阅读短文回答下列问题：Answer the following questions on the Reading Text:

(1) 古波和帕兰卡坐的是什么飞机？

(2) 飞机要起飞了，服务员请大家注意什么？

(3) 广播里汉语说得清楚*不清楚？古波和帕兰卡懂了没有？

(4) 飞机上的服务员怎么样？

(5) 他们什么时候吃午饭？午饭怎么样？

(6) 古波、帕兰卡跟服务员说汉语了没
　　有？他们说了些什么？

7. 先看图回答问题，然后根据这几个问题写一段话：
Study the picture and answer the following questions,
then write a short passage on the picture:

(1) 王英和她爱人去哪
　　儿？

(2) 谁来给他们送行
　　了？

(3) 火车快要开了吗？

(4) 分别的时候，她们怎么样？

(5) 她们在说什么？

六、语音语调　Pronunciation and Intonation

1. 句调(5)　Sentence tunes (5)

(1) 选择问句中，选择部分重读，连词"还是"轻读。全句可
分为两部分："还是"以前的部分读高句调，句尾上升，可稍有停
顿；"还是"以后读低句调，句尾降低。例如：

In alternative questions the two groups of words indicating the choice are stressed, the connective "还是" is pronounced with a weak stress. The whole sentence can be divided

up into two parts. The part before "还是" is uttered in the high-pitch sentence tune, with a rise at the end, and a short pause. The part after "还是" is uttered in the low-pitch sentence tune, with a fall at the end. E.g.

(2) 用语气助词"吧"构成的祈使句或疑问句，一般读低句调，语速较慢，句尾也是缓慢地下降。例如：

Imperative sentences or questions formed with the modal particle "吧" are generally said slowly and in the low-pitch sentence tune, and with the voice falling slowly at the end. E.g.

飞机就要起飞了，你们快走吧!

请大家到楼上看电影吧！

前边是条河，在这儿停车吧？

2．练习 Exercises

(1) 辨别声母 z、zh：Pronounce the following, taking care to differentiate the initials z and zh:

汉字——地址　　知道——杂志

足球——祝贺　　早饭——招待

作家——桌子　　洗澡——照相

(2) 朗读下列三音节词，注意词重音：Read out the following trisyllabic words, paying attention to word stress:

不敢当　乒乓球　茅台酒　葡萄酒

矿泉水　桔子水　服务员　星期日

阅览室　大使馆　图书馆　咖啡馆

朗读下面的成语：Read out the following proverb:

Zhòng guā dé guā,

种　瓜　得　瓜，

zhòng dòu dé dòu:

种　豆　得　豆。

(Plant melons and you get melons,
Sow beans and you get beans—as you sow, so will
you reap.)

汉字笔顺表　Table of Stroke-order of Chinese Characters

1	飞	乁	飞	飞			飛
2	机	木					機
		几					
3	场	圤					場
		勿					
4	别	另	口				
			力				
		刂					
5	愿	原	厂				願
			白				
			小				
		心					
6	离	亩	亠				離

524

		凵			
		内（冂 内 内）			
7	所	戶（´ 厂 戶 戶）			
		斤			
8	步	止			
		少（丿 丷 少）			
9	努	奴	女		
			又		
		力			
10	力				
11	站	立			
		占			
12	緊	収	刂		緊
			又		
		糸	幺（ 幺 幺）		
			小		
13	注	氵			
		主			
14	身				

15	体	亻			體
		本			
16	放	方			
		攵			
17	忘	亡			
		心			
18	过	寸			過
		辶			
19	夏	百	一		
			自（ノ 自）		
		夂			
20	秋	禾			
		火			
21	路	𧾷			
		各	夂		
			口		
22	安	宀			
		女			

第三十课　Lesson 30

复习　Revision

一、课文　Text

布朗太太笑了

帕兰卡　走　了，　布朗　太太　心里　很
Pàlánkǎ　zǒu le,　Bùlǎng　Tàitai　xīnli　hěn

难过。她　请　丁　云　坐　她　的　车，她　要
nánguò.　Tā qǐng Dīng Yún zuò tā　de　chē,　tā　yào

送　丁　云　回　学生　宿舍。
sòng Dīng Yún huí xuésheng　sùshè.

在 车上，丁 云 说："帕兰卡 很
Zài chēshang, Dīng Yún shuō: "Pàlánkǎ hěn

想 去 中国 学习，她 今天 晚上 就
xiǎng qù Zhōngguó xuéxí, tā jīntiān wǎnshang jiù

要 到 北京 了，我 想 她 现在 一定
yào dào Běijīng le, wǒ xiǎng tā xiànzài yídìng

很 高兴。"
hěn gāoxìng."

布朗 先生 说："女儿 很 高兴 的
Bùlǎng Xiānsheng shuō: "Nǚ'ér hěn gāoxìng de

时候，妈妈 心里 很 难过。"
shíhou, māma xīnli hěn nánguò."

布朗 太太 问 丁 云："去年 你 来
Bùlǎng Tàitai wèn Dīng Yún: "Qùnián nǐ lái

我们 国家 的 时候，你 妈妈 愿意 你
wǒmen guójiā de shíhou, nǐ māma yuànyì nǐ

离开 她 吗？"
líkāi tā ma?"

丁 云 告诉 布朗 太太，她 妈妈
Dīng Yún gàosu Bùlǎng Tàitai, Tā māma

开始 很 高兴，给 她 买 了 很 多 东西。
kāishǐ hěn gāoxìng, gěi tā mǎi le hěn duō dōngxi.

528

妈妈 要 她 注意 身体， 努力 学习， 不
Māma yào tā zhùyì shēntǐ, nǔlì xuéxí, bú

要 想 家。 她 走 的 那 天， 快 上 飞机
yào xiǎng jiā. Tā zǒu de nà tiān, kuài shàng fēijī

了， 她 说 "再见"， 妈妈 就 哭 了。
le, tā shuō "zàijiàn", māma jiù kū le.

"是 啊！" 布朗 太太 说。 她 又 问：
"Shì a!" Bùlǎng Tàitai shuō. Tā yòu wèn:

"这儿 离 北京 很 远， 你 妈妈 放 心
"Zhèr lí Běijīng hěn yuǎn, nǐ māma fàng xīn

吗？"
ma?"

丁云 说："我 常常 给 妈妈 写
Dīng Yún shuō: "Wǒ chángcháng gěi māma xiě

信， 告诉 她 这儿 的 老师 和 同学
xìn, gàosu tā zhèr de lǎoshī hé tóngxué

都 很 热情，我 在 这儿 过 得 很 好。
dōu hěn rèqíng, wǒ zài zhèr guò de hěn hǎo.

我 还 告诉 妈妈， 帕兰卡 是 我 的 好
Wǒ hái gàosu māma, Pàlánkǎ shì wǒ de hǎo

朋友， 她 就 象 我 的 妹妹， 她 的 家
péngyou, tā jiù xiàng wǒ de mèimei, tā de jiā

就 象 我 自己 的 家。所以 妈妈 现在
jiù xiàng wǒ zìjǐ de jiā. Suǒyǐ māma xiànzài

很 放 心。昨天 我 又 写 信 告诉 他们，
hěn fàng xīn. Zuótiān wǒ yòu xiě xìn gàosu tāmen,

帕兰卡 快 要 去 中国 学习 了，她 到
Pàlánkǎ kuài yào qù Zhōngguó xuéxí le, tā dào

了 北京 就 要 去 看看 妈妈。"
le Běijīng jiù yào qù kànkan māma."

布朗 先生 说："帕兰卡 认识 了
Bùlǎng Xiānsheng shuō: "Pàlánkǎ rènshi le

一个 中国 姐姐，她 到 北京 以后，
yíge Zhōngguó jiějie, tā dào Běijīng yǐhòu,

又 要 认识 一位 中国 妈妈。"
yòu yào rènshi yíwèi Zhōngguó māma."

布朗 太太 笑 了。
Bùlǎng Tàitai xiào le.

生词 New Words

1. 笑 (动) xiào to laugh, to smile

2. 心 (名) xīn heart

3. 送(人) (动) sòng (rén) to see (or walk) someone home, to see (someone) off

530

4.	女儿	(名)	nǚ'ér	daughter
5.	去年	(名)	qùnián	last year
6.	国家	(名)	guójiā	country, state
7.	东西	(名)	dōngxi	thing
8.	哭	(动)	kū	to cry, to weep
9.	离	(介)	lí	from
10.	远	(形)	yuǎn	far, distant
11.	热情	(形)	rèqíng	cordial, enthusiastic
12.	过	(动)	guò	to live, to get along
13.	自己	(代)	zìjǐ	self

二、注释 Notes

1. "妈妈要她注意身体。"

这是一个兼语句，动词"要"表示要求 某人 做 某 件 事 的 意思。

"妈妈要她注意身体。" is a pivotal sentence in which the verb "要" is used in the sense of "to request" or "to ask".

2. "这儿离北京很远。"

介词"离"和它的宾语所组成的介词结构，常表示空间或时间上的距离，它的宾语可以是表示处所的名词或表示时间的名词。

Prepositional constructions formed of the preposition "离" and its object often indicate distance in space or time, and the object may be either a noun of place or of time.

3. "她的家就象我自己的家。"

代词"自己"常用来复指前边的代词或名词，有强调的作用。如"他自己"、"大夫自己"。

The pronoun "自己" is more often than not used in apposition to the pronoun or noun immediately preceding it for the sake of emphasis, e.g. "他自己", "大夫自己"。

三、看图会话 Talk About These Pictures

1. 请求和禁止 Request and prohibition

可以……吗？

这儿不能……

2. 意愿和可能 Intention and possibility

她会来吗？

她不会来，

她不想……

今晚电影
《大闹天宫》

3. 能力 Ability

能当教练吗？

4. 邀请和接受 Invitation and acceptance

能……吗？

5. 招待 Entertaining a guest

请尝尝
请再吃一点儿……

6. 称赞与回答 Compliments and responses

汉字写得……
哪里，……

7. 谈已作的事情 Talking about something done in the
　　　　　　past

买了……

8．谈将要发生的事 Talking about something that will take place in the future

车要……了

9．谈球赛 Talking about ball games

谁跟谁比赛？

谁赢了？

几比几？

10．送行 Seeing someone off

要开车了，

要注意……

到了……请来信

祝你一路平安。

四、语法小结 A Brief Summary of Grammar

1．四种句子 The four kinds of simple sentences

汉语中带有主语和谓语的单句，按谓语主要成分的不同可分为以下四种：

534

According to the different component parts that make up their predicates, simple sentences fall into four different kinds:

(1) 名词谓语句 Sentences with a nominal predicate

名词谓语句是直接用名词、名词结构或数量词作谓语主要成分的句子。名词谓语句经常用来说明主语的时间、年龄、籍贯等。

A sentence with a nominal predicate is one in which a noun, a nominal construction or a numeral-measure word serves as the main element of its predicete. Sentences of this kind are usually used to state the time, someone's age or native place, etc.

现在三点。

今天星期五吗？

我今年二十岁。

(2) 动词谓语句 Sentences with a verbal predicate

动词作谓语主要成分的句子在汉语中占绝对优势，它的情况也很复杂。我们已经接触到了十种动词谓语句（详见下一节），本书第二册将介绍更多的动词谓语句。

Sentences in which verbs serve as the main element of the predicate occupy a dominant place in the Chinese language but are of a most complex character. Ten different kinds of this type of sentences have been introduced so far (for detail see the following section). More will be introduced in Book 2 of this reader.

我学习汉语。

她妈妈是大夫。

帕兰卡有一个中国姐姐。

(3) 形容词谓语句 Sentences with an adjectival predicate

以形容词为谓语主要成分的句子，从语法特征来看，跟以不及物动词为谓语主要成分的动词谓语句很相似（谓语形容词也可以带状语或补语）。这种句子不需要再加"是"。

As far as their formation is concerned, sentences with an adjective as the main element of the predicate are very similar to sentences with an intransitive verb as the main element of the predicate (predicative adjectives may also take adverbial modifiers or complements). "是" is not used in sentences of this type.

他很努力。

这儿离商店不远。

(4) 主谓谓语句 Sentences with a subject-predicate construction as their predicate

我们已学过的主谓谓语句里，主谓结构中的主语所代表的事物常常是全句主语所代表的事物的一部分；主谓结构对全句的主语起描写、说明的作用。

In sentences with subject-predicate constructions as their predicates we have come across, things indicated by the subjects of the subject-predicate constructions are parts of the things indicated by the subjects of the whole sentences, and the subject-predicate constructions are descriptive of the subjects of the whole sentences.

飞机上人真多。

布朗太太心里很难过。

他工作怎么样？

2. 动词谓语句 (1) Sentences with a verbal predicate (1)

1) "是"字句 "是" sentences

她是中国留学生。

这件衬衫不是新的。

2) "有"字句 "有" sentences

商店旁边有一个餐厅。

他没有哥哥。

3) 无宾语句 Sentences without objects

他来了。

比赛要开始了。

4) 单宾语句 Sentences with one object

我看了两本画报。

古波不认识他。

5) 双宾语句 Sentences with two objects

王老师教他们语法。

丁云送帕兰卡一束花儿。

他告诉你他的名字了吗?

6) 动词或动词结构作宾语句　Sentences with a verb or verbal construction as the object

现在开始上课。

他喜欢打乒乓球。

他会说汉语。

7) 主谓结构作宾语句　Sentences with a subject-predicate construction as the object

你知道他是谁吗?

我想他现在一定很高兴。

你妈妈愿意你离开她吗?

8) 前置宾语句　Sentences with a preposed object

他汉字写得很好。

那本书你买了吗?

9) 连动句 Sentences with verbal constructions in series

妈妈进城买东西了。

我每天下午坐车去图书馆。

她送丁云回学生宿舍。

10) 兼语句 Pivotal sentences

他们让我唱一个歌儿。

我请我朋友吃饭。

布朗太太请丁云坐她的车。

她妈妈要她注意身体。

3. 动态助词"了"和语气助词"了"(1) Aspect particle "了" and modal particle "了"(1)

1) 动态助词"了"和语气助词"了"(1)都用在动词谓语句中。动态助词"了"放在动词之后，强调这个动词所代表的动作已完成；语气助词"了"放在句尾，强调整个句子所表达的某件事或某个情况已经发生。例如：

"了", whether as an aspect particle or as a modal particle, is usually used in sentences with a verbal predicate. As an aspect particle, "了" comes after the verb, emphasizing that the action expressed by the verb has already been completed; as a modal particle, "了" is used to modify the entire statement, always found at the end of a sentence, emphasizing that the event referred to is something that has already taken place. E.g.

① 你看了今天的报没有？

我看了(今天的报)。

② 下课以后你作什么了？

我看报了。

例① 强调"看"这个动作已完成，例② 则强调"看报"这件事确已发生。用动态助词"了"强调动作的完成，但整个事情未必已经发生，如："我下了课就进城。"如果强调整个事情已发生，还需要在句尾再加语气助词"了"，如"我下了课就进城了"。

Example ① stresses that the action expressed by the verb "看" has already been completed; Example② stresses that the event expressed by "看报" has already taken place. If the aspect particle "了" is used to indicate the completion of an action, it usually implies that the entire event may not necessarily take place, as in "我下了课就进城". If it is stressed that the entire event has already occured, it is necessary to add the modal particle "了" at the end of the sentence, as in "我下了课就进城了".

如果在带语气助词"了"肯定某事已发生的句子里，又要特别强调动作已完成，则可以在动词后再加上动态助词"了"。试比较：

In a sentence with the modal particle "了" to indicate that some event expressed by the whole sentence has already taken place, if the completion of the action expressed by the verb is specially emphasized, the aspect particle "了" is necessarily added after the verb. Compare:

① 你吃饭了吗？

我吃饭了。（一般地肯定某事已发生 A simple

statement that some event has already taken place)

② 请在这儿吃饭吧？

谢谢，我吃了饭了。（特别强调动作已完

成 A special emphasis that an action has already been completed)

（或，or)

我吃了。

需要注意的是，如果不强调动作的完成或某事已经发生，只是一般地叙述过去某时的情景，则常常不用"了"。例如：

What should be observed is that "了" is generally not used in simple statement of some past happening, i.e., when there is no need to stress its completion or occurance. E.g.

昨天上午他去中国大使馆办签证，下午看足球赛。

2) 动词后有动态助词"了"又有宾语的句子，必须具备下面的条件之一，才能构成完整的句子：

When a verb takes after it both the aspect particle "了" and an object, the sentence remains an incomplete one except to possess one of the following requirements:

① 宾语前有数量词或其它定语。例如：

The object is preceded by a numeral–measure word or other attributive. E.g.

我喝了一杯葡萄酒。

他买了很多中文杂志。

她参观了我们的宿舍。

② 如果宾语很简单，后面必须另有动词或分句。例如：

The object must be followed by another verb or a clause if it is a simple one. E.g.

明天我吃了饭就去看足球赛。

我参观了工厂就回家了。

③ 句尾有语气助词"了"时，宾语可以是简单的：

The object may be a simple one when the sentence ends with the modal particle "了". E.g.

他吃了饭了。

我看了电影了。

④ 动词前有比较复杂的状语时，宾语也可以是简单的：

The object may be a simple one when the verb is preceded by a complicated adverbial adjunct. E.g.

布朗先生在机场给他们照了照片。

昨天他跟我们一起看了电影。

注意：Points to be noted:

（1）不表示具体动作的动词如"是、在、象、让"等和表示存在的"有"后边不能用动态助词"了"。

Verbs not denoting actions such as "是"，"在"，"象" and "让"，and the verb "有" indicating existence, are never followed by the aspect particle "了".

（2）连动句要表示动作的完成，一般在第二个动词后加动态助词"了"。如"他去商店买了一双冰鞋"，不能说"他去了商店买一双冰鞋"。

When a sentence with verbal constructions in series indicates the completion of an action, the aspect particle "了" is usually added after the second verb, e.g. "他去商店买了一双冰鞋". It is incorrect to say "他去了商店买一双冰鞋".

（3）单音节动词重叠时，动态助词"了"要放在重叠动词之间，如"他尝了尝茅台酒"。

When a monosyllabic verb is reduplicated, the aspect particle "了" should be inserted in between the two verbs, e.g. "他尝了尝茅台酒".

4．能愿动词 Optative verbs

（1）主观上的意愿

To indicate will or volition. E.g.

我要到机场送我朋友。（否定形式："不想"。

The negative form of "要" is "不想".)

你想了解中国吗？

他愿意帮助我。

(2) 具有某种能力和技能
To indicate ability or skill of a certain kind. E.g.

你能翻译这本书吗？

你可以翻译这本书吗？（否定形式："不能"。
The negative form of "可以" is "不能".）

他会滑冰。

(3) 客观上允许或禁止
To indicate ability depending on circumstances. E.g.

明天你能来吗？

明天你可以来吗？（否定形式："不能"。The
negative form of "可以" is "不能".）

能吸烟吗？

可以吸烟吗？

(4) 可能性
To indicate probability or possibility. E.g.

他会去吗？

(5) 事实上的需要
To indicate objective necessity. E.g.

学生要努力学习。（否定形式："不用"。

544

The negative form of "要" is "不用".)

我们应该每天锻炼身体。

练习 Exercises

1. 写出下列形容词和动词的反义词：Give the antonym for each
of the following adjectives and verbs:

新　　　　　　　笑

多　　　　　　　送

大　　　　　　　问

快　　　　　　　教

早　　　　　　　赢

难　　　　　　　来

高兴　　　　　　分别

2. 造句：Make sentences, using the groups of words and
phrases given:

　(1) 请　　帮助

　(2) 坐车　去

　(3) 告诉　地址

　(4) 喜欢　看

（5）听　　念课文

（6）要　　放心

（7）教　　开车

（8）给　　花儿

（9）问　　生词

（10）注意　语法

3. 根据括号中的要求，将下列各句改写成用动态助词"了"的句子，强调动作的完成：Rewrite according to the instructions given in parentheses the following sentences using the aspect particle "了" to indicate that the action has been completed:

例 Example

明天我看电影。(加定语 Supplying an attributive before the noun)

你看不看？

→昨天我看了那个电影。

你看没看？

（1）明天我参加比赛。(加语气助词 "了" Adding the modal particle "了" to the verb)

你参加不参加？

(2) 晚上我作练习。(加别的动词 Supplying another
verb before the verb)

你作不作？

(3) 我办签证。(加语气助词 "了" Adding the modal
particle "了" to the verb)

你办不办？

(4) 明天我看电视。(加地点状语 Supplying an
adverbial of place)

你看不看？

(5) 晚上我作菜。(加定语 Supplying an attributive
before the noun)

你作不作？

(6) 星期天我听唱片。(加状语 Supplying an
adverbial adjunct)

你听不听？

4. 组句: Rearrange each of the following groups of words
and phrases in a right order so as to make a sentence:

(1) 准备 行李 快 得 他 很

(2) 念 应该 课文 我们 常常

(3) 过 你们 好 星期天 吗 得

(4) 还 这个 用 会 生词 不 我

(5) 健康 身体 老师 我们 太 不

(6) 没有 书 了 看 你 图书馆
到 昨天

(7) 多 房间 家 很 他

5. 用介词填空: Put in prepositions in each of the following sentences:

(1) 我想____你们照相。

(2) 他____帕兰卡一起跳舞。

(3) 他们____这儿坐飞机到北京。

(4) 我朋友请我____他买一顶帽子。

(5) 学院____他家不太远。

(6) 我常常____我朋友打电话。

(7) 他说____大家的健康干杯。

(8) 我没有____他写信。

6. 将下列句子翻译成汉语: Translate the following into Chinese:

(1) Can your friend go to the dance tomorrow?

(2) Don't wait any longer. He is not likely to come today.

(3) The doctor said that you should take good care of yourself.

(4) How is he getting along with his studies of the problem?

(5) He told me that he would leave shortly.

(6) Are you willing to help me with my study of French?

7. 下列句子中，正确的画（+），不正确的画（-）：
Mark the following sentences, using (+) for the correct ones and (-) for the incorrect ones:

（1）这是谁的帽子呢？（　）

（2）你想研究不研究中国文化？（　）

（3）我去商店要买东西。（　）

（4）你能用中文写信吗？（　）

（5）我们上了飞机，就飞机起飞了。（　）

（6）这个姑娘法语很好。（　）

（7）我懂汉语语法一点儿。（　）

（8）你们赢了还是输了吗？（　）

（9）昨天我滑冰了，今天我要又滑冰。（　）

（10）他们星期三就要分别了。（　）

8. 改正下面的错句：Correct the following erroneous sentences.

（1）晚上她写了信。

（2）明天我下了课就去看电影了。

（3）昨天我去了他家的时候，他正看电视了。

（4）去年我常常参加足球比赛了。

（5）冬天我没有滑冰了。

（6）他起床了很早。

（7）我想了看中国电影。

（8）他们让了我唱一个中国民歌。

（9）代表团坐了飞机去中国。

（10）有时候我跟他一起钓鱼了。

（11）老师问我了一个问题。

（12）同学们都试试了中国筷子。

9。看图写话：Wtite a short passage based on the pictures。

汉字笔顺表 Table of Stroke-order of Chinese Characters

1	笑	⺮					
		天					
2	东	一	七	车	东	东		東
3	西	一	广	币	丙	两	西
4	哭	吅	口				
			口				
		犬（大 犬）					
5	热	执	扌				熱
		丸（九 丸）					
		⺌					
6	情	忄					
		青					
7	自						
8	己	⺄	⼐	己			

实用汉语课本

（英文译释）

第 一 册

北京语言学院 编

*

商 务 印 书 馆 出 版

（中国北京王府井大街 36 号 邮政编码 100710）

北京语言学院印刷厂排版

北京中科印刷有限公司印刷

中国国际图书贸易总公司发行

（中国北京车公庄西路 35 号）

北京邮政信箱第 399 号 邮政编码 100044

1981 年 5 月第 1 版

2006 年 5 月北京第 21 次印刷

ISBN 7-100-00088-2 / G·13

03300

9—E—1577PA